Teams That Work

TEAMS THAT WORK

The Seven Drivers of Team Effectiveness

Scott Tannenbaum
and
Eduardo Salas

OXFORD
UNIVERSITY PRESS

Oxford University Press is a department of the University of Oxford. It furthers
the University's objective of excellence in research, scholarship, and education
by publishing worldwide. Oxford is a registered trade mark of Oxford University
Press in the UK and certain other countries.

Published in the United States of America by Oxford University Press
198 Madison Avenue, New York, NY 10016, United States of America.

Library of Congress Cataloging-in-Publication Data
Names: Tannenbaum, Scott, author. | Salas, Eduardo, author.
Title: Teams that work : the seven drivers of team effectiveness /
Scott Tannenbaum and Eduardo Salas.
Description: New York, NY : Oxford University Press, [2021] |
Includes bibliographical references and index.
Identifiers: LCCN 2020006697 (print) | LCCN 2020006698 (ebook) |
ISBN 9780190056964 (hardback) | ISBN 9780190056988 (epub) |
ISBN 9780190056995
Subjects: LCSH: Teams in the workplace. | Organizational behavior. |
Organizational effectiveness.
Classification: LCC HD66 .T364 2020 (print) | LCC HD66 (ebook) |
DDC 658.4/022—dc23
LC record available at https://lccn.loc.gov/2020006697
LC ebook record available at https://lccn.loc.gov/2020006698

9 8 7 6 5 4 3 2 1

Printed by Sheridan Books, Inc., United States of America

Dedicated to Becky and Vicki, our "teammates" for life

CONTENTS

ACKNOWLEDGMENTS

Throughout our careers we have worked with, led, and advised all sorts of teams. Like most of you, we have experienced the power of high-performing teams and the angst of struggling teams. It made us want to crack the code. How could we help more teams succeed?

While we were actively trying to help teams become more effective, we were also conducting empirical research and reading studies published by researchers around the globe. We became increasingly excited as we saw the research grow and mature to the point where we felt it could yield practical, evidence-based advice. Teams became our passion, and we developed a conviction that team leaders and members could create better, more successful team experiences, if only they knew about the research. It is that passion and conviction that led us to write this book.

This book is possible because of the efforts of those researchers who have conducted high-quality studies about teams, including members of the industrial/organizational psychology and human factors communities. That research provides the foundation for our framework and advice. Researchers, we alluded to your work throughout the book—we hope we portrayed it accurately and made it accessible to an audience beyond the academic journals. Your work deserves the visibility, and we thank you for what you have done and continue to do to help crack the code.

To the many people who participated in our research, including military men and women, business leaders, astronauts, technologists, flight crews, pilots, air traffic controllers, production team members, healthcare practitioners, and financial professionals—thank you for allowing us to poke and probe and watch and listen to you as we tried to uncover what really drives teamwork. Thank you for opening your cockpits, your operating rooms, your neonatal intensive care units, your plants, your oil platforms, your boardrooms, your air traffic control towers, your work spaces—they provided an invaluable opportunity to ground us and show us how teams try to address real challenges. Thank you!

To our consulting clients, a big thank you for trusting us to work with and advise your teams; we learned a tremendous amount from those experiences. To our research sponsors, noted in the following text—thank you for your commitment to the science we represent. Your partnership made a difference and your belief in us helped.

Prior to writing the book, we delivered many talks and led discussions about the science of teamwork at various companies, associations, and meetings. Audience members asked us questions about and shared examples of their teamwork challenges, which helped us better understand many of the common pain points we address in the book. To those of you who asked us, "Do you have a book on this?" we want to thank you for the encouragement. We can now answer, "Yes we do!"

We'd like to acknowledge the various agencies that have supported our research, including the US Army Research Institute, the Air Force Human Resources Lab, the Army Research Lab, the Office of Naval Research, the NAWC-Training Systems Division, NASA, the Agency for Healthcare Research and Quality, the National Science Foundation, and the Federal Aviation Administration. A heartfelt thank you to our colleagues in those agencies including Jim Battles, Wink Bennett, Bridget Boyle, Colanda Cato, Stan Collyer, Eleana Edens, Jimmy Garrett, Jay Goodwin, Stan Halpin, Kathryn Keeton, Heidi King, Lauren Leveton, Leah Rowe, Lauren Landon, Greg Ruark, and Brandon Vessey. While we are appreciative of the funding you provided, we value your collaboration and input even more.

Over the years, we've been extremely fortunate to have great teammates, collaborators, and partners who educated, challenged, and encouraged us. To our colleagues from The Group for Organizational Effectiveness—including Becky Beard, Jamie Levy, and George Alliger—we are grateful for the support and advice you provided as we worked shoulder to shoulder on many research and consulting projects.

We also want to recognize some of the people who influenced our thinking about teams and who enriched our journey toward the development of this book, including Bill Baetz, David Baker, Wendy Bedwell, Suzanne Bell, Lauren Benishek, Clint Bowers, Art Blaiwes, Mike Brannick, Shawn Burke, Jan Cannon-Bowers, David Carnegie, Michael Castellana, Chris Cerasoli, Deb Cohen, Marvin Cohen, Chuck "DBear" Colgrove, Nancy Cooke, Mike Coovert, Chris Coultas, Leslie DeChurch, Deborah DiazGranados, Aaron Dietz, Dan Dwyer, Jim

Driskell, Tripp Driskell, Erik Eddy, Amy Edmonson, Jennifer Feitosa, Steve Fiore, Jared Freeman, Clay Foushee, Jennifer Fowlkes, Mike Garrity, Megan Gregory, Becky Grossman, Richard Hackman, Mitch Heine, Bob Heilmreich, Barb Hess, Al Holland, Bill Howell, Ashley Hughes, Chelsea Iwig, Florian Jentsch, Joan Johnston, Joe Keebler, Deanna Kennedy, Gary Klein, Steve Kozlowski, Kurt Kraiger, Mike Kukenberger, Christina Lacerenza, Gary Latham, Liz Lazzara, Tammy Lowry, Margaret Luciano, Rebecca Lyons, Gerry Malecki, Travis Maynard, Shannon Marlow, Jen McCuen, Susan McDaniel, Dan McFarland, Mike Mitchell, Bill O'Keefe, Andy Ortiz, Randy Oser, Heather Priest, Carolyn Prince, Joan Rentsch, Dick Reynolds, Bill Rizzo, Mike Rosen, Mary Salisbury, Marissa Schuffler, Diane Selleck, Daniel Serfaty, Kevin Stagl, Kim Smith-Jentsch, Maryanne Spatola, Renee Stout, Eric Thomas, Mark Teachout, Amanda Thayer, Sallie Weaver, Dale Watson, Jessie Wildman, Kat Wilson, Steven Woods, Janis Yadiny, Gary Yukl, Wayne Zachary, and Stephanie Zajac. We'd also like to acknowledge the many graduate students we've interacted with over the years for engaging in conversations that helped us refine our thinking. To Natalie Croitoru, thank you for your assistance tracking down research articles as we wrote the book. And to Amy Callan, thanks for the superb ongoing administrative support.

We want to extend a special thank you to our long-time collaborator and dear friend, John Mathieu. If there is a research problem that John can't solve, we haven't found it yet. John, this book is greatly influenced by our time spent with you.

To our academic mentors, Terry Dickinson, Al Glickman, and Ben Morgan, who challenged our perspectives, critiqued our writing, and encouraged us to think rigorously throughout graduate school—thank you for the great jump start.

Anyone who has written a book recognizes the importance of having the right publisher. Thank you to our colleagues at Oxford University Press and, in particular, Abby Gross, our editor. We greatly appreciate your guidance, support, deft editorial touch, and encouragement. You made the book better.

Finally, on a personal note, we want to express our love and gratitude to our spouses, Becky Beard and Vicki Salas. As we wrote this book you listened to us talk about teams ad nauseam and helped keep this two-man team of authors from killing one another. On a continual basis, you demonstrate how to be both individually excellent and a great team player. *Muchisimas gracias*!

PART I

All about Teams

CHAPTER 1

What Really Drives Team Effectiveness? (And Getting the Most Out of This Book)

You are a member of small team working on an important, challenging mission. Your assignment is dangerous, and there's a nontrivial chance that you or your team members won't survive. You'll be working and living together in a small, confined space for several years. You'll be isolated from your family and friends, and even from "headquarters" (HQ). When you want to talk with the folks at HQ, it will take 20 minutes for your message to reach them and 20 additional minutes for their response to get back to you, so you won't be able to get any real-time guidance from them. Having a bad day? You can't call in sick or go for a walk. You and your team members will be working and living together shoulder to shoulder, every day, for years. How would you feel about being on this team?

Those are the challenges that a long-duration space exploration crew will face in a future mission. You can readily see the teamwork challenges associated with such a mission, and that's why we and others have been conducting research for NASA that will help them choose astronauts who will be good teammates, form a crew with the right mix of capabilities, and prepare the team to withstand and hopefully thrive in adverse conditions.

A trip to outer space presents an extreme teamwork challenge, perhaps a 98 on a 100-point scale of difficulty. We doubt your team faces such an extreme challenge. Most teams don't. But that doesn't mean being on a team is easy. All teams face challenges—even a "simple" project team. Teamwork and collaboration are hard.[1] If you've been working for a while, you've almost certainly experienced a struggling team first-hand. Despite what they sing in the *Lego* movie, everything isn't always "cool when you're part of a team." Being on a bad team can be a painful experience.

THE SCIENCE OF TEAMWORK: THE SEVEN KEY DRIVERS

We've written this book to help you and your colleagues make informed, evidence-based decisions that enable your teams to work well together and produce great results. You'll learn about the science of teamwork and tangible ways to apply that science to be an effective team leader, a great team member, a supportive senior leader, or an impactful consultant.

We're industrial/organizational psychologists (Eduardo is also a human factors psychologist), and for the last 30 years or so we've worked with, provided advice to, and studied teams in a myriad of settings. Some of these teams operate in dangerous settings, such as astronauts, oil rig crews in the North Sea, smoke jumpers (they parachute into fires), and combat teams. Some perform in settings where mistakes can cost people lives, such as medical teams and teams of military aviators. Others do their work in corporate environments, including boards of directors; leadership teams; and sales, manufacturing, finance, and project teams. You'll read about some of our experiences with these teams.

While we've been working with and studying teams, other researchers have been busy as well. There is now a large, growing body of interesting empirical research, much of it conducted by behavioral scientists. We carefully reviewed the research literature and reflected on our experiences, looking for consistent patterns that reveal what truly drives team effectiveness. We discovered seven consistent drivers of team effectiveness. In this chapter, you'll get a high-level preview of the drivers. Subsequent chapters contain a detailed look at each followed by practical tips and tools. But first, let's clarify what we mean by a "highly effective team."

---

1. Technically, teamwork is a specific form of collaboration but throughout the book we use the terms "teamwork" and "collaboration" interchangeably.

HIGHLY EFFECTIVE TEAMS

A highly effective team is, first of all, a "team." We define a team as:

- Two or more people,
- Who interact with one another,
- In situations where at least some members need to rely on other team members at least some of the time,
- Sharing a common (or at least somewhat overlapping) sense of purpose or goals, and
- Are viewed as a unit by others and/or themselves (i.e., some of what they do could be legitimately attributed to them as a unit).

A group of people who work together in the same room is not necessarily a team. Simply sharing workspace or performing similar tasks doesn't constitute being a team. But a team need not be a neatly defined entity with clearly assigned roles, stable membership, and a singular goal fully shared by all team members. Most "teams" in organizational settings are a good bit messier but still meet our definition of a team.

A highly effective team is one that demonstrates sustained performance, team resilience, and ongoing vitality. If a team frivolously expends resources and spends all its "chips" to hit a short-term goal and, in so doing, degrades its future capabilities and performance, we would not consider it highly effective. If a team produces positive results when conditions are favorable but crumbles when things get tough or takes an extremely long time to rebound from negative events, we would not consider it to be highly effective. And, if a team burns out its team members and therefore lacks the vitality needed to adapt, persevere, and innovate going forward, we would not consider it a highly effective team. Short-term results are an imperfect indicator of team effectiveness.

Our focus is on identifying what enables teams to be highly effective and not simply capable of short-term success or performing well only when conditions are favorable.

Team effectiveness, as we define it, has three components:

- **Sustained performance**—Generating positive results over time
- **Team resilience**—Working through challenges and bouncing back from adversity
- **Vitality**—Maintaining energy, vibrancy, and resources needed for future success

---

Table 1.1. Key Questions about the Seven Drivers

Driver	Fundamental Question
1. Capability	Do we have the right people with the right mix of **knowledge, skills**, and other attributes?
2. Cooperation	Do team members possess the right **beliefs and attitudes** about their team?
3. Coordination	Are team members exhibiting the necessary **teamwork behaviors** for team success?
4. Communication	Do team members **communicate** effectively with each other and with people outside the team?
5. Cognition	Do team members possess a **shared understanding** about key factors such as priorities, roles, and vision?
6. Coaching	Does the leader and/or team members demonstrate the necessary **leadership** behaviors?
7. Conditions	Is the **context** in which the team operates favorable for performing effectively (e.g., ample resources, supportive culture)?

THE SEVEN DRIVERS OF TEAM EFFECTIVENESS

What really creates team effectiveness? Seven drivers consistently make a difference. At times, one may be more important than another, but all play a role in the success of almost any team. Table 1.1 lists these drivers along with a fundamental question for each.

Capability refers to the individual and collective competencies that a team possesses. Does the team have the knowledge, skills, personality, and other personal attributes needed to complete assignments, overcome challenges, and adapt as needed to sustain performance? Sometimes we can anticipate how well a team will perform by examining the team's average capability on a key attribute. Other times the best indicator might be the capability of the strongest or weakest team member or if the team has two people with the capability to perform a critical task.

In chapter 4, you'll learn what the research tells us about capabilities, including five fundamental skills and four personal attributes that contribute to teamwork, along with three toxic traits you'll want to avoid.

> **Capability is about having ample horsepower.** If your team lacks critical competencies, it will be difficult to succeed.

Cooperation refers to the attitudes and beliefs that individuals bring to the team each day. What do they think about *this* team and the people on it? Do they think the team can succeed? Do they trust one another? Do they believe they can be "genuine" with other members on the team? Are they committed to the team and the work they do?

People join a team with general beliefs about working on a team, shaped in part by past experiences and in part by their own personalities and propensities. Over time, they learn about their new team and develop attitudes about that team and specific team members. Together these influence their willingness to engage in teamwork behaviors. As we'll see, research shows that mindset matters. For example, when team members collectively believe that their team is likely to succeed, it boosts the team's effectiveness.

In some cases, all that is needed is for team members to be civil with one another and not get in each other's way—yet even that requires a certain mindset. In other instances, far more teamwork is needed, and team members must be willing to step up and work as a team.

In chapter 5, you'll learn what the research tells us about four distinct cooperative beliefs and how you can help them emerge—trust, psychological safety, collective efficacy, and cohesion.

> **Cooperation is about mindset**—beliefs and attitudes about my teammates and my team.

Coordination is at the heart of teamwork; it refers to the teamwork behaviors that a team needs to demonstrate to be highly effective. The exact behaviors can vary from team to team or even across situations, but almost all teams need to maintain situation awareness, back up or fill in for one another, adapt, and manage team emotions.

Some teams struggle because they don't know the teamwork behaviors they need to exhibit. As a simple example, on a senior leadership team, when someone is unable to attend a meeting, who will provide that person with a briefing of what transpired? Is there an awareness that someone needs to fill in for that person and provide a form of backup? Knowing the necessary behaviors is part of the equation, but then the real question is whether team members take those actions on a consistent basis.

In chapter 6, you'll learn what the research tells us about the four most important coordination behaviors and the three things that effective teams tend to monitor.

> **Coordination is about behavior**, teammates demonstrating the right teamwork behaviors. It is about actions not attitudes.

Communication refers to information exchange within a team as well as with individuals and groups outside the team. It is not simply talking to one another; more communication isn't always better. But the way a team communicates drives its effectiveness; poor communications can doom a team. Communications are needed to ensure team members have the information they need and that they maintain proper awareness. Moreover, the way in which a team communicates with outsiders—for example, with its partners, sponsors, and customers—greatly influences relationship quality, so we discuss "boundary spanning" or sustaining relations with key stakeholders in the chapter on communications.

In chapter 7, you'll learn what the research tells us about the importance of communicating unique information, the value of closed-loop communications, and how to be alert for the biggest communication obstacles.

> **Communication is about information exchange**—to accomplish work, maintain awareness, and foster positive relationships both within and outside the team.

Cognition refers to the extent to which team members possess a shared or at least a complementary understanding about key factors. Cognition as described in this book isn't about an individual's attitudes or mindset but instead refers to the overall team. If we were to interview each person on your team separately, what would they say about the team's priorities? About who is responsible for certain tasks or who gets to make certain decisions?

When a team has conflicting or unreconciled points of view on priorities, roles, or how to handle certain situations, it can adversely affect its ability to coordinate and perform effectively. In contrast, when a team possesses what psychologists call "shared mental models," it often results in better performance. Another way to think about cognition is whether your team members are all "on the same page."

In chapter 8, you'll learn what the research tells us about the eight types of shared cognitions and the questions you should want all your team members to be able to answer in a similar way.

> **Cognition is about shared awareness and understanding**—for example, about priorities, roles, the situation, and expectations.

Conditions refers to the context in which the team operates. No team operates in a vacuum, and the environment can be an enabler and/or an inhibitor of team effectiveness. Local conditions such as resource availability, degree of autonomy, work environment, and time availability can influence team performance. And broader conditions can help promote and sustain teamwork or they can inhibit and constrain it. For example, organizational policies and practices, including performance management and compensation practices, create expectations about teamwork. The climate in which the team is embedded also matters. Is the organization one where people typically feel safe speaking up? Is the team being supported by the leadership above them?

Sometimes the cues are obvious. For example, insufficient resources is a powerful signal to a project team that their project isn't very important. Other cues are more subtle. Who gets promoted in the organization? Team players? Selfish people, as long as they produce results? Collectively, the conditions surrounding a team send signals about whether coordination is encouraged, accepted, or discouraged in the organization. It is critical to monitor conditions and, where possible, take actions to ensure they support team success—or at least try to remove obvious impediments.

In chapter 9, you'll learn what the research tells us about six key organizational conditions, three key senior leadership conditions, and four team-specific local conditions that greatly influence team effectiveness.

> **Conditions are about the environment in which the team is embedded**— they send signals that either support or inhibit teamwork and performance.

Coaching refers to leadership. Without question, leadership matters. A good leader can help a team be more successful, and as anyone who ever worked for a poor leader can attest, bad leadership can not only create a huge performance obstacle; it can also make being on a team quite unpleasant (which affects future beliefs about working in a team!). So there is value in understanding the behaviors effective leaders exhibit and the functions they perform, for example, how they provide advice and promote ongoing team learning.

But leadership isn't just for leaders. More and more frequently we see the need for team members to step up and perform some leadership functions, what researchers refer to as "shared leadership." Shared leadership doesn't involve appointing an additional leader but is more about informal behaviors. As organizational structures get flatter and managers oversee larger groups of individuals, a leader can't see everything and won't always be available to give feedback or help her team members—that's why some degree of shared leadership is often needed.

In chapter 10, you'll learn what the research tells us about the seven essential leadership functions that must be fulfilled on a team, along with practical insights from three empirically tested leadership approaches (and one derived from our experiences).

> **Coaching is about leadership**—the leader as well as team members demonstrating effective leadership behaviors.

How do the drivers relate to one another? As shown in Figure 1.1, they are not independent. For example, information sharing (communications) facilitates the development of shared understanding (cognitions), which in turn makes it easier to back up one another when needed (coordination). Research shows that all of the drivers can influence team effectiveness.

We want to emphasize three key points. First, cooperation or mindset tends to emerge from the other six drivers. As a team member, do I think my team can succeed? Do I trust my team members? The emergence of those beliefs depends on the talent on the team, the extent to which we coordinate our work and communicate effectively, the degree to which we have a shared understanding of roles and priorities, our access to resources, and various leadership behaviors. Attitudes such as trust and collective efficacy emerge from doing the other things well. And, in

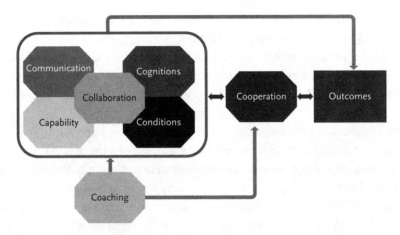

Figure 1.1. How the seven drivers of team effectiveness relate to one another.

turn, those cooperative attitudes can influence the other drivers. For example, when we trust one another, it becomes easier for me to take the time to help you out—and you are more likely to accept my help.

Second, coaching plays a central role in team effectiveness. A key focus for any team leader should be to ensure their team has enough of the other six drivers to be able to sustain effective performance.

Third, the research shows that each of the drivers can directly influence important outcomes such as performance, quality, and innovation. And success begets positive attitudes. When a team is performing effectively and accomplishing its goals, it tends to reinforce positive attitudes. We'll allude to these relationships throughout the book.

GETTING THE MOST OUT OF THIS BOOK

The book is divided into three parts. Of course, we'd like you to read the book cover to cover, but you don't have to.

The first part provides the context for the rest of the book. If you read the next two chapters you'll find evidence with which to make a compelling case that teamwork is a business imperative, be better prepared to avoid five common teamwork myths that can lead to bad decisions, learn how teams differ and why that's important, and be better equipped to understand the research described throughout the book.

The middle part of the book, chapters 4 through 10, describes the science of teamwork. Each chapter highlights one of the seven drivers and is full of research findings and insights, along with examples from teams in action. This section is evidence-based but easy to read—not too geeky but not oversimplified either.

We believe anyone who leads a team, works on a team, or supports a team in any way should know what really drives team performance. That knowledge can keep you from being unduly influenced by what sounds logical (but is wrong), is easy to understand (but is too simplistic), or is consistent with what you have been led to believe (but is actually a myth). So, we hope you'll read the middle part of the book, but if you want to get immediately to the punchline to learn "What I should do?" you can jump directly to the third part of the book. Chapter 11 summarizes key points about the science of teamwork. Chapters 12 through 15 contain role-specific advice for team leaders, team members, internal or external consultants, and senior leaders, respectively. If you choose to jump ahead, we won't judge you! But you'll miss out on learning some really useful things about the nature of teams in Part I and about the science of teamwork in Part II.

If after reading the book you want to share what you've learned with a leader who has a limited amount of time, guide them to read chapter 11 and then either chapter 12 (if they are a team leader) or chapter 14 (if they are a senior leader). At the end of the book you'll also find a set of tools, including a list of desirable team member competencies, tips for conducting a team debrief, questions for reviewing the conditions that foster or inhibit teamwork (e.g., policies, senior leader behaviors, and resources), a quick diagnostic tool, and a matrix with practical ideas for addressing a broad array of teamwork challenges.

One final thought for getting the most out of this book: we encourage you to identify a team you can think about as you read the book. It could be a team you are a member of or one you lead, but having a specific team in mind will be helpful when we guide you to think about key findings throughout the book.

CHAPTER 2
Busting a Few Teamwork Myths

On September 7, 2015 the Boston Red Sox were playing the Philadelphia Phillies on a beautiful sunny afternoon at historic Fenway Park. In the top of the fourth inning, with the Sox leading 6 to 1, rookie Red Sox pitcher Eduardo Rodriguez threw a fastball on the outer half of the plate to Phillies first baseman Darin Ruf. Ruf swung and hit the baseball, hard. The ball launched off Ruf's bat at over 100 mph, headed toward the deepest part of Fenway Park in right center field, a tricky area known as the Triangle, where the bullpen wall juts out precipitously into the field. Five-tenths of a second after the ball left Ruf's bat, Red Sox center fielder Mookie Betts broke into a run, accelerating to a top speed of over 18 miles per hour in 4.3 seconds, and reached up over the edge of the wall, snatching the ball out of the air at the last moment to save a homerun. Red Sox announcers Don Orsillo and Jerry Remy described Betts's basket-style catch as a great individual play, showing "great courage" and "great skill."

Although this appeared to be just a great individual play, a closer look (toward the end of this chapter) reveals how the play was actually the culmination of a series of team-related elements. This is often the case in work settings as well. We should care about teamwork because most business successes involve contributions from various people working together effectively—even when it might first appear that it was simply due to individual excellence.

Perhaps you like to work in a team. According to a survey of 23,000 employees conducted by CEB, a global research and advisory firm, most people say they want to work collaboratively, although obstacles often get in the way. But whether you like or dread being on teams, you'll almost certainly be on many teams in your career—perhaps serving as a team leader. There's a good chance you'll be on more than one team at a time; maybe you'll be on a departmental team while also leading a project team. And looking forward, the odds are that you'll be expected to collaborate and work in teams even more frequently.

Organizations are becoming flatter and more matrixed with fewer layers of management. This type of organizational design heightens the need for teamwork. Over two-thirds of the respondents in the CEB survey reported that collaboration requirements are increasing in their organization. And in a widely cited *Harvard Business Review* article, Rob Cross, Reb Rebele, and Adam Grant reported that time spent in collaborative activities has grown by 50%! Looking forward, in a Deloitte study of over 7000 companies from over 130 countries, business leaders said they expect to use team-based structures even more frequently as an organizational design strategy. Simply stated, there will be fewer opportunities to work alone.

Companies form and disband work teams, cross-functional teams, project teams, and even virtual teams with great regularity. Many of these teams struggle.

- Over 90% of employees believe teams are critical to the success of their organization but less than 25% of them consider their own teams to be very effective, according to Liane Davie, author of *You First: Inspire Your Team to Grow Up, Get Along, and Get Stuff Done.*
- Over 60% of software project teams deliver behind schedule, and almost half come in over budget, as reported by journalist Po Bronson.
- Team-related problems contribute to almost 50% of the failures in business start-ups—either due to the composition of the leadership team or how they work together, as revealed in a series of postmortems collected by CB Insights, a business intelligence firm.
- Teamwork breakdowns are one of the three leading causes of safety problems in hospitals according to an Institute of Medicine study.
- Less than 25% of executives feel confident in their ability to build cross-functional teams, as reported by Deloitte.

Working as a team can have great benefits, but it isn't easy.

Each team experience, good or bad, can make a person more or less eager to be on teams in the future. Having a bad teamwork experience makes you less inclined to take on another team assignment. It starts in school. Remember when the teacher gave you a team assignment? You were told that your team would receive one grade. Freddie, the kid who was loafing and didn't come to any of your team meetings would get the same grade you do. And your teacher probably didn't give your team any advice or training on how to work as a team, although perhaps he told you to "play nice." If your team got a C, you were angry that others who didn't pull their weight hurt your grade. And even if your team received an A+, you might have been resentful that the loafer also received that grade. Bad team experiences can sour you about teams in general. When you subsequently graduate and get a job, your new boss says, "Welcome, here's your desk" and then gives you a team assignment. How enthusiastic are you? You may not be joining that team with the best attitude.

According to a Graduate Management Admission Council survey, less than 15% of US students prefer to learn in team settings (about 20% of Chinese students prefer it, which, while higher, is still a surprisingly low number for a more collectively oriented society). We suspect that team learning may be unpopular because without the right preparation and awareness most student teams don't work well together, so the team experiences aren't positive. Interestingly, when Scott and his colleagues Erik Eddy and John Mathieu helped student teams in the business school at Siena College improve their teamwork, not only did their performance improve, but they were also more interested in being on a team in the future—and they felt more ready to do so. Positive team experiences beget positive attitudes.

Unlike at school, where the worst case is a bad grade, in the workplace a struggling team can cause problems for the business. But in both contexts, it has an adverse effect on individuals. Why is being on a bad team so disconcerting? Psychologists, like Erica Boothby and her colleagues, have shown that sharing an experience with others amplifies the intensity of the experience. Good things seem better and bad things feel worse. The chocolate that you eat in a room with other people tastes better than when you eat it alone. Similarly, failing or succeeding as a team is amplified in comparison with doing so alone. We respond more intensely to team experiences—good and bad.

There are many opinions about what makes teams work. Some are well-grounded; most are pure conjecture. If you've been on a few teams, you almost certainly have developed your own implicit "theory" of teamwork or at least a set of beliefs about teaming. The following are a few beliefs that we've heard recently as we talked with people about their teams. We gave each of these a name:

- "It's really important that we spend time together outside of work and learn to get along" (the **like each other** theory).
- "The key is to talk it out—you can't hold anything back or the team won't improve" (the **openness** theory).
- "It's all about the chemistry. You know really quickly if the team will click" (the **magic** theory).
- "If you leave me alone, I'll get it done" (the **minimize interference** theory).
- "The leader needs to be tough, set the direction, and hold everyone accountable" (the **strong leader** theory).

Do any of these resonate with you? Are any of them valid? As we've alluded to earlier, there's a strong, growing body of research about teams that can inform us and can help us crack the code—so we can move beyond hunches to advice grounded in science. Psychologists, neuroscientists, behavioral economists, sociologists, and human factors experts are producing new research findings about teams all the time. The cumulative findings from that research can guide our actions and help us avoid things that sound clever but don't really drive team effectiveness. The good news is there's an emerging science of teamwork. It's not perfect, and it's still developing, but we do know a lot. For example, we know that the commonly held beliefs above aren't the answer.

The best teams aren't great on day 1. They learn from their experiences and make smart adjustments—they self-correct over time. Research has consistently shown that team adaptation boosts team performance. Knowing what really drives team performance can enable you and your teams to make smart adjustments. That knowledge can help you be a better team leader and even a better team member.

WHAT IS A META-ANALYSIS?

As we describe the research, at times we'll refer to "meta-analysis." In fact, we allude to over 35 different meta-analyses in this book. In case you're unfamiliar with the term, here's a brief description.

Science is conducted one study at a time. A researcher develops a hypothesis, designs a study and gathers data to test the hypothesis, analyzes the data, and then writes up and publishes the findings. After enough research-ers have studied a topic, someone will review all the research and attempt to summarize what it means.

Meta-analysis is a statistical technique for quantitatively combining the results from prior studies. You can think of it as the weighted average of find-ings across studies. It also reveals if the findings are consistent and, if not, why not. Because a meta-analysis is based on multiple studies, it doesn't rely too heavily on any single study. Moreover, while meta-analysis doesn't eliminate subjectivity, it can reduce it. It isn't perfect—for example, a meta-analysis is only as good as the body of research it summarizes—but we are usually more confident when we can make recommendations that are based on a solid meta-analysis. Meta-analyses have been conducted in many fields including medi-cine and psychology; quite a few have examined aspects of team effectiveness. That shows the depth and maturity of the available research on teams.

Before we explore the evidence, let's debunk five false assumptions about teams and teamwork.

MYTH 1: FOCUSING ON TEAMWORK IS A DISTRACTION FROM GETTING REAL WORK DONE

"We don't have time for teamwork. We have a business to run." That is a quote from a leader with whom we worked. His perspective at the time was that teamwork was mainly happy talk and not really related to the work at hand. It made no sense to him to spend any time on team-work. He thought teamwork was about having a team party and going to dinner together. His team was struggling. Why have a party? It was only when he recognized that teamwork is not distinct from getting work done—it is *how* work gets done—that he became willing to focus on boosting teamwork.

There is plenty of evidence that teamwork boosts performance. For example:

- Teams that demonstrate better teamwork processes are 20% to 25% more likely to succeed, as revealed in a meta-analysis by Jeff LePine and his colleagues that combined results from 130 previous studies.
- Team training improves on-the-job performance by an average of 7%. When teams learn how to work as a team they perform better, as shown in a meta-analysis involving 2,650 teams conducted by

Eduardo and his colleagues and in a more recent meta-analysis that examined team training in healthcare.

- Organizations that boosted their collaborative performance had 5% greater annual revenue increases than those emphasizing individual achievement alone, according to a Corporate Executive Board report.

E. O. Wilson, the famous biologist and myrmecologist (he studies ants), suggested that while selfish individuals might defeat altruistic individuals, groups of collaborators are likely to be victorious over groups of selfish people. In his book, *The Social Conquest of Earth*, he intimated that collaboration may be the result of group evolution (analogous to individual evolution). Tribes that collaborated won. The same is seen in the insect world, his primary focus as a researcher; insects that collaborate prevail.

We're not prepared to say that human collaboration is a function of group evolution or that we're intrinsically drawn to collaborate, although it is certainly a thought-provoking concept. But based on the research, we are comfortable saying that when there is a need to work together it makes sense to focus some attention on teamwork—it isn't a distraction; it's a strategic advantage.

> **Fact**: Teamwork boosts performance.

MYTH 2: IF TEAM MEMBERS LIKE EACH OTHER AND MAINTAIN HARMONY, THE TEAM WILL BE SUCCESSFUL

It is certainly more pleasant to work with people you like than with people you dislike. But liking your teammates isn't a prerequisite to team effectiveness. It's how you work together that matters. For example, the venerable team researcher Richard Hackman found that "grumpy" orchestras often performed better. If team members have a clear understanding of and an agreement about how they will perform together, they can succeed, even if they may not appear to be the best of friends.

One team-building trap associated with this myth is assuming that simply spending time together away from work will necessarily make a team better. Google uses teams extensively. Not surprisingly, some of their teams perform better than others, and they felt it was important to find out why. Googlers consider themselves experts in discerning patterns in data, so they conducted a two-year, data-driven study of their teams they called Project Aristotle. One of their hypotheses going into the study was that on the best teams, team members spent more time hanging out together. They found no support for that hypothesis.

In most cases, it won't hurt, but if the problems your team faces are related to issues such as role ambiguity, competing priorities, or insufficient talent, please don't expect a nice dinner together or a weekend retreat socializing to cure it. So, go to dinner with your team, have fun experiences together if you'd like. But please do so with reasonable expectations—it won't resolve significant team performance problems.

Moreover, a little discord isn't always bad. Avoiding conflict isn't the answer. We'll see later how conflict can help a team when it is about the right issues and is handled in the right way. Seeking to perpetually maintain harmony can result in team members being too nice with one another and may prevent the team from acknowledging concerns and making necessary adjustments.

> **Fact:** It doesn't hurt to be friendly with your teammates, but it's not a prerequisite for team effectiveness.

MYTH 3: BEING A TEAM PLAYER MEANS SUPPRESSING INDIVIDUAL EXCELLENCE

It is easy to accept the false dichotomy that I can either look out for myself or be a team player, but I can't do both. That's nonsense. Either–or thinking like that is very "Western"—what is needed is more dialectical thinking about this. You can strive for individual excellence, continuing to boost your own capabilities, while simultaneously caring about your team and enabling your teammates to be successful.

It is also easy to assume that being perceived as a star should boost one's career. But times are changing; in many organizations there is less tolerance of egotistical stars. Most organizations expect people to show they are both personally competent and that they can be team players. NASA is no longer looking for the "right stuff" or individual superheroes. They want astronauts who are individually excellent and also great team players who can work well with others and elevate the people around them.

The flip side is true as well. Most companies acknowledge that teamwork is a critical, desirable competency. But being a team player isn't enough, you need to be individually competent as well.

Michael Jordan is arguably the best basketball player in history, certainly one of the top five all-time greats. At the beginning of his career he posted gaudy individual scoring statistics, but his teams lost. It was only later when he began to elevate his teammates, that the Bulls started winning championships.

There doesn't appear to be a correlation between individual competence and teamwork orientation. Rob Cross and his colleagues reported that about 50% of top collaborators are also deemed to be top performers. So being a great collaborator doesn't guarantee you'll be viewed as a top performer, but it doesn't preclude it either (as long as you don't neglect your individual task assignments). A meta-analysis of over 160 previous studies conducted by Nathan Podsakoff revealed that employees who demonstrate more helpful, supportive behaviors in the workplace (what they referred to as "organizational citizenship behaviors") typically receive higher performance evaluations and are more likely to be recommended for rewards by their boss. You can be both a strong individual contributor and a strong team player—and both can be career enhancing.

> **Fact**: You can be a team player and individually excellent—and should strive for both.

MYTH 4: TEAMWORK CAN OVERCOME A SIGNIFICANT LACK OF TALENT

In 1976, the movie *The Bad News Bears* featured a youth baseball team made up of mostly untalented misfits, who somehow pull together to win despite their dearth of talent. It was funny and uplifting, but it doesn't ring true (not that it was intended to depict reality!). In the real world, sports and business teams with such a large talent deficit almost never win. Competence and capability matter. Teamwork can't overcome a significant lack of talent. For example, if team members are simply incapable of performing their work assignments adequately, better teamwork won't solve the problem. Teamwork can give your team a bump—at times, a big bump—but the team needs at least "sufficient" talent and expertise.

As we'll see later, the relationship between talent, teamwork, and performance is actually a bit complex (spoiler alert: simply adding stars won't always boost team performance). And you shouldn't assume that individual excellence is enough unless you are working on tasks that require no coordination. Teamwork does matter, but so does talent.

> **Fact**: Competence matters. It is difficult if not impossible to overcome a dearth of talent through teamwork. Sometimes you need new team members.

MYTH 5: TEAMS ARE ALWAYS THE ANSWER

By now you can tell that we believe in the power of teamwork. But let's be really clear—teams are not a panacea. Not all work should be performed in teams. We've seen tasks that should have been handled by individuals assigned to committees and task forces with dire consequences. A team is not always the answer. When used inappropriately, teams can lead to suppression of innovation, social loafing, delays, and inefficiency.

We're not advocating the formation of more teams. Don't default to forming a team without ample thought about whether a team is the right solution. When a team is asked to do something that would be better handled by an individual, the experience is likely to be bad, the results are likely to be suboptimal, and people will incorrectly assume that teams don't work. Teams work when they are deployed for the right reasons.

So be smart about whether a team is needed. And when a team is formed, use the key drivers to help ensure the team works as it should.

> **Fact**: Some work is better performed individually or by loose couplings of individuals, not by formal teams.

Throughout the book we share research findings with you from the science of teamwork and examples of some of those principles in action. While the research reveals some universal truths about teams, unfortunately, teamwork is too complex to describe in a handful of "simple truths." Certain recommendations are applicable for some but not all types of teams. So, prior to exploring the drivers of teamwork, we first consider the meaningful ways in which teams differ from one another.

Let's wrap up this chapter by revisiting our opening story about Mookie Betts and the Red Sox. Remember, he made what appeared to be a spectacular, individual athletic play in centerfield. How is this an illustration of team effectiveness and the seven drivers of teamwork?

- **Capability**. There is no doubt Mookie Betts had the skills and ability to make this play. Mookie is a gifted athlete with the speed and hand–eye coordination to perform his job. In 2018, he was named the league's most valuable player. As an aside, he has also bowled seven perfect games and can solve a Rubik's cube in under two minutes. No shortage of capabilities!
- **Cooperation**. On the Red Sox team at that time, there were three young, talented outfielders, Mookie Betts, Rusney Castillo, and Jackie Bradley Jr. They all believed they were capable of being the centerfielder (and we'd speculate probably all wanted to play that position). But their attitude in practice had been to support one another and help each other become better players, even if it meant they weren't chosen to play centerfield. No brooding or griping! They demonstrated solid "teamwork orientation."
- **Coordination**. If you only watched Mookie Betts, it would appear that he was the only active player when the ball left Ruf's bat. But a wide-angle view would show that Rusney Castillo was also running at high speed from left field, positioning himself in the proper place to provide backup if Betts was unable to make the catch and the ball ricocheted off the wall. This allowed Betts to go full speed without worrying about what would happen if the ball evaded him. Incidentally, Castillo had only played left field five times in his professional career prior to this game but he demonstrated perfect, role-specific back-up behavior!
- **Communication**. Rusney wasn't the only teammate who enabled Mookie Betts to make a great "individual" play. The right fielder, Jackie Bradley Jr., also helped tremendously. How? When the ball was hit, he ran toward center field and as Mookie's eyes were focused upwards tracking the baseball, Jackie shouted out how far Mookie was from the wall. Knowing he was 20 feet or 5 feet from the wall allowed Mookie to run at high speed "safely." Betts had suffered an injury on a similar play earlier in the year, so without those communications

about distance, he would likely have become nervous and slowed down to avoid hitting the wall.

- **Cognition**. A good outfield possesses a shared "if–then" mental model about what to do in certain situations. This trio of outfielders knew that "if" the ball is hit in the right centerfield gap, "then" each person has a specific role to play. Bradley's view was that originally he and Mookie "both were attacking it" then he quickly realized that Mookie "had the best angle on it" at which point all three outfielders had a shared understanding of the situation and evoked a synchronized response based on that awareness.

- **Coaching**. Their shared awareness didn't happen by chance. Remember, Rusney Castillo had very little experience playing left field. Fortunately, Red Sox outfield instructor Arnie Beyeler had been working with the outfielders, coaching them on how to handle certain situations, including this particular one. "Those are the kind of things to me that we look at," Beyeler said. "Backing up bases, the little stuff of guys helping each other out, them working as a group, cutting balls off, taking deep angles, holding balls to singles." Coaching prepared the outfielders to make this play in a coordinated manner.

- **Conditions**. This Red Sox team operated within in a culture in which teamwork was the norm. That wasn't always true. There was a time when the Red Sox were known as a group of individuals who didn't play as a team. It was epitomized by the phrase, "25 players, 25 taxis," suggesting that each player went his own way after the game (and, at times, during the game!). When a prior manager (Bobby Valentine) called out a Red Sox player in the press rather than behind closed doors (something that tends to kill psychological safety), another team member said, "That's not the way we go about our stuff around here." The conditions at that time were not conducive to cooperation. In contrast, the play Mookie made was a collective effort, in part enabled by an organizational expectation of playing as a team.

The lesson here: Behind most individual displays of excellence you'll find subtle teamwork contributions that made it possible.

CHAPTER 3

Teams Are Not All the Same

Let's consider two types of teams that you are probably familiar with, a senior leadership team (SLT) and a manufacturing production team. The SLT comes together periodically to establish the direction of the company, make strategic resource allocation decisions, assess progress, and ensure adequate alignment across units. Team members do not work together or rely on one another to perform their jobs on a daily basis. In fact, each member of the SLT is not only a member of that team, but also represents, and is typically the leader of, a different function or business unit.

In contrast, the manufacturing team works together every day, in well-defined roles, to ensure adequate production, quality, and safety levels for their shift. They work shoulder to shoulder and rely on one another to perform their jobs and hit their goals.

Do the same factors drive team effectiveness in these two teams? The answer is yes and no. Yes, because the same seven key drivers impact the effectiveness of both teams. No, because they manifest themselves in different ways.

For instance, one of the drivers is communication. While both teams need to communicate to be successful, their keys to successful communication are quite different. What happens if the SLT meets, makes a collective decision, and then afterwards the chief financial and chief marketing officers communicate conflicting messages to their employees? When members of the SLT spread a message that is discordant with the agreements reached by the team, it creates confusion and intensifies factions. The resulting "us–them" problems that inevitably arise then make their way back up to the senior team, reducing trust, polarizing SLT members, and adversely affecting subsequent team decision-making. In highly effective leadership teams, team members convey a *generally* unified message about agreed upon priorities. Note that we say "generally" rather than "fully" unified because we've yet to see a SLT that didn't slip on occasion!

In comparison, the manufacturing team has less need to communicate a unified message to people outside. Team members work together and rely on each other on a daily basis, so clear, consistent communications within the team are critical. When they do communicate with people outside their team, a primary focus is on sharing information with the next shift, for example, about equipment problems they encountered. These "external" communications are typically handled by designated members of each shift who serve as an information conduit for their team, rather than all team members being responsible for conveying a common message, as was the case for the leadership team. Communication is important for both types of teams, just in different ways. Teams are not all the same.

The research reveals some universal findings about teamwork that apply to any team, and we will share those. It would be great if that was all you needed to know. It that were true, it would certainly make it easier to be a team leader and would make this book much shorter! But unfortunately, it's not that simple. Teams and teamwork are more complex and nuanced.

Teams can differ in countless ways, but a few of these differences are particularly important. Perhaps the most important distinction between teams is the extent to which team members must rely on one another. The research findings are different for teams whose members work fairly independently than for teams with a high degree of interdependency among team members. In the following discussion, we examine this distinction in detail and briefly describe four other ones that will help us interpret the science of teamwork throughout in the book.

It is best to think of these five distinctions as sliding scales, rather than simply "on" or "off." As we describe the reliance, membership stability, work requirements, proximity, and similarity continua we encourage you to conduct a thought experiment. Ask yourself, "Where does my team currently fall on each continuum?"

THE RELIANCE CONTINUUM: FROM INDEPENDENT TO INTERDEPENDENT

The key question here is, "To what extent must team members rely on one another and coordinate with other team members to accomplish their work?" If there are no interdependencies, then it is not a team, simply a group of individuals. But a team can range from fairly independent to highly interdependent (Figure 3.1).

When interdependence is low, team members can perhaps help one another prepare and "cheer" for one another, but when they perform their work, they do so independently. Other team members are generally unable to help them. Many sales teams operate toward the low end of this continuum.

A regional sales team we worked with exemplifies how low interdependency teams operate. Members of this team participate in training together. Periodically they meet to update one another and to share experiences, but most of their time is spent in the field, individually working their territory. When a salesperson is trying to make a sale, she is on her own. Ask any person on the team, "How much have you sold this period" and they can tell you, often down to the decimal point. But they probably can't tell you the total sales for the region. The way the company evaluates the team is also quite revealing. The company determines if the regional sales team met its quota by adding up all the sales from each individual's territory. This is a classic example of a team with low interdependence.

As we move from left to right on the continuum, we find teams in which some members must coordinate with other team members some of the time, but not everyone is required to coordinate with all other team members on a regular basis. Team members may need to rely on one another at certain points in time or in certain circumstances. In teams toward the middle of the continuum, some team members work fairly independently at least some of the time. Think of this as a medium or moderate degree of interdependence.

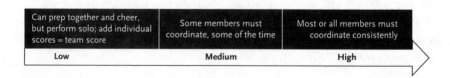

Figure 3.1. The reliance continuum.

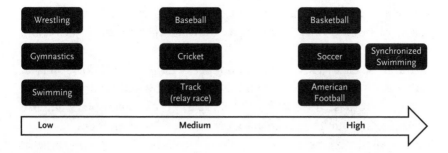

Figure 3.2. Sports teams across the reliance continuum.

Finally, on the right side of the continuum are teams with high interdependencies. In these teams, most, if not all, team members work together on a consistent basis and regularly rely on each other to ensure personal and team success.

At some point in your career you've probably heard the expression, "Business is a team sport." We recently had a great dinner at the Union Square Café in New York. Their feedback card states, "Hospitality is a team sport." A bit trite perhaps, but there is a lot of truth to that statement, and their owner was among the first to do away with tipping and to raise prices so that the full restaurant team, waiters and kitchen staff, could be rewarded as a team.

In a given business setting, what type of team sport are we talking about? A useful way to illustrate the reliance continuum is by considering different types of sports teams (Figure 3.2). Which of these does your team most resemble?

Low Interdependence

On the left end of the continuum are teams such as wrestling, gymnastics, and swimming teams. If we're on a wrestling team together, you can help me during practice but when I'm "doing my job," I'm on my own. And unless we are professional tag team wrestling partners, no one else on the wrestling team can help me while I'm on the mat, other than cheering for me. Let's consider a collegiate wrestling match between Iowa and Penn State universities. How do they determine the winning team? First, the winner of each individual match gets three to six points, depending on whether they pinned their opponent or won by a decision. After all the individual matches are complete, simply add up each of the individual scores to yield team scores. The team with the most points wins. That sounds a lot like that regional sales team, doesn't it?

But to be clear, a low interdependence team is still a team. Golf is an individual sport—no one can fill in for you to hit a difficult shot, there is no one to pass the ball to, and, in fact, no one even plays defense against you! But there can be some team-related elements as well. Jordan Speith is one of the world's best golfers. He has won three of golf's four major championships, including the 2017 British Open, and was named PGA Player of the Year in 2015. Interestingly, he talks about golf as if it more than just an individual sport. In a news conference prior to a major golf tournament, Jordan used the word "we" 29 times to refer to his actions, saying things like "*We* have been improving each year in the major championships." He views others around him as part of his team, a team that shares the goal of helping him become the best player in the world. His team includes his manager, his swing coach, his caddie, and his trainer. He is the only one on the team who plays golf for a living, but his team helps prepare him, and he and his caddie interact on the course. And if his coach, his caddie, and his trainer are not on the same page, it will be reflected in his performance. The world may not view "Team Spieth" as a team, but Jordan seems to. He also recognizes that much of what he does is individual, and he takes responsibility for his performance. You'll probably never hear him say, "*We* missed a putt."

Medium Interdependence

In the middle of the continuum are teams such as baseball, cricket, and relay race teams. On these teams there are times when tight coordination is needed among some, but perhaps not all, of the players. In those situations, a player can't perform his job properly or a task may not be completed effectively unless two or more team members are truly in sync.

For example, let's dissect a play during a baseball game—the Hanshin Tigers are playing the Yomiuri Giants. There is a runner on first base with one out in the bottom on the third inning. A ground ball is hit to the pitcher. He fields the ball and spins toward second base, where the shortstop is already moving to cover the base. The pitcher throws the ball to the shortstop who steps on second base and then fires the baseball to the first baseman to complete the double play. If the pitcher's throw was off line, if the shortstop was late getting to second, or if the second baseman thought he was supposed to catch the throw from the pitcher rather than the shortstop, the team would not have completed the double play. Tight coordination was needed among several, but not all, of the nine players on the field. But in the top of the fourth inning, when the shortstop comes up to bat, none of his teammates can help him. He is performing a solo task. Baseball is a combination of independent performances and brief coordinated interludes.

That balance is highly visible in a 4 × 100 relay race. The team is made up of four runners; each runs a 100-meter leg and then passes a baton to the next runner on the team until the final runner crosses the finish line. It is a sport that relies on purely individual performances (no one can help you while you're running your leg of the race) punctuated by three events requiring smooth coordination between two team members. A dropped baton or a pass that occurs outside the designated area means the team is disqualified. Historically, this has been an event in which US teams often excel. From 1912 to 2008, the US men's teams made the finals of every Olympics except one. But in the 2008 Olympics the US team dropped the baton and was disqualified. Their response was admirable. Runners Darvis Patton and Tyson Gay both said, "I take the blame for this." The US coach, Bubba Thornton, was also willing to accept fault, saying "You can put it right on my shoulders." As Thornton noted, each of the athletes had practiced passing and receiving the baton "a million times" in their careers. But unfortunately, they were unable to practice handoffs in the United States prior to the 2008 Olympics because of an injury to Gay's hamstring. Their independent individual performances were fine, but when coordination was needed between Gay and Patton, they weren't ready, and as a result, they failed as a team.

High Interdependence

At the right end of the continuum are sports teams such as soccer, rugby, football, basketball, and hockey (field or ice) teams. In these teams, all the players on the field need to perform in a coordinated manner on a consistent basis. Teammates need one another and rely on one another to a great extent, play after play. The degree of interdependence among the players is high.

Watch a soccer, football, or basketball game, and you'll probably see a few great, "wow-inspiring" individual plays, performed by a single player. A basketball player will make an acrobatic move to elude his defender and then score on an off-balance, twisting shot over a seven-foot tall center. Or a soccer player will dribble past two defenders and curve an arching left-footed shot around the goaltender. On the surface, these acts are the personification of individual excellence. And it might appear that a basketball or soccer team's performance is determined the same way as it is for a sales or wrestling team. Simply add up the points or goals that each player scored—only one player gets credit for a goal or basket—to determine the team's overall team. But while the scoring mechanics are the same, the underlying phenomenon is quite different. A basketball or soccer player, even a great one, relies heavily on his or her teammates. In basketball, often the reason a player is able to get past his defender is because a teammate set a perfectly timed screen. And the reason another opponent couldn't double team him is because the player he was assigned to guard required his attention. In soccer, even a great goal scorer needs her teammates to pass her the ball in a position where she can do some damage. Of course, there are instances of pure, individual excellence throughout the game, but rarely are such actions as independent as they might appear. Pele, perhaps the greatest soccer player of all time, said it quite succinctly, "No individual can win a game by himself."

Sometimes coordination can be planned. Football teams have play-books filled with diagrams of plays that stipulate who is supposed to go where, often specifying second and third options. Every player needs to know the play—if I think we are going to run the football and you think we are going to pass it, things will go very badly. Perhaps the ultimate example of planned coordination in sports occurs in synchronized swimming. Every team member must know, in advance, exactly where each other swimmer needs to be, as even a misdirected toe is costly. There is no room for improvisation.

In other cases, coordination occurs on a real-time basis. While skating at 20 miles per hour, a hockey player needs to read his teammates and defenders to know where to pass the puck. Defenders on a soccer team need to infer the intent of the attacking team, reaching a common con-clusion so they can spontaneously coordinate their actions and set the opponent offside. Most teams must demonstrate a mix of planned and spontaneous coordination. But even spontaneous coordination is typically founded on shared mental models, which are formed from practicing and playing together. Whether planned, spontaneous, or a combination, a common attribute of teams that fall toward the right side of the continuum is that coordination requirements are continual.

Why Should You Care about the Reliance Continuum?

We need to consider the extent to which team members must rely on one another because the research findings are different for teams that have low versus high coordination requirements. For teams that fall toward the far-left end of the continuum, sometimes all that is needed from a team perspective is for members to be civil with one another and not get in each other's way. In the regional sales team, a few general principles help—don't be a jerk, don't do something that will create a problem for other salespeople in their territories, be constructive in your interactions, and occasionally share a good idea or two during our meetings. That's enough. Perhaps all the team leader needs to do is provide individual feedback when deviant behavior emerges and occasionally host a social event, so team members see each other as real people. But for teams where team members must rely on one another a bit more, they need more than just being civil. They need to be able to pass the baton, know the planned plays, or adjust to one another on the fly. Teamwork and the seven drivers become increasingly critical as we move from left to right on the continuum.

> **Thought Experiment**: Think about your team. To what extent can team members complete their work independently? Using the sports analogy, is your team similar to a wrestling team? Wrestling plus? A baseball team? Baseball plus? A soccer team? Where does it fall on the continuum?

THE MEMBERSHIP STABILITY CONTINUUM: FROM STABLE TO DYNAMIC

Let's look at another way teams can differ from one another. How stable is the membership of your team? Does the composition ever change and, if so, how frequently and how significantly?

Historically, psychologists and other researchers tended to study intact teams with a membership that remained constant throughout the course of the research. While those studies yielded some useful insights, team membership in organizational settings is often more dynamic. A common scenario is for a team to experience periodic changes in membership. The team is formed, and after a few months, a team member is replaced. Another team member becomes unavailable for a period of time, so the team must cover for him, working "one person down," in his absence. Then the team leader is promoted, and a new team leader gets appointed. And when a new task is assigned to the team, an additional person is temporarily assigned to help for a few months. Over the course of a year, a significant proportion of the team's membership has changed. That type of dynamic membership is not uncommon.

The composition of a team can change intentionally, for example, through planned movement such as a promotion, or unintentionally, for instance as the result of unexpected turnover. In some teams, membership changes are continual and can become part of the team's natural rhythm. In other cases, a team's composition may remain quite stable with little or no changes.

A related factor to consider is the life span of the team. Some teams are designed to be ongoing; when formed they don't have an established "expiration date." The senior leadership and manufacturing teams we alluded to earlier are examples of ongoing teams. Other teams are temporary. They are formed for a targeted purpose and expected to disband within a given timeframe. Most task forces and project teams are built as temporary entities, often with an expected life span of weeks or months. The Deloitte study of 7,000 leaders we alluded to in chapter 2 suggests that we can expect to see even greater use of such temporary teams in the future. And some teams are particularly fleeting, such as an airline flight crew or a hospital trauma team. A team is assembled to service passengers flying from London to Hong Kong or to treat a patient who was in a car accident, and after completing their task, they rapidly disband. Such teams are sometimes referred to as "flash teams," given their short life cycle.

Why Should You Care about Membership Stability?

Let's consider one of the seven drivers, cognition. Cognition refers to the extent to which team members possess a common understanding, or a shared mental model, about key factors such as roles, priorities, and individual team member's expertise. Research has shown the importance of these. When team membership is dynamic, it is more difficult to build and sustain shared mental models. If you are leading a team with a rapidly rotating membership or one with a short life span, there are certain actions you may need to take that are different than those you would take leading a stable, ongoing team.

> **Thought Experiment**: Where does your team fall along a continuum of membership stability? Highly stable? Fairly stable? Somewhat dynamic? Highly dynamic? What percentage of people currently on your team were on it six months ago? Will be on it six months from now?

THE TASK CONSISTENCY CONTINUUM: FROM CONSISTENT TO UNPREDICTABLE

The question here is, "How stable and predictable are the team's work requirements?" Does the team perform the same tasks on a consistent basis? Can they establish and rely on stable routines? How frequently and dramatically do work requirements and expectations change? Can they anticipate forthcoming needs?

Why Should You Care about Task Consistency?

When work requirements are constant, a team has the chance to perform key tasks repeatedly, providing many opportunities to learn from experience. A food service crew on board a cruise ship performs a fairly consistent set of tasks. When you are on a cruise, you can probably detect how long the crew has been working together. During an initial "shake out" cruise, when the crew is just starting to work together, service is often quite spotty. But with each passing day that the team works together, if they are receiving constructive feedback, they will work through glitches and build clear and stable shared mental models about roles and "if–then" expectations, and service typically improves.

But many teams work in environments where the task requirements change, either gradually or rapidly. When task requirements evolve slowly over time, a team must make adjustments, but they can typically do so in a planned or orderly manner. In contrast, teams that work in rapidly changing environments experience constant changes to task requirements. Expectations can change unpredictably, so teams that work in a highly dynamic setting must learn to be highly adaptive and flexible.

The degree to which work requirements are consistent or unpredictable has implications for many of the key drivers, including the individual capabilities team members must possess, the extent to which coordinated planning can occur, and the ease with which shared mental models can be formed.

> **Thought Experiment**: Would you describe the work requirements as fairly consistent? Evolving slowly over time? Shifting fairly regularly? Or highly unpredictable? Does the team tend to perform similar tasks over time, or is it more dynamic?

THE PROXIMITY CONTINUUM: FROM CO-LOCATED TO GEOGRAPHICALLY DISPERSED

The primary question to consider here is, "Do team members work in a common location, or are any team members geographically dispersed?" Fifty years ago, it was common for all team members to work together in the same location (e.g., on the manufacturing floor) or down the hall from one another (the SLT), or at least be able to easily meet in the same physical place (all project team members meet in the conference room). Now, that is often not true. Team members may be located across the campus, town, country, or globe.

Why Should You Care about Proximity?

While many technologies can help connect team members who are physically separated, team dynamics are influenced by distance. For example, one of the key drivers is coaching, which we use to refer to leadership. In a geographically dispersed team, the leader is typically unable to see everyone on a regular basis. As a result, a different coaching or leadership approach is often needed, including, for example, a greater degree of shared leadership, a concept we'll explore later in the book.

> **Thought Experiment**. Where along the proximity continuum does your team fall? Are you all working in the same location? Slightly dispersed? Largely or fully dispersed?

THE SIMILARITY CONTINUUM: FROM COMMON TO UNIQUE EXPERTISE/PERSPECTIVE

The key question here is, "To what extent does the team consist of individuals who possess similar expertise?" A team can be "designed" with similar or complimentary roles. When all the positions on the team are quite similar, job requirements are likely to be similar, and team members are likely to share similar educational backgrounds. Some team members may have greater levels of experience and expertise, but the work they perform and the functional expertise required are quite similar. The result is a team that is relatively homogeneous. An example of this is a team of actuaries. Actuaries are involved in measuring and managing risk and uncertainty. All members of an actuarial team possess similar degrees (not likely to include any art history majors), a strong common element that they all bring to the table. That doesn't mean that all actuaries are identical, as they may have grown up in different parts of the world, have different personal interests, etc. But relatively speaking, a team of actuaries is likely to be a fairly homogeneous group.

In contrast, some teams are specifically designed to include people with diverse expertise. In the case of a cross-functional team, team members bring different functional expertise and perspective to the work they perform. That is basically the definition of a cross-functional team. When one of the actuaries becomes a member of a cross-functional task force, she is likely to be working with people who possess competencies and perspectives that are quite different than those of her fellow actuaries.

Similarly, consider a project team we supported recently. The team was focused on developing and testing a new retail banking technology. Some team members were bank employees while others worked for the vendor developing the technology. Even if they were all "technologists," the difference in their primary source of affiliation (customer vs. vendor) produced a fundamental disparity in perspective. The cross-functional team and the banking technology teams were far more heterogeneous in their expertise and perspective than the team of actuaries.

Why Should You Care about Similarity?

A team made up of people with a similar background and expertise are likely to share a common "language." That commonality can have positive and negative implications for team dynamics. For example, coordination is one the key drivers. It refers to the teamwork behaviors teams should exhibit, such as backing up or filling in for a teammate. On a team where people occupy similar roles, have similar training, and possess similar expertise, back-up behavior is easier. When one of the actuaries is unavailable, someone else on the team can often fill in. In contrast, in a cross-functional team made up of a representative from finance, information technology, human resources, and marketing, if the finance person can't attend a meeting, who can back them up and provide a financial perspective?

> **Thought Experiment**: Where does your team fall along the similarity continuum? Is the team quite homogeneous? Somewhat diverse? Highly diverse?

Throughout the book, as we delve into the science of teamwork, we will offer some universally applicable, science-based recommendations. But we'll also highlight where the trick to helping your team succeed may depend on the nature of the team, where it falls along the various continua. So, take a look at Table 3.1, consider the nature of your team, and keep your answers in mind as we proceed.

Table 3.1. Five Important Team Distinctions: How Would You Describe Your Team?

Reliance	Most work performed independently (**mostly independent**)	Split of work done independently and work that relies on others (**even split**)	Most members must rely on or coordinate with others much of the time (**mostly interdependent**)	Members consistently rely on or need to coordinate with others (**fully interdependent**)
Membership Stability	Almost all team members remain the same (**very stable**)	People leave or join the team on occasion (**fairly stable**)	People tend to leave or join fairly regularly (**fairly dynamic**)	People constantly leave or join the team (**very dynamic**)
Task Consistency	Work requirements remain constant over time (**consistent requirements**)	Work requirements change slowly over time (**evolving requirements**)	Work requirements change fairly regularly (**shifting requirements**)	Work requirements change rapidly and unpredictably (**unpredictable requirements**)
Proximity	All team members work in the same or a close location (**full co-location**)	Most of the team work in the same or a close location (**mostly co-located**)	Most of the team work in different locations (**mostly dispersed**)	All team members work in different locations (**full dispersion**)
Similarity	All team members share an overlapping area of expertise (**highly similar**)	Most team members share an overlapping area of expertise (**mostly similar**)	Most team members have unique areas of expertise (**fairly unique**)	All team members have unique areas of expertise (**highly unique**)

PART II

The Science of Teamwork

Understanding the Drivers

CHAPTER 4

Capabilities

It Starts with the Right Expertise

Back in the day, the shorter of the two authors (five foot, seven inches on a good hair day) was on an intramural basketball team made up of graduate students and professors. We'd won our first two games and were feeling pretty good about ourselves. We liked one another. We had no star players, but we were readily willing to share the ball without ego getting in the way. We were okay basketball players, good enough to win a few games to start the season. We were also older than all the other teams in the league, and we weren't in the same shape as the other teams that were composed of 18- to 21-year old athletes. During warmups for our third game, we looked across the gym at the team we would be playing that day. They were dunking the ball during warm up drills and were jumping higher, shooting better, and moving faster during practice than we did during our games. On our side of the gym, a few of our players were "warming up" by smoking cigarettes (don't judge; it was the 1980s!). While their team was dunking, our tallest player could just barely touch the rim with a running start. As Hall of Fame basketball coach Red Auerbach noted, "You can't teach height." We'd love to tell you a story of how our team used our superior "experience" and comradery to steal a hard-fought victory that day. But that would truly be a story. In reality, the game was pretty much over by the end of the first half. We simply lacked the talent to perform at a level that matched our competition.

This chapter covers *capability*, by which we mean the knowledge, skills, abilities, and other attributes that team members possess, such as personality. We're not talking about team member attitudes such as motivation or trust that can wax and wane quite suddenly. We focus on those in the chapter on cooperation. In this chapter we are talking about fairly stable competencies and predispositions, in particular those that have been shown to consistently contribute to or detract from team effectiveness.

When you form a team, you bring together people who possess certain capabilities, and if you choose to, you can further develop your team's capabilities through training, feedback, experience, and coaching. While high capability levels don't guarantee team effectiveness, a lack of capability hurts team effectiveness, and a significant dearth of talent (like having short and slow players on our basketball team) can assure failure. But the effect isn't always linear—adding capability won't always translate into better performance. Let's see what the research can tell us about how capability influences team effectiveness.

Thought Experiment. While reading this chapter on capabilities:

- What are the current strengths and limitations of your team with regard to capabilities? Are your gaps more about **task-related** or **teamwork-related** capabilities?
- Would it be worth trying to boost your team's capabilities? If so, what **capabilities** will you focus on?
- How might you boost capabilities? **Training**? Changing team **membership**?

It can be helpful to think about team member capabilities as falling into two main categories: **task-related capabilities** that individuals must possess to be able to perform their work assignments (e.g., the ability to program in JavaScript), and **teamwork-related capabilities** that people need to work and collaborate effectively with one another and that make someone a better teammate (e.g., communication skills). Let's look at task capabilities first.

TASK-RELATED CAPABILITIES

Not everything that appears obvious is true. But we'll start with an obvious and, in this case, true statement: on average, teams composed of individuals with greater expertise in the tasks they are expected to execute will typically outperform teams with less expertise. We know from research dating back to A. J. Lotka's "inverse square law of productivity" in the 1920s (he studied chemical researchers) up through Herman Aguinis's recent examinations of star performers that highly talented people can make great contributions. Task-related capabilities matter.

But, of course, we can't specify a universally applicable set of task capabilities that every team must possess as, by definition, those requirements are contingent on the tasks the team needs to complete. A silicon chip manufacturing team at Intel performs different tasks than a potato chip manufacturing team at Frito-Lay, and as a result they need different task-related capabilities (although both teams may need to possess quality control skills). Fortunately, it is relatively easy to identify and specify task capability requirements in teams with high task consistency. For example, the task-related competencies needed to be an effective member of a lawn care team include mowing, trimming, planting, and fertilizing, along with customer service skills for those team members who interact with homeowners. However, in more dynamic settings with shifting or unpredictable requirements, for example, in many technology teams, it can be much more challenging to anticipate the task-related capabilities that will be needed next year.

But whether your team experiences high, low, or moderate task consistency, if it is truly lacking key task capabilities, you'll need to do something—add or replace team members, provide additional training, or, in some cases, change the task to fit the team's capabilities. In most cases, you can't just magically "team" away a significant talent deficit.

While it is true that significant capability gaps are a problem and that teams with higher levels of task-related capabilities will usually demonstrate better performance, the research also reveals something less obvious, maybe even paradoxical. You can't always boost a team's performance simply by adding more talent or by bringing in another "star." In fact, research has shown that you can have too many stars.

A team of researchers from France, the United States, and Amsterdam, explored the question, "Can a team have too many stars?" The researchers, led by Roderick Swaab, a professor of organizational behavior at INSEAD, a well-respected global business school, proffered what they refer to as the "too-much-talent" hypothesis. Their hypothesis was based on the assumption that when a team has too many dominant individuals, it can lead to dysfunctional competition and jostling for status. Competing "stars" begin to focus undue attention on their own standing within the team to the detriment of the team. They expected teams with "too much talent" to have more unhealthy disputes, in some cases going so far as to overtly undermine one another.

There is a parallel to this phenomenon in the animal kingdom. When a chicken colony has too many dominant, high-producing chickens, overall egg production declines. Why? Due to intense conflicts. Alpha chickens will attempt to peck their rivals to death and sometimes succeed. This is a literal example of how a highly competitive "pecking order" can hurt performance! But are humans like chickens?

Before they conducted their studies, Swaab and his team proposed that the degree to which team members are interdependent was a key to understanding the "too-much-talent" phenomenon. They believed that when team members are fairly independent or only loosely reliant on one another, adding talent should yield better results ad infinitum. In contrast, when team members rely on one another and must coordinate to produce results, then there may be a maximum threshold for stars. Beyond that point, adding top talent would disrupt teamwork so much that it offsets any potential value associated with greater talent. They hypothesized that beyond the threshold, team performance would decline.

The researchers conducted a series of studies. First, they asked people what they believe about the relationship between talent and performance. They found that the general public sees a linear relationship between talent levels and team performance. In other words, people *believe* that more talent is always better for a team.

But the researchers wanted to examine their "too-much-talent" hypothesis empirically. To do so, they analyzed data from soccer teams (every national team that receives a FIFA ranking), basketball teams (10 years of data from NBA teams), and baseball teams (10 years of data from 30 major league teams). They identified the percentage of "elite" players on each team and compared that to the team's win and loss record. Why did they pick those sports? The answer can be found in our reliance continuum. Soccer and basketball teams fall toward the interdependent end of that continuum, where team performance is highly contingent on teamwork. In contrast, a baseball team is toward the middle of the continuum. The researchers predicted that the "too-much-talent" effect would show up in soccer and basketball teams, but not in baseball teams.

What did they find? In soccer and basketball teams, the relationship between talent and team performance was positive and significant, just as the general public would have predicted. However, that relationship only held up to a point, beyond which performance flattened out (no gain from additional talent) and eventually turned downward (performance declined with additional talent). Basketball and soccer teams with the highest concentration of stars had poorer win–loss records than those with a mixed roster. The apparent inflection point or threshold was when approximately 60% of the team (give or take 10%) were "elite" players. Above that point, additional talent didn't help and could even be detrimental!

But what about baseball teams, where half the game is performed individually (batting), and there are almost no instances when all nine players need to coordinate simultaneously? Baseball teams did not exhibit a similar threshold. The relationship between talent and performance was consistently positive—there was no apparent decline associated with adding another star player.

Collectively, the research tells us that talent matters—significant gaps in task-related capabilities can doom a team—but you can't always boost a team's performance simply by adding more stars. It is important to remember that capability is only one of the seven key drivers. Capability interacts with the other six drivers to determine team effectiveness. Margaret Peteraf, a professor of management at Dartmouth University, suggested that we can't predict the productivity of a Nobel-prize winning scientist without considering the team of researchers around her and the conditions in which she is operating. And even a great actor can appear amateurish when his director, co-stars, stunt double and cinematographer don't do their jobs well. So let's examine some research that considers how task-related capabilities interact with conditions by turning from the world of sports to the high-priced world of investment analysts.

Investment analysts study industries, companies, and investment opportunities. They gather data, perform financial analyses, and offer insights and opinions that can influence very large financial decisions. They issue earnings forecasts, stock recommendations, and detailed company research reports. Star analysts are quite highly compensated. If you can predict when to buy a particular stock, avoid investing in a particular industry, or refrain from acquiring a failing company, you will be paid a great deal of money (top analysts at major investment banks make millions of dollars per year). If you are an investment analyst, making it into the top rankings in *Institutional Investors* magazine can help your career soar and if you happen to appear on the cover you become a celebrity—so get ready to do interviews for TV, cable, and newspapers!

As a result, the industry is notorious for buying (aka "stealing") top talent from competing firms. This mindset is not unique to the financial sector; it is also true for other knowledge intensive industries such as law, consulting, medicine, technology, and accounting. The prevailing wisdom is that you can readily import star talent. This thinking is often applied to sales and insurance professionals as well. You "acquire" them and their book of business, plug them in, and bingo, you've improved your company. Stars in these industries are often perceived as similar to free agents in baseball. Find a homerun hitter and sign him up, and your team is better. But keep in mind, investment analysts and those who work in professions such as medicine and consulting rarely work independently; they rely on those around them, the other members of the team, to produce results.

Boris Groysberg is a professor in the organizational behavior unit at the Harvard Business School and the author of *Chasing Stars: The Myth of Talent and the Portability of Performance*. He and his colleagues have been examining assumptions about star talent for several years. He, along with Linda Eling-Lee and Ashish Nanda, conducted a study that examined data from over 1,000 equity and fixed-income analysts across 78 firms over a period of nine years. This allowed them to examine a few key questions. What happens when a star analyst moves to a different firm? Can you just plug in a star and expect them to perform at the same high level?

The results were dramatic. They found that star analysts who switched employers exhibited an immediate decline in performance. On average, that decline lasted five years! But conditions played a critical role in their effectiveness. Analysts who moved to firms that provided similar levels of support as their prior employer only exhibited a two-year decline. And those who switched to firms with better conditions didn't experience any decline. Moreover, when star analysts moved with other members of their team (e.g., junior and senior research analysts, institutional salespeople, or traders who specialize in the same sector)—in other words, when they brought their support network with them—they exhibited no performance decrements. Interestingly, it also appeared that female analysts fared better in their transition to a new employer than their male counterparts.

Groysberg's research provides a clear picture of how conditions can greatly influence whether capabilities, even elite capabilities, translate into results. Several years ago, we also conducted a study of industry analyst teams for a well-known global company. Within the company, two types of team structures had emerged over time. Some analyst teams were configured with a clear star at the center. The star received all the publicity, and it was clear that the rest of the team was there to make the star successful—to be ranked as a top industry analyst. In contrast, other teams were configured in a more distributed manner. There was still a designated leader, but all the analysts on the team were expected to coordinate with one another, and they all were able to make visible contributions to the team's success. Going into the research, senior leadership told us that they believed the star model was better and they had been looking to find more stars to build teams around. But to their surprise, our research found the opposite was true. By all indicators, including highly credible financial metrics, the star-centric teams did not perform as well as the other teams. The other teams demonstrated greater teamwork and that translated into better results.

The conclusion of our research is not that star-centric teams are bad but rather that talent alone doesn't determine team effectiveness. Boris Groysberg and his colleagues demonstrated that conditions can greatly influence whether task-related capabilities translate into results, and our research suggested that teamwork does as well. Before we leave our examination of task-related capabilities, let's quickly revisit one additional finding from the research on basketball teams.

As you'll recall, basketball teams with too many stars underperformed teams with a mix of talent. That finding was true *on average*, but there were exceptions. The exception was that star-laden teams that were able to demonstrate high levels of teamwork and coordination overcame the "too-much-talent" problem and performed up to their talent level. While teamwork can't overcome huge talent gaps, it may be able to overcome an overabundance of talent—if the stars are willing to flex their teamwork-related capabilities and not worry too much about who is the alpha chicken.

TEAMWORK-RELATED CAPABILITIES

When team members are expected to collaborate with one another, even to a small extent, team members need to possess teamwork-related capabilities—knowledge, skills, abilities, and other attributes that enable them to work together as a team. In team environments, teamwork capabilities supplement task work capabilities. But which are more important, task work or teamwork capabilities? It depends.

All teams need "ample" task work capabilities, and any team that needs to work together needs at least some teamwork capabilities. Both are important but their relative importance is based largely on where the team falls on the reliance continuum.

When team members rarely need to coordinate with or rely on one another, teamwork capabilities are less important. In such teams, there is little need to help or back up one another, so they can get by with less teamwork capabilities. But even in teams where work is performed fairly independently (e.g., many sales teams), a toxic teammate can poison the well and adversely affect team performance. In general, the more team members need to rely on teammates and actively help one another, the greater the need for teamwork capabilities. But every team needs a mix of both task-related and teamwork-related capabilities.

When considering the capabilities required in a team setting, we've found it can be helpful to think about them in a 2 × 2 competencies matrix, as shown in Table 4.1. We first developed this distinction in the 1990s, with our colleague Jan Cannon-Bowers, while we were examining team performance for the US Navy.

The matrix shows that some teamwork capabilities are applicable regardless of the task being performed or who else is on the team. For example, because almost every team experiences conflict on occasion, being skilled at conflict resolution is universally applicable. We refer to competencies such as conflict resolution skills as "transportable team competencies." But other competencies are only applicable when performing a specific task ("task-specific") or when working with a particular set of people ("teammate specific"). Finally, there are a few competencies that are only applicable when performing a particular task with a particular set of people ("situation specific team competencies").

Table 4.1. Generic and Specific Teamwork Competencies

	Teammate Generic	Teammate Specific
Task generic	**Transportable team competencies**: Useful in almost any team performing almost any tasks	**Team-specific competencies**: Useful for working with this team, regardless of the specific task
Task specific	**Task-specific competencies**: Applicable to performing required tasks regardless of who else is on the team	**Situation-specific competencies**: Applicable to working on a specific task with particular team members

We'll focus primarily on transportable team competencies, as these apply to any team.

Transportable Team Competencies

The research suggests that there are a few generic or transportable competencies that can influence team effectiveness in almost any team setting. Some of these are skills that can be trained or developed, while others are more stable attributes that are difficult to change. For example, personality traits and other personal attributes are not very malleable; it is difficult to change a person's personality, so your one opportunity to address this is at the time of hire. If your organization relies on teams, you can attempt to hire people with the "right" personality traits or at a minimum try to screen out those with toxic personalities. It also makes sense to help your employees strengthen those teamwork skills that can be readily enhanced.

Transportable team competencies are useful in any team, but they are even more important in settings where:

- People frequently serve on more than one team at a time, because they can apply transportable competencies in all their teams.
- Team membership is dynamic (i.e., the team scores low on the membership stability continuum), because when teammates regularly change or teams are quickly formed and disbanded, it is hard to develop teammate specific competencies.
- Team tasks are dynamic and unpredictable (i.e., the team scores low on the task consistency continuum), because when task requirements are unpredictable it is more difficult to develop task specific competencies.

If these characteristics are common in your organization or business unit, it is particularly important to find ways to integrate the development of transportable teamwork skills into the various training and learning experiences you provide to your employees.

Most organizations would benefit from boosting their employees' teamwork skills—and we encourage you to invest some effort in doing so. But we also want to emphasize the societal value of developing transportable, fundamental teamwork skills before people enter the workforce. We want to encourage educators to create opportunities for students to learn about and practice teamwork skills throughout their education, starting as children, through high school, and continuing into college and postcollege professional education. Currently, we are advising medical schools about how to foster the development of transportable teamwork competencies in their curricula, to supplement the development of task work skills (of course, doctors should learn how to diagnose a patient, but communication and leadership skills are also pretty important!). Healthcare work is increasingly performed in teams. Teamwork has a significant impact on patient care and safety, so wouldn't it be great if new doctors, nurses, and other health care professionals entered the workforce with fundamental teamwork skills?

We'll step off the soapbox now and continue our exploration of teamwork capabilities. What does the research tell us are the most important transportable teamwork capabilities? Five generic teamwork skills, two related types of teamwork knowledge, and a set of other attributes including personality make a meaningful difference.

If I learn to be a stronger listener and communicator, become more comfortable giving and receiving feedback, develop the capability to deal with conflict constructively, and strengthen my interpersonal skills, I will most assuredly be a more valuable member of my current team. I'll also be more valuable on virtually any other team that I join in the future. The research would suggest that communicating, giving and receiving feedback, dealing with conflict, and interpersonal skills are foundational and transportable skills. Teams that have members who possess these skills are more likely to demonstrate effective teamwork behaviors and to develop cooperative teamwork attitudes such as trust. Later, we explore how these skills manifest themselves as behaviors and attitudes in the chapters on coordination and cooperation, respectively. In addition, because team members are increasingly asked to informally fulfill certain "leadership" functions, we would argue that there is merit in considering a few basic leadership skills as transportable team-related competencies. We'll explore leadership further in the chapter on coaching. The following is a list of five key generic teamwork capabilities along with a few of the behaviors they enable:

- **Communication skills** to provide clear messages, ask effective questions, listen actively, and convey understanding.
- **Feedback skills** to observe and monitor performance, provide constructive feedback to others, encourage feedback from others, and interpret feedback received.

- **Conflict skills** to disagree productively, use constructive conflict styles, diagnose the cause of conflict situations, and defuse and work through conflicts and help others do so.
- **Interpersonal skills** to infer intent/emotions, convey empathy when appropriate, interpret nonverbal cues, regulate one's own emotions, and influence/persuade others.
- **Leadership skills** to constructively hold others accountable, motivate, and encourage teammates; share expertise/teach others; and clarify expectations and priorities.

There is also some evidence that possessing general knowledge about teamwork, or what we refer to as teamwork savvy, is helpful.

> **Teamwork savvy** is knowing what drives team effectiveness and knowing what good team members do.

Mike Campion from Purdue, Fred Morgesen from Michigan State, and Michael Stevens from Weber State University have been studying teams and teamwork knowledge for quite a while. One finding from their research is that teams that possess a greater understanding about teamwork outperform other teams. That seems logical. When an individual knows what really influences team effectiveness (the science of teamwork rather than "myths"), knows how to handle common situations that involve team dynamics, and is aware of what good teammates do, they are going to be more valuable on almost any team. That's why everyone who works on a team should read this book!

There are a few other personal attributes that are typically related to team effectiveness across a wide range of tasks and with different teammates. For starters, team members need adequate cognitive ability not only to perform their tasks but also to acquire new knowledge and skills, to communicate effectively, and to contribute to effective team decision-making.

> **Cognitive ability** refers to the capacity to perform higher mental processes of reasoning, recalling, understanding, and problem-solving. It doesn't refer to what someone knows.

Rory Brown, the former president of the *Bleacher Report*, believes that as a leader, "If you are the smartest person in the room, you haven't hired well." In general, that may be true. But we'd say the key is that your team needs *ample* cognitive ability given the nature of the work they perform. Inadequate cognitive ability to do the job is a problem, but simply assembling a bunch of really, really smart people won't guarantee team effectiveness.

The research also provides insights about a few relatively stable personal traits that enable people to be better teammates. One such trait is collective orientation.

> **Collective orientation** is an underlying belief about working in teams. Individuals who are high in collective orientation typically prefer working in teams and think "team first." They are generally predisposed to promote their team's interests. In laymen's terms, we might refer to them as "team players."

Suzanne Bell is a professor at DePaul University and one of the leading researchers of team composition. Like us, she has studied how a team's make-up influences their teamwork and performance. She has examined this in many settings, including teams at NASA, and we've had many interesting conversations with her. She conducted a meta-analysis of "team composition" effects from almost 90 previous studies. One of her findings was that teams with higher levels of collective orientation and preference for teamwork demonstrate higher levels of performance. Interestingly however, this relationship only occurred in studies conducted in real field settings, not in studies conducted in a laboratory. We think that may be because lab studies tend to be fairly short in duration, so there is less opportunity for people to use their collective orientation for the team's benefit.

Other studies suggest that collective orientation benefits a team because it makes it easier to share information and to fill in for teammates. If I think "team first," I'm more likely to share what I know and less likely to hoard information. I'm also more likely to step in to help a colleague in need. Naturally, collective orientation is more critical in teams where members rely on one another more heavily. When team members are predominantly independent contributors, then being respectful and civil may be adequate—and you don't need high collective orientation to be civil.

In our consulting work, we have observed that it appears a team needs "enough" people with a collective orientation, but not every team member must be a strong team player. There is probably some lower threshold of collective orientation below which teams are more likely to struggle. We'd like to be able to tell you that magic number; but currently research isn't available to specify the inflection point.

Because collective orientation is a relatively stable trait, the primary opportunity to address this is when you are choosing people for the team. It is hard to change someone's fundamental beliefs about teams, at least in the short term, so it makes sense to assess the teamwork orientation of your job candidates. Keep in mind, however, that whether a trait such as collective orientation results in subsequent teamwork behaviors is greatly influenced by the other drivers. In our own research using the Team Role Orientation and Experience (TREO) tool, we found that people who are predisposed toward being a team player (i.e., who see themselves as someone who calms or motivates other team members and seeks to maintain a positive team environment) do in fact demonstrate more teamwork behaviors. However, that isn't always the case. For example, if trust is low, roles are unclear, and the leader is viewed as selfish, even someone with a high level of collective orientation is unlikely to demonstrate a high degree of teamwork.

You may get the impression that collective orientation means subjugating yourself. It doesn't. Collective orientation does not mean being saintly or selfless. Consider research conducted by Scott Gayton from the Australian Army and James Kehoe from the University of South Wales. They studied applicants for the prestigious Australian Army Special Forces. One of the top predictors of who would make it through the rigorous Special Forces training was having a preference for teamwork. Virtually all their recruits are personally driven, physically fit, and mentally tough, or else they wouldn't be trying out for the Special Forces. These are not bashful, wilting violets. So, while there was no shortage of toughness and personal drive in the candidate pool, it was the trainees who were also team players who thrived. In fact, applicants who viewed themselves as "team workers" were 2.6 times more likely to make it through the training! We see a similar mix of individual excellence coupled with a strong teamwork orientation in NASA's astronaut program. In the early days of space flight, the goal was to hire tough individuals with the "right stuff"; collective orientation wasn't on the radar screen. Today, NASA fully understands and appreciates the powerful duality of individual excellence and team orientation.

You can find people who are high in collective orientation and are also great individual contributors, perhaps even "stars." Smokey Robinson is one of the all-time greats of Motown and a musical legend, but behind the scenes he has consistently demonstrated his collective orientation. On Oprah Winfrey's *Master Class* television show, he talked about his experiences at Motown. While each musical act ("team") was competing for visibility and resources, he approached his work collaboratively. "It would be nothing for us to go into the studio and help one of our competitors with a song that they were working on, with an artist that we were working on," Smokey says. "We all did that, for each other." For example, he wrote one of his most famous songs, "My Girl," specifically for the Temptations, not for his group, Smokey Robinson and the Miracles. We believe he wasn't the only one who cared deeply about the larger team at Motown, but we suspect that not everyone did. That isn't a statement about Motown or the competitiveness of the music industry; it is simply a recognition that there are significant individual differences in collective orientation. It is highly unlikely that every artist and producer at Motown shared Smokey Robinson's underlying beliefs about teamwork.

In addition to collective orientation, three other traits are often associated with heightened team effectiveness. One is adaptability. Given the rapid pace of change in most organizations, most teams experience change quite regularly, so team members typically need to be flexible and adaptive.

Two other traits to consider are conscientiousness and agreeableness. The most prevalent framework for understanding personality is referred to as the Big Five, and these are two of the Big Five. In general, these traits can be helpful in team settings, but unlike the skills we discussed earlier, more is not always better.

Adaptability is the willingness and ability to adjust to fit changed circumstances; being flexible rather than rigid.

Conscientiousness is a tendency to be dependable, organized, and dutiful. People with this trait typically prefer planned rather than spontaneous actions.

Agreeableness is the tendency to be trusting, helpful, and cooperative rather than highly competitive and suspicious of others.

You can see the benefit of having team members who are high on conscientiousness, as they tend to be quite reliable. But if the team needs to regularly adjust on the fly, and adaptability is essential, we'd be a little concerned if all members scored very high on conscientiousness.

It is also easy to see how having team members who score higher on agreeableness can facilitate teamwork, although we would speculate that if everyone scores extremely high on this trait, the team may lack constructive friction. The research suggests that simply knowing your team's average agreeableness isn't the key here. Based on Suzanne Bell's meta-analysis, it appears that to understand the influence of agreeableness, we need to look at the person with the lowest score. If that person scores very low on this trait, they are likely to be a disruptive element.

While we should be looking to hire and promote people with desirable teamwork capabilities such as collective orientation and communication skills, it is also very important to know which attributes to avoid. Let's switch our attention to the dark side of team capabilities.

The Dark Side

Unfortunately, you've probably had the misfortune of being on a team with someone who is "toxic." We suspect you know what we mean when we say toxic, but in case you don't, Rebecca Bennett and Sandra Robinson conducted a series of studies on deviant behaviors in the workplace. They found seven common behaviors that are consistently considered to be deviant: making fun of someone, saying something hurtful, making an inappropriate ethnic or religious remark, cursing at someone, playing mean pranks, acting rudely, and publicly embarrassing someone. Toxic employees are prone to these behaviors. In addition, they notoriously withhold effort, are continually pessimistic, and let others know about their anxiety and irritation. Clearly you want to avoid hiring toxic employees, but how can you predict if someone will be toxic?

The work of Ernest O'Boyle, a researcher at the University of Iowa, can help. He and his colleagues conducted a meta-analysis of 245 prior research samples that examined what has been referred to as the "Dark Triad" of personality traits—Machiavellianism, narcissism, and psychopathy.

Someone with a **Machiavellian** personality believes manipulation is effective and acceptable, has a cynical view of human nature, and possesses a moral outlook that places expediency above principle.

Narcissism is typified by an overinflated sense of self-worth, inaccurate beliefs about control and success, and a strong desire to have their self-love shared and reinforced by others. They typically see themselves as superior, even when others do not.

Characteristics associated with **psychopathy** are a lack of concern for others, high impulsivity, and a lack of remorse after harming others. They are often great "impression managers" and can be charismatic.

You may know someone who has exhibited some of these traits. Perhaps you've been exposed to Dark Triad personality traits in your company, or maybe you've seen a politician on the news who has shown these characteristics (feel free to pick a country and political party of choice; there seems to be plenty of exemplars from which to choose). If so, you have seen the Dark Triad in action. These personality traits are certainly annoying, but do they really make a difference? O'Boyle and his colleagues found that Machiavellianism and narcissism (and to a lesser extent psychopathy) were consistently associated with counterproductive behaviors at work. These folks aren't just annoying; they are truly disruptive. So, as you think about assembling a team that possesses all the necessary task-related and teamwork-related capabilities to succeed, also give a little thought to the capabilities you really want to avoid—traits that can derail your team and make you miserable! Hiring and coddling team members with Dark Triad personality traits or extremely low levels of agreeableness can adversely affect the entire team, in part because their negative emotions can spread to others.

How can negative emotions spread? Through emotional contagion. Researchers across the globe have been studying whether emotional contagion is real and, if so, how it works. *Emotional contagion* is a term psychologists use to describe how one person can "catch the emotions" of another person, in a way that is analogous to catching a cold.

Workplace rudeness can spread. Even low-level negative emotions can be contagious, as shown in a series of studies by Trevor Foulk and his colleagues in the United States. Exposure to negative emotional expressions appears to activate different parts of the brain than exposure to positive expressions, according to Tokiko Harada from the National Institute for Physiological Sciences and a team of researchers from the School of Medicine at Nagoya University in Japan. To make matters worse, negative emotions can spread not only from person A to B, but person C can "catch" the emotion from person B, without ever seeing person A! Guillaume Dezecache and a team of researchers in Paris showed that negativity gets passed along more widely than we might anticipate. And if you are hopeful that exposure to positive emotions could help "cure" narcissists, we have disappointing news. People who are high in narcissism are less prone to emotional contagion, as seen in research by Anna Czarna and others, perhaps because narcissists are less empathic. Somewhat ironically, it appears that narcissists can infect you with their negative emotions, but are less likely to catch your positive ones!

These studies on emotional contagion are an interesting example of how scientists around the world are trying to understand an important psychological phenomena. Collectively, they reveal one of the ways that someone with a toxic personality can "infect" other team members. We encourage you to do your best to "quarantine" your team from people with Dark Triad characteristics as much as possible.

The following box contains a list of the 11 transportable team capabilities and provides a reminder about a few toxic traits. You'll find a nice summary of these capabilities, along with some additional information about task- and team-specific competencies in the Tools section at the end of the book.

SUMMARY: TRANSPORTABLE TEAM CAPABILITIES

Fundamental skills: Giving/receiving feedback, communicating, conflict resolution, leadership, and interpersonal skills

Teamwork savvy: Understanding team dynamics and how to be a good teammate

Personal attributes: Cognitive ability (adequate), collective orientation (enough), adaptability (particularly in dynamic settings), conscientiousness (but not everyone must be high)

Toxic traits to avoid: Machiavellianism, narcissism, psychopathy, and very low levels of agreeableness

---

We wrap up this chapter on capabilities by providing a few brief thoughts about team profiles, followed by a few practical implications of this chapter.

It is easiest to think about capability as a purely individual attribute: Sarah knows how to program in Python, Lakshmi has strong financial skills, Bill knows how to speak Spanish, and Sophia is an excellent communicator. But to take appropriate actions to improve a team, you may also need to consider a team's collective capabilities. How does the profile of current capabilities match up against the capabilities the team needs? Using a task-related competency example, if everyone on the team needs to speak fluent Spanish, but 30% of the team only possess basic skills, it doesn't matter that most of the team members are fluent, or even that one team member is "world-class." Unless some adjustments are made to the team's capability (e.g., by training or changing members), the team is likely to struggle or fail.

Sometimes it is enough to have one expert in a given area, but in other cases a team's performance can be better predicted by knowing the team's average capability or by examining the capability of the weakest team member (remember the research about agreeableness). For example, how likely is an Olympic relay team to be victorious if a slow, five-foot, seven-inch author is running the anchor leg? There aren't three people on the planet who are fast enough to make up for that!

Researchers have begun studying how a team's profile of teamwork-related competencies affects teamwork and performance. Research led by our friend and long-term collaborator John Mathieu showed that a team's profile can predict team performance beyond that accounted for by individual competency levels alone. As a result, he started using that thinking with student teams in the University of Connecticut's MBA and Executive MBA programs. Students complete a TREO survey designed to assess each person's own team role propensities, uncovering the type of team role they typically gravitate toward when on a team (e.g., challenger, organizer, doer, team builder, and innovator). John then assigns students to teams to optimize their team's profile (e.g., ensuring a mix and not having too many challengers on the same team) and noticed that thoughtfully composed teams did much better than when he randomly assigned them to teams.

When you are going to add or replace a team member, consider the current mix of capabilities on the team and identify the gaps. On the task side, is there someone on the team who has the skills needed to fill in for a key team member? On the teamwork side, do you have enough people with a collective orientation? Enough team members who are conscientious and can be counted on to get things done? A team's profile of capabilities matters!

IMPLICATIONS

- Make sure your team has sufficient task-related capabilities to perform their own jobs—while a team can overcome small deficiencies, if the gap is significant enough you won't be able to magically "team" it away.
- Consider how important teamwork capabilities are for your team—these merit more attention if your team members must rely on and coordinate with one another to succeed.
- If your team operates in a highly dynamic environment, where task requirements change frequently, or people move quickly from team to team, focus attention on hiring people with solid, transportable teamwork competencies.
- Be sure your team has *enough* people with a collective orientation—not everyone must have this orientation, but you need enough.
- Avoid hiring people with toxic attributes—don't be fooled by their charisma or apparent task capabilities. You won't change their personality and they are rarely worth the trouble.
- Adding "elite" talent can help, but when the need for coordination is quite high, too many stars can hurt a team's effectiveness.
- You may be better off building your own stars than hiring them, but if you hire one, consider having them bring other team members with them—or at least prepare the environment for their success; "plug and play" often won't work with stars.
- Before you add someone to your team, give some thought to the current mix or profile of your team. What are the task- and/or teamwork-capability gaps you want to fill?

CHAPTER 5

Cooperation

Attitudes and Beliefs that Emerge from the Other Drivers

In 1996, a team attempted to ascend Mount Everest via the South Col route in Nepal. The expedition was led by two of the world's most skilled and seasoned climbers, Rob Hall and Scott Fischer, both of whom had successfully led prior expeditions to the top of Everest. The team also had four experienced guides, several skilled Sherpas, and 16 paying clients. Tragically, five of the climbers perished during the expedition—including the two team leaders. How could this have happened to such a skilled, "capable" team?

At the beginning of the mission, the leaders established a plan; they agreed they needed to reach the mountaintop by 2 PM, or they would turn back and abandon the climb. The agreement was, "No matter how close," if they weren't at the top by the designated time, they would begin their descent. But during the climb, the team fell behind schedule. When it became clear they wouldn't reach the top by 2 PM, Rob Hall made the decision that they would continue. At that point, four of the team members chose to return to the base, but everyone else continued the climb. Many had serious reservations, yet they continued to climb. When a severe storm set in, visibility declined, and temperatures dropped. Climbers ran out of supplemental oxygen, became disoriented, and lost their bearings. During the decent, five died, and others barely survived.

While the ultimate cause of death for these climbers was likely asphyxiation or hypothermia, the underlying cause as we see it was a lack of "psychological safety," or the belief that you can speak up, admit concerns, and offer a dissenting opinion.

Team members felt that they couldn't speak up without being ostracized by the leader. They started to form this belief well before the climb. According to Jon Krakauer's personal account of the expedition (as described in the book, *Into Thin Air*), Rob Hall, the mission leader, told the team before they began, "I will tolerate no dissension up there. My word will be absolute law, beyond appeal. If you don't like a particular decision I make, I'd be happy to discuss it with you afterwards, not while we're up on the hill." He made it clear that they shouldn't feel comfortable speaking up.

Hierarchical teams often struggle with psychological safety—less powerful team members feel they should do what they are told. The climbing team had a clear hierarchy: leaders, then guides, and then customers. There was even a hierarchy among the guides. One guide, who knew he was paid less than the others, felt his opinion wasn't valued. He had serious concerns about proceeding beyond the designated turnback time, but he had learned to "not be argumentative." He, like all but four members of the expedition, was afraid to offer an opposing point of view. The consequences were deadly.

This chapter is about cooperation, the term we use to describe the attitudes and beliefs that team members have about their team. These attitudes and beliefs are formed based on experiences with the team (and with previous teams), and they are influenced by team member capabilities and personalities, teamwork behaviors (or lack thereof), communications, conditions, shared understanding (or misunderstanding), and leadership. In other words, cooperation "emerges" from the other six drivers. And, in turn, cooperative attitudes and beliefs can help some of the other drivers.

Cooperative attitudes and beliefs are driven by perceptions, and perceptions don't always match reality. That is why you can't "make" someone trust you; you can only take actions that increase the likelihood that they perceive you as trustworthy. There are no guarantees, but taking the "right" actions improves your odds.

Cooperation is what psychologists refer to as an "emergent state," which is simply a way of noting that it develops over time and is dynamic in nature. Cooperation isn't like a skill or personality trait that you take with you from team to team. And it isn't about your general attitude towards teamwork, but rather how you currently think and feel about *this team*. And those attitudes and beliefs can change over time. Do I believe this team can "win"? Is my team leader trustworthy? Is it acceptable to offer a dissenting point of view? Answers to those questions can change quite rapidly. And when you join a different team, a whole new set of attitudes and beliefs about that team will emerge over time.

The research is clear—four cooperative attitudes and beliefs can greatly influence team effectiveness, so it's important to keep an eye on them (Table 5.1). You can think of these four as a form of warning system—when they decline, performance problems are likely to follow (or may have already started). If you take actions that boost them, there is a good chance performance will improve.

Table 5.1. Four Key Forms of Cooperation

- **Trust**—Do I expect my teammates to *do the right thing*? Do I believe they have positive intentions?
- **Psychological safety**—Do I feel I can *be genuine and openly share my perspective*? Do I believe my teammates will give me the benefit of the doubt?
- **Collective efficacy**—Do we believe *our team can "get it done"*? Are we confident that our team will "win?"
- **Cohesion**—How do our team members feel about the team and our work? To what extent are we attracted or *committed to the team and the task*?

Of course, people form many other attitudes and beliefs while on a team. But we focus on these four because there is clear evidence that that they make a meaningful difference. They are all backed by solid meta-analytic research results that indicate they drive teamwork and team effectiveness.

Thought Experiment. While reading this chapter on cooperation, ask:

- What are the current **strengths and limitations** of your team with regard to cooperation?
- Would it be worth trying to improve your team's attitudes and beliefs? If so, which of the four forms of **cooperation** should you focus on?
- What **actions** could you take?

TRUST

Trust Is a Business Imperative

An old Irish proverb says, "When mistrust comes in, loves goes out." Everyone knows it is hard to maintain a happy, healthy personal relationship without trust. When we trust someone, we assume that they are operating with positive intent, we expect that they will do what they say, and we believe they have our best interests at heart. These beliefs allow us to accept some vulnerability and forego some personal control because we "trust" they will do the right thing.

While no one will say trust is unimportant at work, some people believe it is merely nice to have, that you can get by without high levels of trust if you hire smart, hard-working people and establish clear rules and consequences. But the research would suggest that they are wrong. Trust is a business imperative.

When team members trust one another (intrateam trust), they consistently demonstrate better team performance, even after accounting for how much they trust their leader and how effectively they performed in the past. This is based on a meta-analysis of 7,700 teams conducted by Bart DeJong and researchers from the Netherlands, the United States, and Australia. Their findings, published in the *Journal of Applied Psychology*, were the same for temporary and for ongoing teams. But are there any situations where trust is particularly important?

DeJong and his colleagues found that trust was even more strongly related to performance in highly interdependent teams (those that fall on the high end of our reliance continuum), when authority is more centralized, and when team member skills are more dissimilar (on the low end of our similarity continuum). This all makes sense. If we rely on one another to get the job done, we must trust each other to provide help when needed. In a more centralized team, people with the authority to make decisions must trust the rest of the team to feed them accurate information, and individuals without that authority must trust that those in power will make decisions that benefit the team. And when team members possess dissimilar expertise, they must trust that their teammates know what they are doing and are making contributions, since they lack the expertise to readily assess if that's true. DeJong et al. uncovered three situations where trust is particularly important, but they found that even in low reliance situations, when authority isn't centralized, or when team members possess similar skills, trust is positively related to performance.

What about when team members work in different locations? Does proximity make a difference? DeJong's meta-analysis suggests that trust is somewhat more important in virtual teams, but Christine Breuer and her colleagues also conducted a meta-analysis, and they didn't find any differences. In the big scheme of things, it probably doesn't matter whether DeJong or Breuer is correct. What does matter is that they both confirmed that trust is needed in virtual and in co-located teams—so it is important to build and sustain trust in both settings. But because it can be more challenging to build trust when you don't have the opportunity to physically interact with your teammates on a regular basis, we'd suggest that a little extra attention may be warranted when team members work at a distance.

We've been discussing trust within a team, between team members. What about trusting one's team leader; does it matter if I believe that my leader will do what she says? The short answer is, Of course. You'll hear more about this in the chapter on coaching, but for now, here's a little evidence that trust in your leader matters. Employees who trust their leader perform better and are more committed to the organization according to a meta-analysis conducted by Kurt Dirks and Donald Ferrin. In addition, those employees are much more likely to go above and beyond their specified job duties—they are often better "corporate citizens." And trusting one's immediate team leader was more important than trusting senior leaders.

Tony Simmons showed how this translates into economic payoffs in an interesting study of 6,500 hotel employees. Simmons found that in hotels where employees believed their manager regularly followed through on commitments, profits were higher. His analysis showed that a one-eighth of a point improvement in a hotel's "behavioral consistency" score (on a five-point scale) could be expected to boost a hotel's profitability by 2.5% of revenues. That translated to more than $250,000 per year, per hotel. Trust is a business imperative.

Why Do We Trust or Distrust Others?

Trust might be a little more important in certain circumstances, but the findings are quite robust—when it comes to team performance, trust matters in almost any team. What can the research tell us about how trust is formed? Why do we believe one person is more trustworthy than another?

Three Key Judgments

Researchers have been contemplating this question for decades. Back in the mid-1990s, Roger Mayer and his colleagues developed an influential theory to address that question. Based on previous work, they proposed that perceived trustworthiness is a function of three judgments about the person. The first judgment is related to perceptions of capability ("can he do"), and the last two are related perceptions of character ("will he do"). The three judgments are as follows.

Do I believe this person:

- Is capable of doing what he said he would? (ability)
- Wants to do what is good for me? (benevolence)
- Adheres to an acceptable set of principles or values? (integrity)

Mayer thought that judgments about ability, benevolence, and integrity would determine whether someone is deemed trustworthy. While that sounds logical, does it reflect how trust really works? Fortunately, there's a meta-analysis that can answer that question!

When Jason Colquitt, Brent Scott, and Jeff LePine were at the University of Florida, they meta-analyzed results from over 130 prior research samples to test Mayer's theory. They found that, as Mayer proposed, all three factors play a significant role in determining who we trust, even after controlling for a variety of other possible explanations. When deciding whether to trust someone, the research suggests that you consider whether that person has the ability to deliver on their commitments. You might not trust someone to deliver, even though they have positive intentions, because you don't believe they have the skills or authority to "make it so." You also consider how they feel about you; do you think that they are truly going to look out for your best interests, and not just their own or the company's interests? And you consider the person's general character; for example, are they generally fair and do you believe they possess virtuous values.

In addition to those three judgments, Colquitt and his team considered another factor. If you ask your "trusting" Aunt Mabel (some might call her gullible) if you can borrow $20, will you get the same answer as the one you'd get from your cynical cousin Mitch who doesn't seem to trust anyone? Aren't some people simply more trusting than others? Could that explain why someone trusts you?

The research confirms that some individuals are generally more trusting than others. We learn whether to be trusting from our life experiences. Some psychologists refer to this inclination to be more or less trusting as "trust propensity" and consider it to be similar to other fairly stable personality traits like conscientiousness; people take their general propensity to trust with them wherever they go.

So what matters more, general trust propensity or our current judgments about a person's ability, benevolence, and integrity? It turns out that both predict trust, but current judgments are stronger determinants. We bring our general propensity with us, but each interaction provides us with new information about the person, which we interpret, and that often overrules our initial tendencies.

Of course, when you first join a team, you only have your general trust propensity to guide you (and perhaps some stories you heard about your new teammates or leader). But as you interact with your team and you see how individuals behave, you begin to make judgments about the trustworthiness of your new colleagues. In essence, you are adding and subtracting points from each teammate's trust score. You probably aren't explicitly asking yourself, "Is she able to deliver on that" or "Do I trust her values," but as a human you are naturally processing how much you can trust each person.

The Role of Prior Experiences

Judgments of trustworthiness don't happen in isolation. Prior experiences influence the way people perceive and interpret new experiences. We filter and interpret new experiences through the lens of our prior experiences. Trust tends to beget trust, and distrust contributes to distrust. Here is an illustration.

We were providing consulting advice to several oil exploration and production teams in the Gulf of Mexico. Each team was made up of an offshore group and an onshore group. The offshore group worked on an oil platform in the Gulf, accessible only by helicopter. They lived in tight quarters, performed dangerous hands-on work, and handled the daily operations of the rig. The onshore support group worked in Houston and went home to their families after work. They were mostly white-collar experts in various engineering-related disciplines and they were there to support and at times guide the offshore team—the person with the most authority was located onshore. The company decided to set up an ongoing video connection between the control room on each rig and the meeting room of their respective teammates in Houston. Let's examine how two teams who performed similar work but on different rigs responded to the new video capabilities.

Team 1's response was very positive. They immediately used the video connection to engage in more frequent conversations with their onshore counterparts. Team 2's response was far less positive. In fact, at first, Team 2's offshore team members put an actual hard hat over the camera lens so Houston couldn't watch them at work.

Why Did the Two Teams Respond So Differently?

Based on past experiences, Team 1 had a high level of trust in the onshore leader and in their teammates in Houston. They had been getting good advice from them and felt that the onshore group was looking out for them. The way they interpreted the decision to add a video connection was, "Excellent. Now we have easier, faster access to Houston to get support and advice." In contrast, Team 2 had a rockier relationship with their onshore counterparts. They felt that they were continually being evaluated by their colleagues onshore. They believed onshore was competent, but they didn't think they shared common values. "Houston doesn't understand the pressure we are under and the way work gets done out here. If they see us cursing and spitting, they'll think we're not being professional. We have enough problems to deal with without them judging how we look all day."

The onshore leader of Team 1 was already viewed as trustworthy when the video concept was introduced, so the offshore group interpreted it as an additional means of support. The leader of Team 2 began with a negative trust score; therefore, the same action was viewed by that team as "big brother" will be watching.

Each interaction we have with teammates can add to or detract from our trust score with them. As we saw in the example, it is harder to make up a deficit than to operate with a surplus. And in all relationships, at work and at home, there are times when we need to spend a few trust chips, and so we should be looking for ways to build trustworthiness when possible.

A Few Tips about Trust

As we noted before, because trust is based on perceptions and interpretations, you can't "control" it, you can only "influence" it. Sometimes people will unfairly distrust you. Perhaps their perceptions are an inaccurate reflection of your intentions. Perhaps they view you as similar to a former teammate whom they didn't trust. Or, if you are in a leadership role, sometimes an unpopular organizational action (e.g., a downsizing) will affect your team's perceptions of you, even if you weren't involved in the decision. You can't make someone trust you, but you can act in a manner that increases the likelihood that they will.

- **Monitor your "trust score."** Look for signs that indicate how much people trust you. Do they seek your input? Voice their concerns to you? Those are signs of trust. We all like to think that we are perceived as trustworthy, but be alert for signs to the contrary.
- **Try to put yourself in their shoes**. Avoid defaulting to what you believe a person "should" think. Ask yourself, How else might they interpret what I'm saying or doing—how might they perceive my ability, benevolence, and integrity? Their perceptions could be different than your intentions.
- **Avoid making commitments you may not be able to keep**. For example, if the final decision about a problem is outside your control, it is better to say that you will "look into it" rather than saying you will fix it. Failing to live up to commitments is a huge trust killer and is often perceived as a sign that you lack the ability to deliver.
- **Own your mistakes**. We all make mistakes. If you do something wrong, admit it and take responsibility for it. Be clear about what you will do going forward and then live up to those commitments. Admitting a mistake can make a contribution to the "character" element of your trustworthiness.
- **Recognize that "trust but verify" doesn't build trust.** Ronald Reagan is often cited as evidence that "trust but verify" is a good way to operate. In some instances, that may be true. But recognize that each time you do that, you are sending the signal that you really don't trust the person, which may adversely affect the way they perceive your benevolence. Of course, there are times when you must verify "the truth," for example, when peoples' safety may be at risk ("I'll verify that my parachute is packed properly"). But if you verify every little thing, don't expect to have many trust points in the bank when you need them later.
- **Take an action that is clearly not in your best interest.** Being perceived as selfish costs you points. In contrast, taking actions that are in the best interest of another person and not necessarily best for you shows that you care about them. That's the definition of benevolence. Be honest—Do you do this enough or are you always angling so you "win?"

The second of the four key cooperative beliefs is psychological safety. Psychological safety is a big deal and not just when climbing a mountain.

Think about what we expect from most work teams. Of course, we need them to be productive, but given the dynamic, uncertain, and challenging nature of work, we also want teams to be adaptable, to learn, and to innovate. For that to happen, team members must be willing to speak up, offer their point of view, vocalize dissent, provide feedback, ask questions, and share expertise. They need to be open to try new ideas and ways of working, admit what they don't know, seek feedback and assistance, and learn from mistakes. What do these behaviors have in common? They all involve some degree of personal risk. Telling your boss that you disagree with her involves risk. Admitting a mistake involves risk. Experimenting with a promising but unproven approach involves risk. No one wants to be seen as pushy, incompetent, or reckless. We don't want our reputation to be tarnished. So most people are unwilling to take interpersonal risks at work unless they believe there is psychological safety. That's why psychological safety is a big deal.

The concept of psychological safety was first introduced in the 1960s by two highly respected organizational scholars, Ed Schein and Warren Bennis. They proposed that psychological safety facilitates peoples' willingness to learn and change. Amy Edmondson, a professor in the business school at Harvard University, has built upon and extended their work in meaningful ways. Edmondson is perhaps the world's leading expert on psychological safety (and the author of book, *The Fearless Organization: Creating Psychological Safety in the Workplace for Learning, Innovation, and Growth*). She has used the term to describe the extent to which people perceive their work environment as conducive to taking interpersonal risks. In a psychologically safe work environment, people believe that they won't be penalized, rejected, or thought less of when they demonstrate behaviors such as speaking up or asking for help. She has also done a nice job of distinguishing psychological safety from trust. She notes that trust is giving the other person the benefit of the doubt and psychological safety is believing that others will give you the benefit of the doubt.

We see psychological safety as the belief among team members that they can "be themselves" at work. It isn't feeling that we are all friends; it's not comradery. It isn't safety in the sense that there is an absence of pressures—there can very well be pressure to deliver results on time.

And it isn't feeling secure that no one will ever disagree with you or provide you with feedback. It isn't a license to be unprepared or to be a jerk. Instead, psychological safety is the belief that if we speak up, admit a weakness, or any of the other behaviors we previously noted, we won't be judged harshly.

As you would imagine, working in a strong hierarchy can strain psychological safety. A study of over 5,000 mountain-climbing expeditions revealed that teams with more members from countries with strong hierarchical cultural values had higher mortality rates. Perceived hierarchical power differences can discourage people from speaking up.

It is normal to feel threatened or exposed when working with someone who is in a position of greater power than you. We witnessed this first-hand in a medical setting. We were helping train teamwork skills at a sophisticated simulation center where teams could practice handling surgical cases with realistic, state-of-the-art patient mannequins. One simulated case involved a normal hernia operation that morphed into an emergency situation when the patient started to show signs of a possible heart attack. Each team, made up of a surgeon, anesthesiologist, nurse, and scrub tech, needed to work together to save the patient. When the simulation was over, the team would huddle up and conduct a debrief of what happened. During one debrief, we asked the surgeon, who was the de facto team leader, if he had encouraged the team to speak up. He said, "I didn't do anything to discourage them." At that point the scrub tech asked if he could say something. He was the lowest ranking and least powerful person on the team. To his credit, he said the following:

> Sir, with all due respect, we are scared of you and all the surgeons. When one of you shuts us down during a surgery, we probably won't speak again for a month. Imagine that you just parked your car at the mall, and on the way in, you pass a person getting out of his car. You notice that his lights are on, so you gently say, "Excuse me you left your lights on." If he responds, "They're automatic lights, you idiot," when you return to the mall tomorrow and notice someone else who left their headlights on, will you say anything? That's why if you want us to speak up, you need to encourage us. Without that we probably won't feel comfortable doing so.

Personally, we want everyone in the operating room to be willing to speak up and say, "Isn't the procedure supposed to be on the patient's *left* leg" or "Are you done using the sponge that is currently still in the patient's body cavity?" Fortunately, the healthcare community has recognized the importance of psychological safety and the challenges of creating it in a hierarchical culture. And the good news is that they are making some progress in that area—although there is clearly room for further improvements.

What's the Evidence regarding Psychological Safety?

You just read a story about psychological safety in the medical world, but a story is not evidence. What can team science tell us?

Lance Frazier from Creighton University and a team of four other researchers published a meta-analysis on the predictors and consequences of psychological safety. They analyzed the results from 136 prior research samples, based on data from almost 5,000 teams. As expected, they found that psychological safety is strongly related to task performance, information sharing, learning behaviors, and job satisfaction at both the individual and team level. In other words, psychological safety enables the types of behaviors teams need to demonstrate in dynamic, challenging environments. The impact of psychological safety is so strong that, even after controlling for personality, trust in leadership, work design, peer support, and job engagement, it predicted performance.

At every company, some teams outperform others. At Google around 2011 or so, it was viewed as a puzzle they needed to solve—and they decided to conduct their own study. The Google People Operations group, their equivalent of human resources, initiated an investigation around the question, "What makes a team effective at Google?" They had a few hypotheses. For example, they believed that assembling the right mix of team members, "one Rhodes scholar, two extroverts, etc.," would yield a great team. They would just need to uncover the right recipe. They also thought that the best teams socialize and hang out together. So perhaps the way to solve the puzzle was to find the magic algorithm to create a strong team and then encourage them to hang out together to boost their sense of togetherness.

They launched Project Aristotle, which was code-named after Aristotle's quote, "The whole is greater than the sum of its parts." They assembled a research team of some of their best statisticians, organizational psychologists, sociologists, and engineers. Over a two-year period they interviewed more than 200 people and analyzed data from over 180 high- and low-performing teams, examined over 250 attributes, and tested over 30 different statistical models to explain what makes a team effective at Google. At first, the results weren't clear cut. "At Google, we're good at finding patterns," project leader Abeer Dubey told the New York Times. "There weren't strong patterns here."

But they persevered and eventually figured it out. For starters, they concluded that at Google, certain factors did not predict team effectiveness. For example, working in the same location, levels of extroversion, seniority, team size, team member tenure, and even individual performance didn't predict team effectiveness. Who was on the team was less important than how they worked together. We'd speculate that one reason for that finding is that Google is able to hire highly competent people, so very few of their teams suffered from talent gaps. It is likely that almost all their teams were composed of capable people. So, if team composition didn't matter, what did?

The top predictor of team effectiveness at Google, by far, was psychological safety. Teams with higher psychological safety were rated as effective twice as often as other teams, and they brought in significantly more revenue. Members of those teams were also less likely to leave Google and more likely to tap into diverse ideas from teammates.

Prior research had already demonstrated the importance of psychological safety, but Google didn't waste time reinventing the wheel. It was important for them to know what works in their culture. Local evidence carried a lot of weight for them. And it was also useful for them to clarify what didn't matter—to dispel their local myths. Too often companies have "hypotheses" and then act on those hypotheses as if they are the truth, without any evidence. The Google-centric research effort allowed them to disconfirm some hypotheses and focus attention on a few key drivers. Going forward, they won't be wasting their time pushing teams to "hang out" together a certain amount of time or finding an extravert to put on each team. Instead, they could focus on how their teams work together. Their research is driving evidence-based actions in their company; for example, they conducted scenario-based workshops to teach the behaviors that hurt and promote psychological safety. Their study makes us even more confident that psychological safety plays a central role in enabling team effectiveness.

One Caveat

Psychological safety is a key ingredient for team success, with one caveat. There are times when psychological safety makes it easier for unethical behavior to surface and spread. In a study of management students, Matthew Pearsall and Aleksander Ellis allowed teams to "self-evaluate" a piece of work, making it easy for them to cheat. Which teams cheated? It mainly occurred in teams with high levels of psychological safety. Of course, not all the high safety teams cheated, but when a team did cheat, someone was comfortable raising the possibility of doing so because they believed they wouldn't be ostracized or turned in for bringing it up. And there is some evidence that when one person feels comfortable enough to act in an openly unethical way, others may start to feel that it is acceptable as well. Perhaps that is what happened at Enron in the early 2000s.

There can be a dark side to psychological safety. As you become more aware of the best ways to promote psychological safety, please use it for the forces of good and not evil! And as a team leader or team member, recognize that you don't need to tolerate unethical, illegal, or immoral behavior in the name of maintaining psychological safety. When someone crosses the line, they need to be called out.

A few Tips for Promoting Psychological Safety

Two of the top predictors of psychological safety in Frazier's meta-analysis were leadership behaviors and peer support (another was role clarity, which we will discuss in a later chapter.) The following are 10 tips that leaders and peers can adopt to promote a psychologically safe work environment for their team. Remember, you can't make someone feel safe, but you can help create an environment of psychological safety.

TIPS FOR PEERS AND LEADERS

- **Thank people for offering their point of view**—particularly when you disagree with them. It reinforces that speaking up is expected in your team and that it is safe to offer a dissenting view.
- **Summarize what other people have said**—convey that you "get it." This tells teammates that you are listening to them and that their perspective matters.
- Be careful about your **facial expressions.** When you roll your eyes or look "pained," your face may be conveying that the person

is incompetent or pushy. That can not only shut her down but may squelch other team members too.

- Focus on **"what's right"** not **"who is right"**—you don't need to win every disagreement. It is easier to generate innovative ideas and engage in a creative discussion when you don't feel like you must defend your position at all costs.
- **Don't tolerate a teammate saying disparaging things** about another teammate. When a teammate is criticized behind their back, other teammates wonder, "Is anyone saying bad things about me too" and "Would my teammates stick up for me?"

TIPS FOR LEADERS

- **Admit that you don't know something**, don't understand something, or made a mistake. When a leader does this, it makes it much easier for everyone else on the team to do so too.
- **Keep an eye on how often team members speak up**, voice dissent, provide feedback, ask questions, admit they don't know something or made a mistake, seek assistance, and try out new ideas. These are the behaviors exhibited in psychologically safe teams, so consider this a pulse check. If your team isn't doing these enough, then talk with team members one on one to find out why.
- **Ask a team member to share his thoughts and opinions**—and **respond respectfully** when he does. Some people, particularly junior team members, need encouragement to speak up. When they do so, the reaction they get will determine if they do so again.
- **Be clear about nonnegotiables and negotiables**—what can't be changed and everything else where their input is valued. When the team knows which topics are "off limits" and which decisions can't be changed, they are less likely to bring them up. And later, if you do need to redirect the discussion away from those issues, they will understand why you are doing so.
- **Focus more attention on what can be learned from a mistake** ("Do differently next time") and **less on assigning blame** ("You really messed up this time"). A learning-oriented focus allows people to acknowledge their mistakes and ask questions without feeling threatened.

The third of the four key cooperative beliefs is "collective efficacy." A useful way to understand collective efficacy is by comparing it to a few related concepts.

We're all familiar with self-confidence. While psychologists some-times debate its precise meaning, self-confidence can be thought of as a general personal belief in one's capabilities and a general, transport-able sense of self-worth. In contrast, self-efficacy is more specific. It is the belief that you can execute effectively in a specific situation to get desired results. Self-confidence is more general—I'm confident that I'll be successful. Self-efficacy is specific to a task or situation—I believe I can get an A in this chemistry class. (See Table 5.2).

There are parallels at the team level. *Team potency* is a term used to describe a team's overall belief in their team's capabilities. It is the equiva-lent of team confidence—"Our team is strong." Collective efficacy is more specific, like self-efficacy. It is a shared belief among team members that the team can perform specific assignments well or can be effective in specific situations or contexts—"Our team is capable of completing this project on time and within budget." Team potency and collective efficacy are shared beliefs, not simply an individual's belief. It isn't just that I have confidence in my team. It is that our team, collectively, shares that belief.

Over the years, we've interviewed people from teams in almost every major industry. In doing so, we've uncovered many teams made up of individuals with high self-efficacy ("I can do my job well") but low collective efficacy ("I don't believe my team can be very effective"). Unfortunately, if team members must rely on one another for the team to be successful, self-efficacy is insufficient. Teams with high self-efficacy and low collective-efficacy usually struggle to succeed.

Table 5.2. Confidence and Efficacy Defined

	Self	Team
Confidence (general)	**Self-confidence**: A general sense in my self-worth and overall belief in my capabilities	**Team potency**: A general belief that our team is capable—confidence in the team
Efficacy (specific)	**Self-efficacy**: A belief that I can perform a particular task well or handle a particular situation	**Collective efficacy**: A belief that our team can succeed in a particular task, mission, or situation

As with trust and psychological safety, collective efficacy is a judgment based on perceptions and interpretations. It emerges based on experiences with team members and can fluctuate over time and across situations. At times, collective efficacy judgments may be artificially inflated (imagine a team full of narcissists!) or deflated, but even when they are inaccurate, they influence performance. All things being equal, a team's probability of success is greater when they have higher collective efficacy. That doesn't mean that a team that lacks key capabilities will be effective simply because they believe in themselves. But it does mean that they are likely to perform better than another team with the same capabilities and low collective efficacy.

What Does the Research Tell Us about Collective Efficacy?

Alexander Stajkovic, Dongseop Lee, and Anthony Nyberg conducted a meta-analysis of almost 100 studies based on data from over 6,000 groups. They examined the relationship between team potency, collective efficacy, and team performance. Team potency (general team confidence) and collective efficacy both predict team performance. But collective efficacy was the stronger predictor. The belief that "We're good *at this*" is more powerful than the belief that "We're good." Both potency and efficacy matter, but efficacy matters more.

The meta-analysis also revealed that team potency typically operates through collective efficacy. In other words, general confidence in our team is useful because it can often help boost our team's efficacy when a specific situation arises. But if potency doesn't lead to efficacy—for example, if the specific challenge we face is clearly insurmountable—potency alone is unlikely to give our team an advantage.

Stajkovic's meta-analysis, as well as one conducted by Stan Gully and his colleagues, confirmed that collective efficacy is more important in teams that are higher in interdependency. Think of it this way. When I'm working alone, I need self-efficacy. If I don't believe I can do it, my probability of success is lower. When I'm on a team that mostly involves independent work but also some interdependent work, then self-efficacy is still quite important, but collective efficacy starts to matter a bit. As the degree of reliance increases, collective efficacy becomes increasingly important. Highly interdependent teams benefit from collective efficacy more than self-efficacy.

There is solid evidence that collective efficacy boosts team performance, but why? How does having a sense of efficacy improve performance? If you've ever taken a psychology class, you probably read about Albert Bandura from Stanford University. Among Bandura's many accomplishments, he is considered one of earliest and most influential researchers and theoreticians in the area of self-efficacy. His work sparked a long line of research that helps reveal why efficacy matters and how it works. When efficacy is high, we are more likely to:

- View a difficult task as a challenge rather than an insurmountable obstacle.
- Set more challenging goals.
- Exert more effort to learn and execute tasks.
- Sustain effort when "the going gets tough."
- Bounce back from setbacks, failures, and disappointments.

Efficacy enables a team to feel they can exercise some control or influence over their environment. This feeling is often referred to as a sense of "agency." When team members lack a sense of agency, they are far more likely to give up and less likely to exert effort and persevere.

Efficacy also helps a team be more resilient. A resilient team is able to withstand and recover from challenges, pressure, and stressors. Over the last several years, along with our colleagues George Alliger, Becky Beard, Chris Cerasoli, Deanna Kennedy, Jamie Levy, John Mathieu, and Travis Maynard, we've been studying team resilience for NASA and the US Army. Our research confirms the importance of team resilience and suggests that the relationship between resilience and performance grows stronger the longer a team works together. Team resilience is a function of the team's capabilities (Does the team have ample skills, staffing, resources, sleep, etc. to handle challenges) and attitudes (Does the team believe it is ready to overcome challenges and bounce back if needed). Collective efficacy boosts performance in part, because it provides the "attitude" portion of the resilience recipe.

Tips for Boosting Collective Efficacy

Collective efficacy can be a competitive advantage for a team because it boosts agency and team resilience. Here are a few ways to increase your team's collective efficacy.

- **Discuss and occasionally celebrate the team's successes**. If the focus of every discussion is on solving problems, the team can start to forget about their successes. Discussing successes can boost team potency and collective efficacy.
- When faced with a challenge, **draw a line of sight between the current challenge and a time when the team overcame a somewhat similar challenge.** The greater the similarity, the more this will boost collective efficacy (otherwise, it can still boost team potency).
- If you are the leader, **take actions to improve or remove persistently low-performing team members**. Try to help them to improve. If that doesn't work, manage them out. When team members see poor performers on the team and no signs of improvement, collective efficacy drops precipitously.
- When the **team's capabilities** have been improved, communicate that to the team. For example, when you acquire a better piece of equipment, get an infusion of capital, or add a team member with a key skill set, be sure the team understands how this tangible improvement can help them succeed.
- **Focus attention on what the team can influence or control**. When a team spends too much time discussing things they can't influence or control, they lose their sense of agency and can develop learned helplessness. It is okay to allow a little time to "wallow" when something bad happens, but then switch the team's attention to "what can we do about this." Knowing there is a plan to remove obstacles creates a sense of agency.
- **Engage in team debriefs** that culminate with an agreement about how the team will handle similar challenges effectively in the future. This helps the team feel they can tackle future problems and speeds their recovery time.

COHESION

The last of the four cooperative beliefs is cohesion. You can think of cohesion as a form of glue that induces a team to remain united.

Researchers acknowledge that cohesion is a bit more ambiguous than the other cooperative beliefs. Outside of the research realm, the term *cohesion* has been used to describe anything and everything related to teamwork. While there is some debate about what cohesion really means, most researchers agree that there are at least two components to it: social cohesion and task cohesion. Social cohesion refers to a shared interpersonal attachment among team members (but not in a creepy way!). Task cohesion is the belief that the work the team is performing is important, so team members feel committed to the task.

For example, at NASA almost every team has a strong sense of task commitment because they believe they are supporting an important mission. Some teams at NASA also have a sense of interpersonal attachment to their teammates, but as is the case in most organizations, social cohesion can vary greatly from team to team.

What the Research Tells Us about Cohesion

Daniel Beal, now a professor at Virginia Tech, conducted a meta-analysis with several other researchers. They found that both task and social cohesion were positively related to team performance, with task cohesion appearing to have a bit stronger influence. Two Canadian researchers, Francois Chiocchio and Helene Essiembre, reported similar results in their meta-analysis. The research also shows, as it did with the other cooperative beliefs, that the more team members must rely on one another, the more cohesion matters.

We want to alert you to a potential cohesion killer—fault lines. Researchers define a fault line as a hypothetical dividing line that splits a group into two or more subgroups. When team members identify more closely with some members of their team due to shared characteristics—age, gender, ethnicity, education, nationality, occupation, physical location—the stage is set for the formation of subgroups. For example, we worked with teams from a technology company that had teams made up of members from Israel and Asia. Those teams had three potential fault lines: cultural differences, geographic differences, and functional differences (engineering vs. customer service).

A fault line can be active or dormant. Dormant fault lines can be triggered to life by an event that makes it more visible and activates it. Table 5.3 provides a few other examples that we've observed.

The research suggests that fault lines are more likely to create problems when:

- There are strong perceived similarities among members within each subgroup and greater perceived differences between the subgroups.
- When the team is neither very large nor very small.

Table 5.3. Examples of Fault Lines

The Team Members Were ...	Faultline Based On ...	The Trigger That Made It Active
Doctors and other staff on a medical team	Education	A case where a nurse needed to speak up to an attending physician
Senior and junior officers on a military team	Authority	Where they are required to sit during meetings (who gets chairs with wheels)
Members of the company's founding family and others	Family	A promotion decision
Younger and older members of a work team	Age	How technology should be used to communicate with one another
Project team members in the US and Europe	Geography	Deciding when to hold the weekly phone meeting

- When there are fewer subgroups (e.g., splitting into two subgroups is usually more detrimental than three).
- When team members are less open to experience and diversity of perspectives.

Almost all teams have potential fault lines. The goal is not to form homogenous teams—that will stifle creativity and lead to group-think. Rather, the goal is to ensure that a diverse group of people don't splinter into "in" and "out" subgroups but instead operate as a unified, cohesive team.

A Few Tips about Fault Lines

If you are concerned about potential fault lines in your team, what can you do if you are the team leader? Here are a few tips to consider based on the research and our experiences.

- When launching a team, start by focusing on what the team needs to do and accomplish collectively. An early focus on task requirements tends to emphasize commonalities and de-emphasize demographic differences.
- After task requirements and roles have been established, you can shift toward building and sustaining relationships

- Establish and emphasize shared goals that all team members can embrace.
- Use "connectors." In this context a connector is someone who shares something in common with both groups (e.g., a salesperson who worked as an engineer in the past). Research shows that having even one connector can help reduce the detrimental effects of a fault line.

IMPLICATIONS

- Four cooperative beliefs consistently have an impact on team effectiveness: trust, psychological safety, collective efficacy, and cohesion. Keep an eye on them as they can serve as a form of early warning system. If you see signs that they might be dropping, take prompt action—particularly if your team members must rely on one another for the team to be successful.
- Cooperative beliefs are based on perceptions and interpretations, so they aren't always an accurate reflection of reality. They emerge based on experiences with team members and can fluctuate over time and across situations. You can't control other people's beliefs, but you can take actions that may influence them in a positive way.
- Remember that people will judge your trustworthiness based on how they perceive your ability, benevolence, and integrity. Take actions that build your trust score (e.g., avoid making commitments you aren't sure you can keep; do something that clearly isn't in your own best interest). You'll need those trust points later!
- Psychological safety is a big deal. Bad things happen when team members aren't willing to speak up, admit mistakes, offer a dissenting view, seek feedback, etc. Psychological safety won't happen by accident, so try to model the right behaviors.
- All things being equal, when team members believe the team can "get it done," the team is more likely to succeed. So, don't spend all your time focusing on problems. Be sure to allow some time to discuss successes and remind the team that they are capable.
- Be careful about potential fault lines that can fracture your team. To maintain unity and cohesion, when possible emphasize shared goals. And look for "connectors" on your team who can relate to and bridge the gap between two "subgroups."

CHAPTER 6

Coordination

Teamwork Is about Behaviors

S cott was on a business trip that would last a few days longer than originally planned, so he needed to purchase clothing for the unexpected portion of the trip. Here's what happened.

He went to the local Nordstrom store looking for socks, underwear, a few dress shirts, and a pair of pants. He started in the men's underwear section. As he began to examine the underwear, a salesperson emerged. "Hello, my name is Sue. How may I assist you today?" Scott told her about his trip being extended and what he needed. Sue looked conspiratorially to her left and right and then in a low voice said, "You can purchase anything you want, but I must tell you that you are holding an old man's brand of underwear. I think you would be much happier with a more modern style." When he thanked her, she said, "I'll start a collection of the things you are interested in, so you can keep your hands free while you shop. Let me show you where you can find some of the other items you're looking for." As he continued shopping, about 10 minutes later, another salesperson approached him. "Hi, I'm Stewart, I noticed you were working with Sue earlier. She is tied up with another client, so she told me what you were looking for. I hope you don't mind, but I've pulled a few items that I think might be of interest to you. Would you like to take a look at them?" Stewart continued, "I also checked with our tailor. Alterations normally take a few days, but once he heard your story, he assured me he could have any pants you select altered by the end of the day, and we could have them sent to your hotel." In this example, Scott experienced seamless coordinated teamwork, with monitoring, back-up behavior, and adaptation clearly on display.

Let's contrast that with a different shopping experience, which took place at a well-known, high-end store on New York City's Fifth Avenue. Scott was looking for a nice suit. The salesman showed him several beautiful (and expensive) suits, but the one he really liked was too large, and they didn't have his size in stock. The salesperson said, "We employ the most amazing tailors from Europe. They are magicians. Let me bring you to Antonio, he's one of our best, and he'll take some measurements, make some alterations, and your suit will look awesome." Scott went to see Antonio. Almost immediately Antonio started shaking his head and mumbling under his breath. He was trying to be a good soldier, but it was clear that something was troubling him. Scott finally asked him, "Antonio, what's wrong?" In heavily accented English, he said, "This is no good. This is a beautiful suit. The nicest cloth. It should lie just right across the shoulders. But it is too big. I can make it look okay, but not how it should look." When Scott called over the salesperson, the salesperson and Antonio got into a heated discussion, just out of earshot. Scott didn't need to hear what they were saying to get the gist of it. Needless to say, he didn't buy the suit or anything from their store that day (or since). Unlike the first example, he didn't experience seamless, coordinated teamwork. They didn't demonstrate teamwork behaviors or handle conflict constructively; instead, they set each other up to fail.

This chapter is about coordination, or the behaviors that underlie effective teamwork. It is often what we might think of when we use the term *teamwork*. Whenever team members must rely on one another in any way, teamwork behaviors matter. Of course, as we explored in prior chapters, how people feel and the skills they possess are also important, but the rubber meets the road when we see if they are exhibiting the right teamwork behaviors.

Thought Experiment. While reading this chapter on coordination, ask:

- How effectively does your team maintain situational awareness—of teammates' needs and what's going on that can affect the team?
- How well do team members back up and support one another? Do they adapt effectively to challenges?
- How do they handle conflict? Is their approach more competitive (my idea must win) or collaborative (the best idea should win)?

Let's start by turning to our trusted resource, the meta-analysis. Jeff LePine and his colleagues examined this question by meta-analyzing 138 prior research samples involving over 3,000 teams. They found that teams with better coordination demonstrated consistently higher levels of performance and were more satisfied and cohesive. Teamwork behaviors certainly matter. Moreover, teams can learn how to coordinate more effectively. In a meta-analysis of team training interventions conducted by Eduardo and two of his colleagues, Diana Nichols and Jim Driskell, the most potent training strategy was one that focused on improving team coordination and adaptation.

A study conducted in the United Kingdom illustrates how coordination can save lives. Dimitrios Siassakos and his colleagues studied medical teams dealing with simulated obstetrics emergencies, specifically eclampsia. Eclampsia is a potentially catastrophic complication during pregnancy, where high blood pressure produces seizures. They found that medical teams that demonstrated better teamwork administered magnesium to the patient 2.5 minutes faster and oxygen 25 seconds faster than teams with less coordinated teamwork. In cases like these, a delayed response can prove to be fatal. While team coordination isn't always the difference between life and death, in medical cases, it can be! In other instances, it can determine whether a project is completed on time or whether someone has a positive shopping experience and becomes a repeat customer.

Not surprisingly, LePine's meta-analysis also revealed that coordination is increasingly important when team members must rely on one another to accomplish the team's goals. At one extreme, a fully independent worker has little concern with coordination. Consider James, an artist who paints still-life imagery, specializing in bowls of fruit. James only has to coordinate briefly with a supplier to ensure he has the brushes, paints, and canvas he needs and then with an art dealer afterwards, to arrange to sell his work. While he is working, he works alone. Any monitoring and adjusting is done by James. If James was painting a human model, then a tad more coordination would be needed, but fruit bowls are very acquiescent and are never late for work.

In contrast, consider a team involved in producing and performing a play. The director, the actors, the stagehands, and everyone else involved in the process rely on each other continuously to produce a great experience for the audience. Team coordination is essential to their success.

The level of reliance within a team dictates how important coordination is for the team's success. In addition, coordination may be more challenging, but no less important when:

- There are continual membership changes (when the team is low on member stability).
- Task requirements are dynamic and varied (low on task consistency).
- Team members work from different locations (low on proximity).
- Team members possess different areas of expertise or experience or use different languages or terminology to communicate (low on similarity).

WHAT FORMS OF COORDINATION MATTER MOST?

After reviewing the large body of research on teamwork and observing countless teams in a myriad of settings, we've identified four of the most universally applicable and consistently important teamwork behaviors. These are:

- **Monitoring (maintaining situation awareness [SA]):** Remaining cognizant and aware of what is going on within and outside the team that might affect their success.
- **Providing back-up/support:** Providing advice, support, or filling in for a team member when needed.
- **Adapting**: Learning from experience and making adjustments to address needs and improve performance.
- **Managing team emotions and conflict:** Dealing with conflicting points of view, managing team members' emotions, and taking actions that maintain morale.

Monitoring (Maintaining Situation Awareness)

LePine's meta-analysis examined ten different types of teamwork behaviors. One of those behaviors was monitoring. They found that teams that were better at monitoring demonstrated consistently higher levels of team performance. This confirms what we know intuitively— that a team is better able to perform effectively when its team members are alert and aware, are watching out for one another, and have an accurate sense of what's going on that might affect the team.

Human factors experts often use the term *situation awareness* to reflect this understanding of what is going on that may affect performance. One of the early proponents of this term was Mica Endsley, the first woman to serve as Chief Scientist of the US Air Force. Endsley developed a comprehensive model and theory about SA that involves perception, comprehension, and projection.

Perception is being aware of what is going on. It involves being alert and attuned to challenges in the environment and what your teammates are experiencing. Comprehension is interpreting that in a meaningful way. It is like the concept of sensemaking, which the venerable Karl Weick wrote about extensively. Looking back on what we've been seeing, hearing, and experiencing, how do we explain what is really going on? Sense-making has been referred to as a "way station" on the path to action. While sense-making is a backwards look to explain what happened, projection is a forward look. Projection is trying to anticipate what is likely to happen, allowing a person or team to take appropriate actions.

Perception, comprehension, and projection can happen individually or collectively. For example, if I uncover a rumor that one of our competitors may be launching a new product, that's individual perception. When I share that information with other members of my team and they add what they have been hearing, that is collective perception. When together we interpret what that information means and the potential implications of it, we are engaging in collective comprehension and projection. In a team setting, collective SA often leads to better quality decisions and actions, because typically, no individual can see and understand everything that is going on—even the leader.

Effective monitoring or SA is what allows teams to initiate the other coordination behaviors. As depicted in Figure 6.1, it enables them to

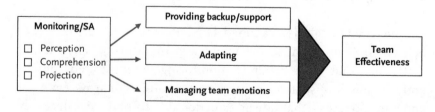

Figure 6.1. Cooperative behaviors and team effectiveness.
SA = situational awareness.

provide backup/support, make constructive adjustments and adaptations, and effectively manage team emotions. In a study of simulated combat teams, Michelle Marks and Frederick Panzer confirmed this relationship—monitoring enables other forms of coordination, which, in turn, boosts team effectiveness.

What Do Effective Teams Monitor?

While the details vary from team to team and setting to setting, in general, effective teams monitor three things. They monitor (a) one another, (b) team performance, and (c) the conditions in which they operate. The following is a list of questions that a team with strong SA can probably answer:

- **One another**
  - How are my teammates doing? How are they feeling?
  - How effectively are they performing their own work and coordinating with one another?
  - Is anyone struggling or in need of assistance? Do I need assistance?
- **Team performance**
  - How well is our team performing? How strong are our results?
  - Where are we making progress and where are we struggling? Are our adjustments working?
  - What merits additional attention or a potential adjustment?
- **Conditions**
  - What is currently going on that could affect the team? What may be coming up that we should be aware of?
  - Have there been any change in demands, expectations, workload, task requirements, needs, or resources? Are any likely to happen in the near future?
  - Given the situation, what changes should we be making or be prepared to make if needed?

To be fair, you can't expect each team member to monitor everything, all the time. That type of hypervigilance is an unrealistic expectation that will collapse under its own weight. Monitoring is often distributed, but collectively, as a team, could you answer the previously noted questions about one another, the team, and the conditions? If so, your team is probably doing an effective job of monitoring.

Monitoring is an enabling coordination behavior; without it, it is difficult to support one another and adapt effectively. But conversely, monitoring without subsequent actions such as filling in for someone, making an adjustment, or dealing with an emergent conflict is insufficient.

Tips for Improving Your Team's Situation Awareness

If you believe that your team can do a better job of maintaining SA, you can help boost their SA by identifying where the potential problem lies:

- If important things are going unnoticed, then you may want to
  - Allocate time for scanning and pulse checking.
  - Clarify expectations about what "we need to keep an eye on."
  - Designate people to pay attention to specific areas of interest.
- If team members are noticing things but are not sharing their observations, you may have a psychological safety issue and should take some of the actions we recommended in chapter 5.
  - As a starting point, be sure that everyone knows who they should communicate with when they perceive something that may affect the team.
- If you think the team could be better at interpreting the signs, engage the team in periodic, "What might that mean" conversations to boost their collective understanding.

PROVIDING BACKUP/SUPPORT

In highly effective teams, you'll often see team members providing backup or support to one another. Sometimes this is a required response, for example, when triggered by a leader request. But highly effective teams also provide what can be thought of as discretionary support, triggered by team members, without a formal requirement to do so.

Backup can take several forms such as (a) providing advice or feedback to help someone perform a task more effectively, (b) assisting or lending a hand while the team member works on the task, and (c) completing a task or filling in for someone, for example, when they are overloaded or distracted.

In the Nordstrom story at the start of this chapter, we saw effective back-up behavior between two sales reps. Offering and seeking support, at the right times, are two clear keys to team effectiveness. So, what do we know about back-up behavior?

Whether someone will offer to support or back up another team member is a function of three factors:

- **Monitoring**—Am I in a position to recognize that you may need support?
- **Expectations**—Do I believe that I am supposed to help out (and am I willing)?
- **Capability**—Do I have the competencies (and time) needed to support you constructively?

Whether someone will seek assistance operates in a parallel manner:

- **Monitoring**—Do I recognize that I may need assistance?
- **Expectations**—Do I believe that it is acceptable to seek help?
- **Capability**—Do I know who has the necessary competencies to help me?

A deficiency in any of the three factors can lead to inaction or ineffectiveness. Here's a rather extreme example from one of the authors. Scott was scheduled to take a short commuter flight from Albany, New York, to Boston, Massachusetts. He arrived at the airport in his business suit (not purchased on Fifth Avenue!) and went to the gate, where the eight other passengers were waiting. The flight was delayed, and the passengers started chatting. It was clear from the conversation that Scott was not a pilot and not a member of the airline, just another business guy with a meeting in Boston. Finally, the pilot, who was standing by the gate in uniform during this time, said they were ready to go and led the passengers to a small, 10-seat, propeller-driven plane. There was no co-pilot or flight attendant. While boarding, Scott asked the pilot, "Do you mind if I sit up front," and surprisingly, the pilot said, "No problem."

I want you to imagine that you are one of the passengers. You spoke with Scott in the terminal and know he's not a pilot. Now he is sitting in the cockpit. How confident are you that he can provide effective backup if the pilot suffers a heart attack? Scott was in a position to monitor the pilot, as he was seated just two feet away. He seemed willing to help, as the pilot kept saying things like, "Don't touch that." But he clearly lacked the capability to fill in (his entire flight experience to date had consisted of flying and crashing an F-16 jet simulator). Despite his careful monitoring and his apparent willingness to help, we should not expect effective back-up behavior from Scott in this instance. He lacked the necessary competence.

What Influences Whether Effective Backup Occurs?

It is easier to back up and fill in for a teammate when you share similar skills, terminology, and job responsibilities. Having a common perspective and skill set eliminates one potential barrier to providing assistance. For example, when a waitress stops by your table to explain the evening's specials because she noticed that your waiter is busy with another table, she was able to do so quite easily because she shared the same knowledge as your waiter. She is even more likely to do so if she has a higher level of collective orientation—if she is someone who tends to think about the team and not just herself.

We also know that backup happens more naturally when team members are familiar with one another. Eduardo and our colleagues Kim Smith-Jentsch, Kurt Kraiger, and Jan Cannon-Bowers, studied air traffic controllers (ATC). I think we can all agree that we really, really want ATCs to avoid mistakes. We want them to seek help when they are overloaded and fill in for one another when they see a potential problem emerging. The researchers in this study examined 51 commercial ATC teams and found that teammates who had spent more time working together sought and accepted back up more frequently from each other than those who had less experience working together. This occurred in part because the ATCs knew who to turn to when they had a particular need. Knowing who has knowledge and expertise on your team is called *transactive memory*, and we'll examine that further in the chapter on cognitions. In that chapter, we'll also explore why some team members can provide seamless backup and support without saying a word to one another.

We can all agree about the potential value of back-up behaviors. We want the nurse or scrub tech to step up when the surgeon who is operating on us needs something. We want someone to help the overwhelmed ATC who is guiding our airplane into a busy airport. But we would be remiss if we didn't mention that there is a downside to backup behavior. A team of researchers, led by Chris Barnes, conducted a series of lab studies to examine the potential "costs" of providing back-up support.

They found that, as expected, back-up behavior is usually beneficial to the person receiving the support. However, team members who receive continual back-up support may start to decrease the amount of work they do over time. In some instances, persistent back-up behavior may lead employees to engage in social loafing, because they assume that someone will fill in for them if needed. In addition, there are times when helping someone else can result in neglecting one's own work. They found that when workload was evenly distributed, for example, when everyone on the team is very busy, then taking time to help someone else may cause you to drop the ball on your own work. It appears that back-up behavior is easiest when there is uneven work distribution, for example, when someone has the time to help. Overall, you should certainly encourage and prepare your team to back up and help one another. But you should also be alert for any unintended consequences.

Tips for Improving Back-Up Behaviors

If people on your team aren't offering to help because expectations aren't clear (or perhaps teammates don't know one another very well),

- Clarify the situations when you expect team members to back up one another.
- When you see the need, actively guide someone to step up and help out.
- Thank people when they help out.

If it isn't clear where and when backup is typically needed,

- Conduct a "team coordination analysis" which answers the following questions:

  - Who might need support and for what?
  - Who should help out and should they help by providing advice, active assistance, and/or filling in?
  - Do they have the skills and capacity to do so and if not, how can we prepare them?

If people aren't offering to help because they lack the skills (or people aren't asking for help because there isn't anyone skilled enough to help),

- Conduct targeted cross-training, which is simply training another team member(s) to be able to perform a part or all of another job.

If people aren't offering to help because they aren't motivated to do so,

- Modify your reward and recognition practices. Are you inadvertently sending the message that doing your own job is all that matters? Do you recognize people when they help out?
- When you hire new team members, look for people who have a strong collective orientation—they are more likely to provide assistance naturally and can help change the "norms" within the team.

If people aren't asking for help when they should,

- Uncover why they are unwilling or uncomfortable doing so.
- Examine the consequences of seeking help. A lack of willingness to ask for help may yet again be a result of insufficient psychological safety!

ADAPTING

The best teams are rarely great on day 1. They become great by maintaining SA, learning, and adjusting. Adaptation is essential for any team that doesn't live in a completely static environment. And, really, who lives in a completely static environment? We probably don't need to convince you about the importance of team adaptation but recall that the most effective team training approach is one that helps teams adapt effectively. And a failure to adapt can have terrible consequences.

The September 11th attacks is a catastrophic example of what can happen when teams don't adapt. The 9/11 Commission Report highlighted how teams in the intelligence community failed to adjust to changing threats. Despite warning signs to the contrary, teams continued to engage in practices that were designed to protect against large, governmental adversaries rather than more dynamic terrorist threats. No one can say whether the September 11th attacks could have been averted, but the Commission concluded that an inability to adapt contributed to the failure.

There are an endless set of adaptations that teams can make. Stewart, the salesperson at Nordstrom, adapted when he recognized a need and filled in for Sue. You can probably think of any number of adaptations or adjustments that your team has made in the last week. We find that it can be helpful to differentiate between two ways that teams adapt, both of which begin with effective monitoring.

Some adaptations are triggered by an event or cue. For example, in a medical case, when the patient starts to show unexpected problems during a routine surgery, the team needs to recognize what is going on and switch from their normal routine to emergency mode. That is an example of a real-time, event-driven adaptation. Many of these adaptations occur when a team experiences a "nonroutine" event and needs to make a quick, on-the-fly adjustment. A real-time need emerges, the team recognizes it, interprets what is going on, and anticipating what might happen next, decides whether to make an adjustment to address the situation. A real-time adjustment might be to quickly reprioritize, dedicate additional (or fewer) resources or attention to a task, do a quick "work-around," fill in for somebody, switch roles, initiate a different procedure, etc.

Other adaptations occur through reflection and are driven by the recognition of a gap, a change in the environment, or simply an awareness that the team may be able to do something better than they have in the past. The adaptation could be a process improvement, a change in strategy or in the "plan," the introduction of an innovation, or just a targeted "tweak" to how the team works together based on a consideration of the past. You can think of those adjustments as more reflection-driven, learning adaptations. Michaela Schippers, Michael West, and Jeremy Dawson studied 98 primary healthcare teams in the United Kingdom and found that teams that overtly reflect on their work processes demonstrated higher levels of innovation, particularly in challenging work environments.

Some teams operate in dynamic environments where real-time adjustments are commonplace and frequent; for example, a combat team must continually adapt to changing conditions. Other teams— for example, on a manufacturing production line—operate in more stable environments. Regardless, effective teams make both real-time, event-driven adaptations and reflection-driven, learning adaptations, as needed. Jessica Christian and her colleagues from the Universities of North Carolina and Georgia completed a meta-analysis of team adaptive performance and found that teams that engage in "stimulus-specific actions" (e.g., event-driven) demonstrate better performance, as do teams that engage in "learning behaviors" (e.g., reflection-driven).

So how does team adaptation work? Here are a few things we know.

The Challenges Vary, but the Process Is Similar

Not surprisingly, teams respond to different types of challenges in different ways. Currently, we are studying how teams that live and work in isolated, confined environments adapt to challenges. We are examining how deep-sea saturation dive teams adapt to challenges. These are teams that install and repair equipment hundreds of feet below the surface of the sea. They live in a small hyperbaric chamber for around 28 days at a time, leaving the chamber in a dive bell to perform their work in rotating eight-hour shifts. We have also studied the adaptation behaviors of teams living and conducting research in an isolated, confined habitat called HI-SEAS on the side of a volcano in Hawaii. Once a HI-SEAS team enters the habitat, they remain there for eight months, only leaving to perform tasks near the habitat in hazmat suits. And we've been conducting research with teams that live and work in a small NASA habitat called HERA, similar to what a team might live in on Mars. HERA teams perform multimonth missions that are designed to be similar to what future astronaut teams will experience.

The type of challenges that require attention in these isolated environments are quite different than those that teams typically experience in corporate environments. For example, the deep sea, HI-SEAS, and HERA teams that work and live together in tight quarters must adapt to some of the same challenges you may have experienced if you shared a dorm room in college. What do you do when your teammates have a different perspective regarding cleanliness, noise, or privacy? And at the other extreme, the saturation dive teams must occasionally adapt to challenges that, left unabated, could be life-threatening.

Despite their differences, extreme teams and typical corporate teams share a similar foundation. They are more effective when they maintain SA, make sense of what's going on, recognize when adaptation is needed, and make adjustments to fit the conditions—on a real-time basis and by periodically pausing and reflecting on their work.

A Few Leader Behaviors Can Make a Big Difference

Leaders can greatly influence whether and how a team adapts. The research shows that when leaders empower their teams, team learning is greater. This was confirmed in a meta-analysis conducted by Shawn Burke and her colleagues at the University of Central Florida. In our work with teams, we've often seen how micromanagement, or an unwillingness to empower the team, suppresses learning and adaptation.

While empowerment is important, we'd advise leaders to let their team know where adaptation is encouraged and where it is unacceptable (or requires explicit approval). Empowerment is rarely limitless. Knowing the boundaries makes true empowerment feasible. When a team leader doesn't specify the "nonnegotiables," a team member can inadvertently get in trouble for making an unacceptable adaptation. When that happens, the entire team may erroneously conclude that they are not allowed to adapt and innovate.

And, of course, we'd be remiss without emphasizing the central role that psychological safety plays in adaptation. Why didn't the team of mountain climbers adapt their plan in response to deteriorating weather conditions on that fatal climb in the Himalayas? Because the team leader didn't create a sense of psychological safety. Leader actions that build psychological safety provide the foundation for subsequent adaptations.

Too Much Agreement Can Derail Adaptation

We want agreeable people on our team. Who doesn't? But be careful about too much "agreeableness." At times, team members need to ask, Why are we continuing to do things the same way? Teams need people who are willing to challenge the status quo and suggest adjustments. We've noticed that some long-tenured, highly successful teams fail to generate alternative perspectives. For example, we worked with a board of directors that experienced almost no turnover for a decade. Members of the board developed a fairly homogenous perspective and rarely offer dissenting perspectives. The organization is thriving, but our sense is that any significant organizational adaptations will need to be generated by the management team rather than the board. Interestingly, the board recently recognized the concern and started to discuss board succession practices to avoid stagnation.

Learning Is Good, but Too Much Emphasis on "Learning" Can Be a Problem

A learning goal orientation is one that values increasing competence (Let's get better) more than avoiding failure (Let's not make a mistake). In general, teams that have members with a stronger learning orientation should be more open to trying out new things. For instance, Jeff LePine found that teams staffed with people who possess a strong learning orientation were much more likely to adapt to a changing situation. But several researchers, including J. Stuart Bunderson and Kathleen Sutcliffe, who studied management teams, have shown that *over*emphasizing team learning can result in an undue focus on "process" that can compromise short-term performance. We acknowledge this is possible, but in our experience, teams are more likely to underemphasize than overemphasize learning, particularly when they are busy. It is easy to get caught up in deadlines and to-do lists and continue to "plow ahead" with blinders on, when a little bit of targeted reflection would have allowed the team to tackle their challenges more intelligently.

Team Debriefs Are a Simple, Powerful, Inexpensive Tool for Promoting Team Adaptation

A proven method for promoting team reflection and adjusting is the team debrief. During a team debrief, team members reflect on a recent experience or how they have been working together. They discuss what happened, uncover problems and areas for improvement, confirm successes, and reach agreements about any adjustments they intend to make going forward. A debrief can range from a quick 10-minute check-in to an elaborate postproject, half-day, after-action review.

The research in this area is clear and compelling; teams should make time to conduct periodic debriefs as they accelerate learning, enable adaptation, and improve team performance. Scott and his colleague Chris Cerasoli published a meta-analysis showing that teams that conduct debriefs outperform other teams by an average of 20%! And in a study Scott, Kim Smith-Jentsch, and Scott Behson conducted for the US Navy, teams led by leaders who were trained to conduct effective team debriefs performed up to 40% better. Why? Because debriefs enabled the teams to adjust and self-correct over time.

We've run debriefs with all sorts of teams, for example, with manu-facturing teams that make potato chips and other snacks (Cheetos taste great fresh off the assembly line!), senior leadership teams that make billion-dollar business decisions, medical teams that affect patient's lives, military teams (the military were the first to embrace the con-cept of after-action reviews), and even astronauts in training. When conducted properly, all these teams found debriefing to be a positive experience. Since we know team debriefs work and are well-received, we want to strongly encourage you to conduct them.

Dan McFarland was a coach for the Scottish National Rugby team and now leads the Ulster Rugby team in Ireland. He is a thoughtful consumer of team science. He has been using different forms of team debriefs to prepare his team for international competition, refining their approach to debriefing over time. He's particularly focused on ensuring his players are actively engaged during their debriefs and not passively listening to the coaches. As he told us, "during a game or practice I can *see* what they are doing, but only they can *feel* it," so everyone needs to share their perceptions if we want to learn from the experience and con-tinue to improve.

You'll find a set of detailed tips for conducting effective debriefs along with a session outline for leading a quick team debrief in the Tools sec-tion at the end of the book.

MANAGING EMOTIONS (AND CONFLICT)

Team coordination isn't just about backing up one another and making adjustments. It is also about taking appropriate actions to manage team member emotions and deal effectively with conflict when it arises. That requires a specific type of monitoring, keeping an eye on your teammates and periodically taking the pulse of the team. How is Joe feeling? Is the team up or down? Who needs a little additional atten-tion? What types of disagreements are arising and are we addressing them constructively? We'll focus on the last question and examine what the research can tell us about how effective teams deal with conflict and disagreements.

Conflict isn't inherently good or bad. But when conflict is handled poorly, it generates negative emotions, hurts morale, and degrades team performance. On the other hand, if team members never disagree, you are unlikely to see enough innovation or adaptation. It is also likely to be a sign of other problems, for example, a discomfort in voicing a divergent point of view. Teams need properly directed and well-handled conflict to sustain long-term success.

Fortunately, there is a solid body of research on conflict that can help guide us toward the positive end of the destructive—constructive conflict continuum.

How Does Conflict Affect Team Performance?

A team conflict begins when one or more team members perceive that their interests or point of view are being opposed (politely or otherwise) by another team member. All teams experience conflict, but not all conflicts are the same. Researchers have distinguished between task conflict (about work content and outcomes), interpersonal conflict (about personal issues), and process conflict (about work logistics; e.g., who gets assigned certain tasks). Karen Jehn and Jennifer Chatman, professors at the University of Melbourne and the University of California Berkeley, found that in higher performing teams, a greater proportion of their conflicts are task-related than in lower performing teams. They also identified that when team members perceive different amounts of conflict on the team, troubles can ensue. If I believe that there are no conflicts, and you think that I'm constantly disagreeing with your point of view, it is unlikely that we are handling conflict effectively.

The three types of conflict affect team performance differently. Frank de Wit (Leiden University), Lindred Greer (University of Amsterdam), and Karen Jehn conducted a meta-analysis of team conflict research. Their analyses, published in the *Journal of Applied Psychology*, combined the results from 116 prior studies and were based on data from over 8,800 teams. They found that when teams experienced high levels of interpersonal or process conflict, team performance was consistently lower. But the results for task conflict were more complex. Task conflict does not necessarily degrade team performance and at times can be beneficial. So what influences whether task conflict is constructive?

Feeling safe matters. As you know by now, psychological safety is a shared belief among team members that it is okay to take some interpersonal risks and speak up without being punished, ostracized, or embarrassed. Bret Bradley from the University of Oklahoma and several of his colleagues conducted a study of 117 project teams and found that psychological safety is a major determinant of how task conflict affects team performance. Their results are clear. When psychological safety is high, task conflict generally boosts performance. If people feel safe speaking up, the team can disagree about work issues openly and make useful adjustments. If voicing a different opinion leads to a backlash, not only do people feel worse, but the team's performance also suffers.

The composition of the team matters. Bradley and his team of researchers also examined how team personality influences whether task conflict will be beneficial. They found that teams made up of individuals who scored higher on "openness to experience" or on "emotional stability" (two of psychology's Big Five personality factors) benefited from task conflict, while teams that scored low on those factors were adversely affected by task conflict. In fact, the pattern of results from this study implies that teams with high openness and emotional stability might need "ample" amounts of task conflict to attain high levels of performance. Some teams are composed of people who are inherently more ready to deal with task conflict constructively. And while research shows that teams made up of very similar individuals find it easy to work together, Clint Bowers and his colleagues at the University of Central Florida found that when teams are working on complex tasks, too much similarity can be a problem. Diversity of experience and perspective can be helpful.

The status of the person disagreeing matters. Nale Lehmann from the University of Amsterdam and Ming Chiu from the Education University of Hong Kong conducted a detailed analysis of almost 900 conversational disagreements during team meetings. They examined these conversations word for word and found that disagreements started by higher status individuals were more likely to result in subsequent agreements, in part because other team members were more likely to acquiesce. That is one reason why it is important for team leaders to avoid being the first to offer a point of view if they want their team to engage in a healthy discourse about a problem. Interestingly, they also found that disagreements were 35% less likely to begin after the prior speaker laughed.

The way conflict is handled matters. How a team interacts when disagreements emerge also determines whether task conflict ends up being constructive or destructive. Leslie DeChurch, Jessica Mesmer-Magnus, and Dan Doty conducted a meta-analysis of 45 prior studies with over 3,000 teams. They found that the way a team handles conflict can be more important than what the conflict is about. Teams that deal with conflict by competing (each person lobbying for their own idea to "win") or by trying to avoid the conflict are likely to suffer. In contrast, teams that use a collaborative or open-minded approach to conflict, where the intent is for the best idea to win, are more likely to improve as a result of the conflict. Uncovering concerns, openly discussing issues, constructively challenging the feasibility of solutions, and integrating ideas leads to better outcomes.

Managing Conflict: Tips for Team Leaders

Every high-performing team that we've worked with has its share of disagreements and conflict. And for that matter, we've never seen a dysfunctional team that was conflict-free either. Given that conflict is ubiquitous, here are ten research-based tips for anyone who is a team leader:

Recognize that conflict is normal. It is not feasible or healthy to avoid conflict. Humans will disagree with one another. They will have different points of view about tasks, about how tasks should be assigned, and about people. And let's face it, we simply like some people more than others. Conflict is going to happen. It is not a sign of failure, and suppressing it is not a viable option. It hasn't gone away; you just aren't seeing it, and your team's effectiveness is probably suffering.

Take the time to address interpersonal disagreements between team members. The research shows that interpersonal conflicts can hurt a team's performance. Unchecked, they can also erode psychological safety, in turn, making it difficult to have constructive disagreements about work-related issues. A team leader told us that an ongoing conflict between two of his team members "was their problem." We advised him that "their" problem affects the team, and so, although he'd rather not deal with it, it was also his problem.

Some conflicts are best handled in private. When two team members have an interpersonal conflict, it should typically be handled in private. If it surfaces in a team setting, find a time to talk with each person individually and then together, but not in front of the entire team. In contrast, when psychological safety is high, a team discussion about a task-related conflict can be quite useful.

Surface and discuss concerns. Conflicts sometimes emerge because small concerns go unchecked. Talk with your team to surface irritants before they become bigger problems. In the research we are doing with NASA, we find that helping teams uncover and discuss potential irritants (for them, it's about issues such as privacy, sleep, and meals) before they become a source of conflict is helping them avert problems later in the mission. Establish a pattern of identifying and discussing concerns openly and "conflict" can boost performance.

Make "deposits" to create a sense of psychological safety. The team leader greatly influences the degree to which a team feels safe. If you are the leader, look for opportunities to set the right tone. How? When a team member offers a dissenting point of view, thank him for speaking up (to encourage others to speak up). Be constructive when you disagree with someone (to model how to disagree effectively). Admit your own concerns or mistakes (so team members become comfortable voicing theirs). In contrast, want to know the easiest way to shut down a team? Punish someone for voicing a dissenting opinion.

Frame disagreements so they are about the work and not about the person. Disagreements that seem "person-related" are perceived as interpersonal conflict. You can take an opposing view about a work idea without sounding like you are opposed to the person offering the idea.

Recognize that "process conflict" has a cost. The research showed that process conflict (e.g., disagreeing about how work is assigned) is negatively related to performance. But at times the leader may need to assign or schedule work in a way that is not universally popular. That's part of the leader's job, but don't assume that it will simply be seen as a "business decision." The research hints that this can be viewed as personal, so if you're the leader, take the time to explain your rationale to a team member who might feel slighted and ensure that they at least feel they have been heard.

Choose your team wisely. When you have the chance, select people for your team who are open to experience and emotionally stable. That alone will improve the chances that differing points of view about work will boost rather than hurt your team's performance.

Know your team. Some people are more comfortable with conflict than others. And there are cultural differences as well. Countries have differing norms about the appropriateness of speaking up. And even within a country there can be differences. In the United States, we facilitated a meeting in the Midwest where people are very nice and tend to be somewhat conflict averse and then went to a meeting in New York where people tend to readily vocalize disagreements, although not always constructively! Be aware of your team's preferences and encourage them to speak up or coach them to be more constructive, as needed.

Know yourself. How do you feel about conflict? Both of the authors generally enjoy task conflict—you would probably have gotten a chuckle watching the two of us debate aspects of this book. And while we like to believe that we promote "constructive friction" in our teams, we suspect not everyone sees it that way! Knowing your tendencies can enable you to tone it down or amp it up accordingly.

IMPLICATIONS

- Coordination involves teamwork behaviors, including monitoring the team and environment, helping teammates, making adjustments, and managing emotions. It is where the rubber meets the road.
- Coordination is more difficult when team membership is frequently changing, task requirements are dynamic, people work in different locations, or team members have diverse capabilities and perspectives. If your team has any of these characteristics, you are likely to have coordination challenges and may need to attend to promoting coordination more consciously.
- Better SA enables better coordination. SA involves perception (what's going on), comprehension (what it means), and projection (what is likely to happen). Teams perform better when there is a collective sharing or assessment of those elements since typically, no team member can see everything.
- Effective teams monitor one another, their team's performance, and the conditions around them. If your team can't answer the nine "What do good teams monitor?" questions posed in this chapter, that's a sign that there is room for improvement.
- Backup can take several forms such as (a) providing advice or feedback to help someone perform a task more effectively, (b) assisting or lending a hand while the team member works on the task, and (c) completing a task or filling in for someone, for example, when they are overloaded or distracted. If you aren't confident that your team knows when they should seek and offer to provide backup, consider conducting a coordination analysis and clarifying expectations. Don't assume they know!
- The best teams become great by making ongoing adjustments including both real-time, event-driven adaptations and reflection-driven, learning adaptations.

- A team debrief is a simple, powerful, inexpensive way of promoting learning, identifying useful adaptations, and improving performance. Schedule time to conduct short, periodic debriefs. Follow the tips in the Debrief Tool at the end of the book and try to avoid the common pitfalls.
- Conflict is natural and normal, but when teams experience a great deal of interpersonal or process conflict, team performance typically suffers. But task-related conflict can be constructive, particularly if your team adopts a collaborative approach to handling disagreements ("Let's try to find the best solution") as opposed to a competitive approach ("Everyone is lobbying for their idea to win") or trying to avoid conflict.
- You'll notice a recurring theme in this and prior chapters. Psychological safety is a big deal. A lack of psychological safety can inhibit people from sharing what they see, from seeking or offering to help, from suggesting necessary adjustments, and from getting benefits out of disagreements. In other words, it can greatly inhibit teamwork, so pay attention to building and sustaining psychological safety.

CHAPTER 7

Communication

More Is Not Better; Better Is Better

A t the time of his passing in 2018, Joel Rubuchon had accumulated more Michelin stars than any other chef. If you've never been to L'Atelier, his restaurant at the MGM Grand in Las Vegas, we recommend you go there. Request a seat at the counter that surrounds the kitchen, order the tasting menu, and watch and hear the culinary crew in action. You'll enjoy a great meal and, if you're alert, might glean some interesting insights about teamwork and communication.

A typical evening at L'Atelier is a busy affair. On one particular night, the restaurant was full. Given the reputation of the restaurant, each dining party expected a smooth, impeccably prepared meal, with multiple courses of complexly designed food arriving on-time—often paired with different wines. The team had to coordinate many moving parts to meet high customer expectations. Yet interestingly, the amount and volume of communications emanating from the kitchen were quite low. Despite a continuous flurry of activity, the kitchen was surprisingly quiet. There was no superfluous conversation; mostly short, quiet, targeted requests and confirmations along with the occasional gentle "bell" rung by a kitchen expeditor.

Throughout the evening, team members kept an eye on one another, often sliding over to help someone else with a task such as wiping the rim of a plate or adding a garnish to keep things moving and ensure that quality remained high. There didn't appear to be a defined pattern of when this occurred; rather, team members seemed to make small, real-time adjustments to help as needed.

Late in the evening a boisterous party of six arrived with an unusual request that the staff could not handle through the same quiet coordination they had been demonstrating. The special request involved incorporating large portions of shaved white truffles in an "off-the-menu" manner. White truffles are expensive, and this appeared to be an important table, so what did the team do? A few of them quickly huddled up and brainstormed solutions. It appeared that the people with the most expertise, regardless of their role on the team, were involved, and a person who knew a lot about truffles did a larger share of the talking. At one point the team reached out, and a gentleman in a suit and tie joined the huddle (we jokingly wondered if it might be their accountant to help calculate the price!). Once a solution was reached, they confirmed that everyone understood the plan and quickly shifted into execution mode, shaving truffles and creating the dish. The kitchen returned to its quiet efficiency.

This culinary team illustrated how a well-trained, coordinated, high-performing team can communicate. Note that they communicated efficiently when performing standard tasks (more communication isn't always better!), recognized the need to change the way they communicated when deviating from routine conditions (huddling up and increasing communication), listened to the team member who had unique information to address the challenge, reached outside the team to bring in additional expertise when needed ("boundary spanning"), and confirmed that everyone understood the plan ("closed-loop"). In this chapter, we'll learn more about these and other aspects of communication and will surface some of the most common communication risks.

This chapter is about communication, or the sharing of information and knowledge to enable effective team performance. Of course, communication is essential for effective teamwork, but it isn't as simple as telling your team to "communicate more." When it comes to communication, quality is more important than quantity.

Thought Experiment. While reading this chapter on communication, ask:

- How **well** do your team members communicate with one another?
- Do they communicate **enough? Too much**?
- Are they sharing **unique information** with one another?
- What are the biggest communication **risks** they face?
- How well are they communicating with people **outside** the team?

One of the most prevalent requests we get from leaders is to help their teams communicate better. For some of them, communicating and teamwork are almost indistinguishable. An unstated inference is that if their team members would just communicate more with one another, then magically their teamwork and performance will improve. But what does the research tell us about communication? Does communication really boost team effectiveness, and if so, how does it work?

At a minimum, we know that communication breakdowns make teams vulnerable. This is quite evident in healthcare. Hopefully you never experience a "sentinel event," an unanticipated mishap that results in death or serious harm to a patient, unrelated to the natural course of the patient's illness. The Joint Commission, an institution that advocates the use of patient safety measures, the measurement of performance, and the introduction of public policy recommendations, reviewed all reported sentinel events. They found that from 1995 to 2005, communication problems were a root cause in nearly two-thirds of all mishaps and remained one of the top causes of sentinel events from 2010 to 2013 as well. Communication is clearly critical in healthcare.

A particularly scary example of a subtle communication breakdown was seen in the case of Thomas Eric Duncan, the first person diagnosed with Ebola in the United States. In that case, the emergency room nurse used a Centers for Disease Control–supplied checklist to screen Duncan for signs of Ebola, accounting for his feverish symptoms and recent travels. Collectively, the cues associated with his case suggested that he was an Ebola risk. The nurse duly documented this information but, unfortunately, did not communicate it to the rest of the team. As a result, the patient was simply treated for a standard stomach virus. An opportunity for early diagnosis and containment was missed.

Communication failures also contributed significantly to the loss of lives when the Costa Concordia cruise ship overturned after striking an underground rock off the coast of Italy in early 2012. Among the many failures exhibited that day, at least three were directly related to poor communications. First, the bridge crew didn't warn the captain that they were too close to shore (a failure to speak up); second, after the ship ran aground, when the Italian Coast Guard's Gregorio DeFalco called the Concordia's bridge, the ship's officers told DeFalco, "It's okay; it's just a technical problem" (a failure to share unique information about the problem); and third, the communication to the crew and passengers to evacuate was unnecessarily delayed, so the ship was listing too severely at that point to deploy the lifeboats successfully (a failure to communicate in a timely manner). As in many team failures, communication wasn't the only issue. Most of the Concordia's crew were entertainers or service staff rather than qualified mariners, and the passengers hadn't received their safety training yet, so a lack of capabilities was also a contributing factor during the evacuation.

Contrast the Concordia tragedy with what happened during USAir flight 1549 on January 15, 2009. On that day, Captain Chesley "Sully" Sullenberger and his crew were forced to land their Airbus A320 jetliner in the Hudson River after the plane struck a flock of Canadian Geese, disabling both its engines. The crew had only met three days before teaming up for a four-day flight schedule, but they communicated and coordinated seamlessly during this unanticipated emergency.

When the captain announced, "Brace for impact," the crew immediately knew they had to switch to emergency mode and prepare passengers for a water landing. The crew quickly shouted out instructions to the passengers, "Brace, brace, brace, heads down, stay down." Captain Sullenberger and co-pilot Jeff Skiles each understood what the other needed to do, so the cockpit was relatively quiet—there were no superfluous communications. Skiles helped reaffirm the captain's decisions as he was making them and called out the plane's speed and altitude, which enabled Sullenberger to focus on landing the plane as smoothly as possible.

These contrasting examples illustrate how communication can influence a team's ability to handle an emergency. A great deal of empirical research supports that contention, and it also reveals that communications are important even under routine conditions. Jessica Mesmer-Magnus and Leslie DeChurch conducted a meta-analysis that examined findings from 72 prior studies, and Shannon Marlow and her colleagues (including Eduardo) conducted another one that analyzed findings from 150 studies and almost 10,000 teams. Collectively, these two meta-analyses confirm what we assume to be true: communication influences team performance and cohesion. In general, if a team fails to share information that needs to be shared (about a hole in the ship or about a simple delay in a customer's order), team effectiveness will suffer. Which means that, as a bare minimum, a team needs to communicate *enough*. But contrary to popular wisdom, simply communicating more does not necessarily improve team performance.

A key lesson from the meta-analyses is that communication quality is far more important than communication quantity. Encouraging your team to "talk to one another more frequently" may not yield the results you're hoping for. In many cases, that will simply create noise. Research shows that in high-performing teams, the quantity of communications can be lower than in poor-performing teams, as we saw in both the top-performing kitchen crew in Vegas and in the heroic USAir cockpit. Instead of trying to boost the total amount of communications, what we should be striving for is higher quality communications. Let's take a closer look at what "higher quality" really means.

WHAT DOES HIGHER QUALITY COMMUNICATION LOOK AND SOUND LIKE?

Let's start with the basics. Quality communication means sharing useful information clearly, accurately, and on time to the right people. Of course, a communication that would be considered necessary, clear, and timely in one situation may be superfluous, confusing, or late in another situation. That doesn't make those factors any less important; it just means that something like timeliness can only be understood in context.

Unique Information

So let's look beyond the basics. One consistent finding is that it is the sharing of unique information that drives team performance. By unique, we mean information and knowledge that other team members do not currently possess or may not fully understand but could benefit from knowing. In the case of the quiet kitchen, one or two of the kitchen staff knew things about truffles that the other chefs did not, and the guy in the suit probably knew more about food costs than anyone else. That team was able to make a better decision because the unique information they possessed was shared with others. In the Ebola case, only the nurse knew about the patient's history. An opportunity was missed because that unique information wasn't shared. Unique information can be related to an area of expertise (e.g., truffles or accounting), the status of a situation (e.g., the hole in the hull is creating flooding), or an action that is needed (e.g., brace for impact). In the prior chapter, we discussed the importance of maintaining situation awareness. Communicating unique information is what enables situation awareness to be shared among team members.

While it can be helpful to remind teammates about things they already know, if all that is being communicated is redundant information (and not unique information), it doesn't matter if we double the amount of communications within the team, performance is unlikely to improve. Unique information doesn't have to be complex. It isn't necessarily based on deep expertise. It can be very basic. A statement as simple as, "The service request is waiting for your approval," can be unique information. Communicating that information helps ensure that the request gets fulfilled.

We've worked with many senior leadership teams (SLTs). The members of an SLT typically come from different functional backgrounds, and while they are supposed to represent the overall enterprise, on a day-to-day basis, they all lead their own teams. Each SLT member typically possesses unique expertise as well as a deep understanding of the area for which their own team is responsible (e.g., a function, product area, or region). They are aware of things that no one else on the team knows about. Unfortunately, when they fail to share that information in a timely manner, the team can't make a well-informed decision. This happens with great regularity in SLTs.

Closed-Loop Communications

Another key element that can drive team effectiveness is the use of closed-loop communications. A teammate may share unique and valuable information with me, and she may do so "on time," but if I misunderstood what she said, that misunderstanding can adversely affect our performance. And the risk is even greater if the message sender incorrectly assumes that I understood. George Bernard Shaw supposedly said, "The single biggest problem in communication is the illusion that it has taken place." If he didn't say it, he should have!

Closed-loop communication is a way to avert that type of communication breakdown. It involves three quick steps: (a) the call out (initial communication), (b) the check back (the recipient conveys their understanding of what they heard), and (c) the close (the message sender either confirms or corrects what was conveyed). Research shows that closed-loop communication is associated with higher team effectiveness. For example, Clint Bowers and his colleagues found that high-performing flight crews use closed-loop communications more often than low-performing teams.

A team of researchers at the Hofstra School of Medicine examined videotapes of 89 pediatric trauma cases, looking for instances of closed-loop communications. While you might think that the time it takes to go through the three steps would delay speed of response, the researchers found that tasks were completed 3.6 times *faster* when communications were closed-loop. Not only do the three steps reduce miscommunications, when treating trauma patients, they also increase task efficiency.

Medical teams and aviation crews usually have a clear leader, and specific requests for actions are quite common ("Hand me the scalpel"), so training programs in those fields often teach closed-loop communication techniques. But how does closed-loop communication play out in other, less structured work settings?

The "Convey"

In any setting, the part of closed-loop communication that is readily within everyone's control is the second step in the process, the check back, or what we like to call "the convey." You can't control if the other person communicates a clear message, but you can control whether you convey. Conveying involves reflecting your understanding of the other person's opinion, point of view, or even their feelings, allowing them to confirm or correct your understanding. There are two types of "conveys"—intellectual (head) and emotional (heart). Intellectual conveying shows you are aware of the person's position ("So the deadline next Friday can't be changed"). Emotional conveying expresses your understanding of what they are feeling ("And you're under a lot of pressure to deliver"). Both types of conveying can be valuable.

Conveying isn't the same as expressing agreement; it is just an attempt to communicate your understanding of the other person's intent. In fact, when you need to disagree, conveying is particularly important. If you disagree without conveying first, anything you say may be perceived as, "You obviously don't get it." You can often tell that is happening because the person you are talking with repeats his position, slower and louder, as if you each speak a different language.

People are troubled when they think others don't "get them," so when they feel that way, most of what they say is intended primarily to make their view and opinions very clear. Until they feel understood, they may continue to pound away, repeat what is already known, and re-emphasize their point. Conveying is a simple, powerful way to break through that common, but counterproductive response.

The motivation to be understood can be even more powerful than the motivation to convince others. In a well-designed study, Nadira Faulmüller from the University of Oxford and colleagues in Germany showed that when people feel understood, they spend less time communicating information in support of their position. That allows everyone to focus on problem-solving and determining what's best, rather than rehashing what they've already said.

Our observation is that everyone conveys on occasion. However, most of the time, rather than verbalizing what they've heard, people reflect and summarize inside their head. Their inside voice is doing a great job of conveying, but on the outside, they are simply nodding their head or saying something like "I understand." Unfortunately, that doesn't assure the other person that they really do "get it," and it certainly doesn't give the other person a chance to say, "That's not what I meant." Conveying is a simple, proven communication technique, so we encourage all team leaders and members to use it a little more often. You might also want to try this technique at home. It generally works well with spouses, less so with teenagers.

Boundary Spanning

We've focused on communications within a team, now let's take a moment to also consider communicating with people outside the team. Psychologists like to use the term *boundary spanning* to refer to communicating and maintaining relationships with people outside the team, both within their own organization and with outsiders such as customers, suppliers, or regulators. Some of the earliest research in this area was conducted by Deborah Ancona and David Caldwell, who observed that two of the most common purposes served by boundary spanning are to be an *ambassador*—for example, convincing people in authority to provide the team with resources—and to *coordinate tasks* with other people or units. Other researchers have since noted a third purpose, which is to *seek input* and expertise.

The way work is performed in most organizations, almost all teams need to communicate beyond their borders. Most teams can't be insular.

A meta-analysis by Shawn Burke and her colleagues revealed that in better performing teams, leaders demonstrate higher quality boundary-spanning behaviors. Leaders often play a significant role in boundary spanning, particularly when ambassadorship is needed. But other team members can engage in boundary spanning as well, for instance, to coordinate tasks and seek input.

Earlier in the book we noted that teams vary on the degree to which team members rely on one another to get work done, from low interdependency (like a wrestling team) to medium (like a baseball team) to high (like a soccer team). Similarly, you can think about the extent to which a team must rely on others outside their team. For example, if a team must first receive work products from another team to complete their work, there is likely to be a strong need for clear, ongoing, communications between the teams. In contrast, when a team is working fairly independently, boundary-spanning communications are less critical. A skunkworks team working in isolation on a secret new product won't need to focus as much attention on outward communications.

What makes for effective boundary-spanning communications? The main ingredients apply—clear, timely, closed-loop communications of unique information is needed. But in cross-team communications, you'll often need greater clarity about the "touch points" than you do in day-to-day communications within your team. If your team relies on (or impacts) people outside the team, it is worth allocating time to answer the three following questions, first among your team members and then in conjunction with key outsiders. With boundary spanning, it is usually insufficient to identify who needs to know what; you also need to clarify who will be responsible for providing it:

- Who does our team need to communicate with outside the team?
- What do we need to communicate about? What types of information should be shared?
- Who will be responsible for communications on both sides of the boundary?

Note that some research suggests that incessantly engaging in boundary spanning on top of other job responsibilities can lead to individual burnout. So you need to think carefully about which people are being asked to fulfill this key responsibility and ensure they have the capacity, information, and role clarity they need to handle it. Distribute some boundary-spanning responsibilities among team members, if needed.

OBSTACLES AND CHALLENGES TO EFFECTIVE COMMUNICATIONS

At one level, communicating seems straightforward. It's not about how much the team communicates; it's about the quality of their communications. To ensure quality, we need team members to share unique knowledge and information, with the right people, in a timely manner. And we should periodically convey our understanding back to others so they can affirm it or correct us, if needed, before we do something based on false assumptions. If it's so simple, then why are communication breakdowns so common in team settings? Because people have human limitations, and teams work in situations that create communication challenges. The better you understand these limitations and challenges, the better you'll be to deal with them.

Humans Are Human

After a lack of communication created a problem, have you ever thought, "Why didn't he just tell me about that?" Sometimes it can appear that a person is intentionally withholding information from us. While occasionally that's true, usually the omission is inadvertent.

One unintentional reason why someone doesn't share a useful piece of information is a common cognitive bias that can be thought of as the "everybody knows" bias. It is a very human attribute to assume that because we know something, others know it as well. Research has shown that even when someone has been told that they are the only person who knows something, they still interact with teammates in a manner that would only makes sense if everyone else knew what they knew! It may seem irrational to act that way, and perhaps it is, and yet people often fail to consciously recognize that they have distinct knowledge that others might not possess.

If you start to look for the "everybody knows" bias, you'll see that it's quite common. Most important, be alert that you, as a human, are prone to it as well. It is natural to assume that others know what seems like common knowledge to you. But what seems common to you may not be as common as you think. One simple tip can help mitigate this risk. We teach team members to develop a habit of asking themselves and their teammates, "Who else should know this?" This simple question can immediately reduce a common cause of communication breakdowns.

While we are all prone to "everybody knows" bias, people with deeper expertise sometimes fail to communicate their unique knowledge for another reason—automaticity. Do you remember when you first learned to ride a bicycle or drive a car with a stick shift? Initially, it was cognitively demanding and required all your attention. But after performing the task for a while, something clicked, and it became far easier. You no longer had to think about releasing the clutch as you stepped on the gas or how to balance to keep from falling off the bicycle. You became enough of an expert to perform the task without thinking. You developed automaticity.

A different part of your brain is activated while you learn a task than when you perform that task after developing automaticity. As an oversimplified analogy, automaticity is as if several lines of computer code have been compiled into a subroutine, and your brain evokes the subroutine without having to look at each line of code. The good news is that automaticity frees up cognitive capacity. The bad news is that it makes it difficult to access details quickly. That's why experts sometimes fail to share unique, detailed knowledge with their teammates. They don't need to think about the details to do what they do. When you ask an expert, "How did you do that," she may provide a superficial response. Please recognize that she isn't being difficult on purpose; she just wasn't able to quickly access the compiled code and, as a result, couldn't share a detailed explanation at that moment.

There is a useful way to help reduce communication risks associated with automaticity. When working with an expert, be prepared to ask "dig deeper" questions and, at times, rephrase a question that originally yielded a superficial answer. This approach, when applied patiently, helps the other person begin to "unpack" their automated expertise. Interestingly, Korrina Duffy and Tanya Chartrand from Duke University found that people who ask more questions, including more follow-up questions, are perceived as more responsive and likeable—if the questions are relevant and not rude. By asking more questions, you not only help an expert unpack their unique information, you'll also be more likeable—and there's nothing wrong with that!

In addition to human limitations, a variety of factors commonly create communication risks for a team. One is a lack of psychological safety, a recurring theme in this book. When psychological safety is low, people are reluctant to speak up, appear wrong, voice an opposing position, acknowledge that they don't know something, or ask questions that might make them appear unknowledgeable. Unfortunately, that reluctance to engage keeps them from sharing important information and reduces the opportunity to correct false assumptions. We talked about psychological safety extensively in the chapter on cooperation, so we'll simply note here that applying the tips we shared previously to build psychological safety can also improve team communications.

A second risk factor relates to rewards and recognition. What happens when you're the only person on the team who knows something? Are you treated as a hero, even if others would have benefited from you telling them about it previously? When you do share your expertise, are you then considered expendable, because others can now do what you do? Is knowledge treated like a currency that loses value when given away? When these things happen, it isn't irrational for people to hoard what they know. When information hoarding is rewarded more than information sharing, whether subtlety or overtly, team members will learn to hoard. We discuss this further in the chapter on conditions.

Teams are also more susceptible to communication breakdowns in the following situations:

- **When team membership is dynamic.** When new people join a team, they are unfamiliar with how information is typically shared, and they don't know who to go to on the team to get the information they need. Due to the "everybody knows" bias, existing team members often fail to provide information to those new team members, particularly information that is known by all the "long-timers."

  We've noticed that this is particularly prevalent when the new team member is highly experienced. An assumption, often erroneous, is that because that person is experienced, they are "ready to go," as if their knowledge is fully transportable from the old to the new team. In reality, however, when someone joins a new team, they require more communications for a period of time, even if they are highly experienced. On the other side of the equation, when an experienced team member leaves the team, she may take unique information with her, creating a knowledge void.

- **When tasks are changing.** When a team performs the same task for a while, in a relatively stable manner, they can develop a shared understanding of how things work. But when work requirements and conditions are more dynamic, the shelf-life of any shared understanding is shortened. As a result, there is usually a greater need for ongoing communications in highly dynamic work environments—it is harder for the team to operate like that quiet kitchen in Las Vegas. There is a greater need for situational updates to maintain a shared awareness of what's going on.

- **When team members work at a distance.** When team members are all co-located, there are more opportunities for informal, unplanned conversations. When team members are dispersed, they can't rely on spontaneous communications as much. It is also easier to pick up on nonverbal communication cues in person. Such cues are invisible via phone or email and not always apparent when communicating over video.

    When team members are split between two or more locations, each location builds its own "common set of knowledge" and is less aware of what's known in the other locations. As a result, each location should get in the habit of asking, "Who might need to be aware of this in the other locations?" In general, there is a need for greater intentionality in communications when team members are working at a distance.

- **When team composition is heterogeneous.** A team made up of people with different backgrounds—for example, a cross-functional team—is prone to certain types of communication problems. People who possess similar educational and work experiences or who share similar expertise and cultural backgrounds can initially find it a little easier to communicate with one another.

    For example, people with the same training and expertise can often use jargon and "shorthand" in their communications without creating confusion. Automaticity is less likely to interfere with communications between experts in the same field, since they implicitly understand why things are being done. But in a more heterogeneous team, the use of jargon and a failure to provide details and explanations can create ambiguity. In those teams, the use of the "convey" and the ability to ask "unpacking" questions are even more important.

- **When there is a clear hierarchy in the team.** A clear, hierarchical power structure can create an obstacle to communications within a team, particularly for communications up the hierarchy. Junior team members or those with less power may be fearful of being perceived as "questioning authority" or asking a question that might indicate they don't know something. We've seen this happen quite often not only in military and medical teams that are inherently hierarchical, but also in corporate teams that operate in hierarchical environments or in national cultures that skew toward deference to authority.

  In such teams, it is not unusual for the team leader to do most of the talking when the team is together. That can be a problem if, as a result, team members fail to share unique information that the team leader doesn't possess. And let's face it, a leader rarely sees and knows everything.

  In hierarchical teams, leaders must work hard to sustain their team's sense of psychological safety, because without it, most team members will be reluctant to speak up. It is insufficient in such teams for the leader to "allow" team members to speak up. We've had leaders tell us that they want their team to speak up, but team members don't seem to have anything to say. We tell them that they need to actively ask team members for their input, and they need to consistently encourage team members to share their perspective and ask questions. In hierarchical teams, "allowing" is insufficient.
- **When handoffs need to occur.** When work responsibilities are passed from one person or subteam to another, communications are needed to avert coordination breakdowns. Handoffs are high vulnerability points. An example of this is when a team member is expected to execute a plan that they weren't involved in establishing. When they are told only "what" to do and not "why" to do it, the recipient is often ill-equipped to handle any unexpected challenges that might emerge.

  Handoffs can also happen across team boundaries. When a shift change occurs, the team that is wrapping up for the day often has a very limited window of opportunity for communicating what transpired to the next team, including any problems or items that need attention. The quality of that communication can greatly influence how well the next shift performs. It is important to recognize that any handoff creates a vulnerability.
- **When deviating from routine conditions.** Remember the quiet kitchen example, where a stable, qualified team was able to perform

their jobs effectively with relatively minimal conversations? That worked until an atypical request emerged. In their case, it was a boisterous group of demanding customers. That was an inflection point, where the team needed to shift from normal mode to a nonroutine mode. More severe examples include when the cruise ship hit the rock and when the airplane lost both its engines. But teams also experience subtler "deviations," like when the CEO tells your team that she needs a report two days sooner than originally planned. No one will lose their life in that instance, but the pressure and stress still rise significantly, and with that comes the risk of a communication breakdown.

The type of communications that works well when things are proceeding normally may not work when an unusual situation or emergency arises. Sometimes, the deviation requires the team to communicate with people they don't talk with during normal times (e.g., the food expense expert, the Italian Coast Guard). Other times, a temporary increase in communications may be required to ensure all team members know what is going on and to establish a coordinated response that may diverge from standard operating procedures. In many team settings, a quick team huddle can help. Given the heightened urgency associated with emergencies, emotions run higher and misunderstandings become more common. In nonroutine situations, closed-loop communications can help avert some of those misunderstandings.

When your team experiences any of these risk points, it is more susceptible to communication breakdowns. We encourage you to anticipate the risks your team is most likely to face and discuss how you plan to handle them when they arise.

Chicken or Egg?

One question we've been asked is whether trust leads to better communications or if quality communications produces higher levels of trust. The answer we give is "yes."

The relationship between communication and trust is best thought of as a cycle that can spin up or down at any point. When team members openly share what they know, it helps build trust. Higher trust makes it is easier to communicate in a genuine manner, and so on. When working that way, trust and communications reinforce one another and create a virtuous cycle. But a breakdown can convert that into a vicious cycle. If something happens that adversely affects the trust level among team members, then team members become reluctant to share potentially sensitive information. If a team member learns that one of their colleagues withheld information, they may start to distrust that person, and so on. While it is hard to say which one comes first, we can say that improvements can begin by encouraging communications or by taking actions that build trust.

IMPLICATIONS

What should be the goal when it comes to team communications? The goal isn't to ensure that everyone gets to speak an equal amount of time or that all opinions are weighed equally. Rather the goal should be to ensure that everyone is comfortable speaking up and asking questions, that communications are understood, and that unique information and expertise are shared.

- Since quality is more important than quantity, saying "Let's communicate more" is not a helpful way to boost team effectiveness.
- Quality communication means sharing useful information clearly, accurately, and on time to the right people. Of course, a communication that is necessary, clear, and timely in one situation may be superfluous, confusing, or late in another situation.
- What drives team effectiveness is communicating unique information and knowledge that others may not possess or fully understand. That builds shared awareness among team members. Unique information can be related to an area of expertise, the status of a situation, or an action that is needed. It doesn't need to be complex or highfalutin.
- Engage in closed-loop communications. Use the "convey" to express your understanding of the other person's intent and allow them to correct you if needed. Convey out loud and not just in your head!
- Be alert for a few common human limitations that degrade team communication quality, such as "everybody knows" and "automaticity." Combat "everybody knows" by getting in the habit of asking, who else needs to know this? Combat automaticity by asking more follow-up questions to help experts unpack what they know.

- If your team needs to engage in boundary spanning, be clear about what needs to be communicated to whom, and who will be responsible for doing so. Effective boundary spanning often requires more intentionality that communicating within the team.
- If you are the leader of a hierarchical team, recognize that it is typically insufficient to "allow" your team members to speak up and ask questions; you need to actively encourage them to do so.
- Anticipate and plan for some of the common communication risk points, such as changes in membership, working at a distance, and when handoffs occur. Identify which ones your team are most likely to experience and discuss how to mitigate or overcome them.

CHAPTER 8

Cognitions

Are We on the Same Page?

One Sunday during the NFL's 2018 season, the Los Angeles Rams head coach Sean McVay called a running play for their star running back, Todd Gurley, the NFL's reigning Offensive Player of the Year. Gurley was supposed to take a handoff from quarterback Jared Goff and then cut to the left. His offensive line, a group of five men who collectively weighed 1,600 pounds, were tasked with moving potential defenders away from Gurley's intended path. The team's receivers, whose primary role is catch passes, were also expected to block on this play. As is true on almost every football play, all 11 offensive players needed to coordinate to make the play a success.

Of course, the 11 defenders on the opposite side of the line of scrimmage had other ideas. As reported by Vince Bonsignore, a sports journalist who does a fine job covering the Rams, the defenders observed the Rams formation and made an adjustment prior to the snap, moving in a way that could thwart Gurley's progress along the intended path. If the Rams didn't adjust, Gurley would be tackled for a loss. If Gurley deviated from the planned play on his own, and the linemen didn't also adjust, they might push defenders directly into Gurley's new path. But somehow, the Rams all adjusted in a synchronized manner. Gurley faked to his left after he took the handoff, but then immediately veered to the right, through an unscripted gap in the defense that had been cleared by his blockers, enabling him to scamper for a first down.

If you watched the play at full speed, you might not have noticed the nuanced, coordinated adjustments that the Rams made. In fact, you might have thought that was how the play was planned. But it wasn't scripted that way. When observed again in slow motion, you could notice the way both Gurley and his blockers read the situation and rapidly adapted as a unit. Several 300+-pound linemen nimbly adjusted, simultaneously, while being pushed by equally large defenders. It appeared magical. But it wasn't magic, and it didn't happen by chance. It was an example of how shared cognitions enable team effectiveness. And it was made possible by actions that took place before and during the play.

Who usually gets the recognition on a football team? On offense, it is typically one of the so-called skill positions, a quarterback, running back, or receiver. Offensive linemen often toil in relative anonymity, at least until they miss a block or are called for a penalty. But the players all know that without a strong offensive line, the skill players can't flash their skills. As quarterback Jared Goff said about his offensive linemen, "Without those guys, we're nothing and we know that," adding, "It all starts up front."

Throughout this chapter, we explore how shared cognitions drive team effectiveness, including some of the elements you read about in the Rams example. The players had prepared together to develop a shared understanding about their respective roles and about if–then contingencies. They understood the "why" and not just the "how." As right tackle Rob Havenstein told *The Athletic*,

> We're not just running plays to run plays. We have meetings where all 11 (positions) are involved . . . and it's like, "What do we want to accomplish? How does some other position affect our position which affects another position?" It's not just the individual groups. It's the O-line and receivers. The quarterbacks, the running backs.

As the play unfolded, the team members all read the "situational cues" in a similar way. "It's especially important with Todd because, I mean, I need to have a feel for where he is," Havenstein said.

> So feeling how a defense plays, where guys can almost say, "As soon as I got this look, I knew [Gurley would run] behind me because that's our read." And I can do this, which will make that happen. And that will (lead) to a good play because I know everyone else is doing their job. And a result, there's a hole right here.

What was the "magic potion" that enabled them to adapt and evoke a set of coordinated responses on the fly? The team possessed a set of shared cognitions.

Thought Experiment. While reading this chapter on cognitions, ask:

- If we interviewed each of your team members separately, would they give similar answers about the **team's goals, priorities, and vision**?
- Do team members have a collective **understanding about their role and the role of others** on the team? Where might there be role ambiguity or conflict?
- Do they know **who knows what** on the team? Who possesses certain expertise and knowledge?
- Think about a potential challenge that your team might face in the next month. Are you confident that all team members would know **what to do if that happens**?

DO SHARED COGNITIONS REALLY MATTER?

In a team sport such as football, it seems obvious that everyone needs to be on the same page. But is that true outside of sports? Do shared cognitions really matter at work?

Psychologists like to use the term *shared mental model* (SMM) to refer to a shared and accurate understanding among team members. Eduardo and Jan Cannon-Bowers were early advocates for studying SMMs. Researchers have also studied and written about *transactive memory systems* (TMS; we admit that researchers, ourselves included, don't always choose the most understandable or user-friendly terminology!). You can think of a TMS as complimentary knowledge that is distributed among various team members and the extent to which team members understand who knows what. A functional TMS enables knowledge to be stored and transferred among team members, when needed.

We use the term *shared cognitions* (or *team cognitions*) to refer to both SMMs and TMSs. Team cognitions are the shared, accurate, and complementary understandings that a team possesses. It doesn't mean everyone on the team knows exactly the same thing, but that collectively they share a common "enough" understanding and they know who on the team possesses relevant knowledge and skills. In this context, you can think about "shared" as meaning more than one person possesses it (as in "Team members share this understanding"), as well as meaning it is distributed among team members (as in "Sharing the load"). Both are appropriate.

Why should you care whether your team possesses shared cognitions? Leslie DeChurch and Jessica Mesmer-Magnus conducted a meta-analysis of 65 studies that examined team cognitions. They found that teams with stronger shared cognitions demonstrated better motivation, more teamwork behaviors, and stronger performance than other teams. Comparing their meta-analytic results with results from other meta-analyses suggests that shared cognitions may be even more important than team cohesiveness. Shared cognitions clearly help work teams succeed.

One example of the research on shared cognitions was conducted by John Austin, who studied cross-functional teams in an apparel and sporting goods company. Each of the teams was responsible for assuring the profitability of a unique product line. They established purchasing and manufacturing levels for their products and recommended new product ideas. These teams, made up of 8 to 11 people with different types of expertise, played a critical role in the overall success of the business. Austin found that teams performed better when team members had a clear, shared understanding of who on their team possessed particular expertise and knew which teammates maintained strong relationships with key people outside the team. In other words, the teams that possessed a shared understanding of who knew what were the more effective teams.

Shared cognitions drive routine and ongoing team performance. But what about nonroutine conditions, when adaptation is required? Jessica Christian, Michael Christian, Matthew Pearsall, and Erin Long from the Universities of North Carolina and Georgia pondered that question. They conducted a meta-analysis of studies that examined team adaptive performance, or how well a team performs after experiencing a change or disruption. They found that shared cognitions, particularly a knowledge of who knows what, were positively related to team adaptive performance.

We've also seen first-hand how shared cognitions can influence performance in extreme conditions. We've conducted research with and advised teams that must work well under highly stressful conditions. When these teams make mistakes, people can die. For example, we've studied military aviation crews (getting ready for combat), cruise ships (preparing for abandoning ship), forward surgical teams (who treat patients near combat zones), oil rig crews, deep-sea saturation dive teams (who work hundreds of feet below sea level), astronauts, smoke jumpers (who parachute into fires to put them out), and coal miners (preparing for evacuation). We've noticed a few common elements in these teams. When confronted with extreme stressors, they need to be able to coordinate seamlessly as a unit. They must maintain a shared picture of what's going on and make continual adjustments, sometimes without the ability to communicate as fully as they would like. They can only succeed if the team possesses shared cognitions, some of which must be developed long before dealing with the actual stressors. Most of these teams practice, in simulated conditions, how to handle anticipated problems, such as a ship evacuation, a parachute malfunction, a fire on the rig, or a mine collapse. Their training helps them build a shared understanding about what to do when the manure hits the fan.

For example, we studied coal mining crews with our colleagues Jamie Levy, George Alliger, Rebecca Beard, Sterling Wiggins, Chris Cerasoli, and Mike Keeney. The research, conducted for the US Office of Mine Safety and Health Research, was intended to understand how crews of coal miners can successfully survive a coal mine collapse. As part of the effort, the research team examined task and competency requirements needed for successful evacuation and conducted a cognitive task analysis to better understand what people think about during an emergency. One of the conclusions was that the team needed a shared understanding of the nature and criticality of the problem, the role of leadership, and the decisions that need to be made during an evacuation.

Teams benefit from shared cognitions in routine situations, in situations that require small adaptations, and in extreme life-threatening situations. But more specifically, what do they need to have a shared understanding about? What types of shared cognitions are needed? Let's look at that next.

SHARED COGNITIONS ABOUT WHAT?

We've identified **eight types of shared cognitions** as shown Table 8.1. Some may be more important for a particular team or at a particular time, but all eight can influence a team's ability to coordinate, adapt, and perform well together.

As we describe these, imagine that we will ask each of your team members questions related to the various types of shared cognitions.

Table 8.1. Eight Types of Shared Cognitions

Question Answered	Related to . . .
Where to?	Vision, purpose, goals
What's important?	Priorities
Who should?	Roles
How to?	Tasks, norms, interdependencies
Why to?	Rationale
Who knows?	Expertise
What if?	Contingencies, if–then
What's up?	Situation, cues

Would your team members provide similar answers ("shared")? Would their answers match reality ("accurate")?

- **"Where to"** is about the team's sense of direction and what it is trying to accomplish. This can be about the team's vision, purpose, and/or goals. Failing to share a common understanding about where the team is headed creates long-term problems, as team members are likely to start pulling in different directions.
- **"What's important"** is about the team's priorities. What's more important, and what's less important? When team members have different perspectives about priorities, it often leads to conflict and distrust, in part because decisions may appear capricious or inconsistent with what some members think is important.
- **"Who should"** is about role clarity. Who is responsible for doing X? Who should be consulted before hand? Several years ago, in collaboration with Rebecca Beard, we reviewed the research on team-building efforts. We found that efforts that were designed to clarify roles ("who should") were among the most effective because role conflict and ambiguity can be so detrimental.
- **"How to"** is about the work. How are we supposed to perform certain tasks and handle certain situations? What are our team's norms about how work gets done? What are our "standard operating procedures?" Not everyone on the team needs to know everything about every task. But all team members who work on a task together need to have a shared understanding about it.
- **"Why to"** is the rationale for how to. Sometimes referred to as conditional knowledge, it is a deeper understanding that explains the underlying reasons for particular actions or expectations. It can be

hard to deviate from a standard operating procedure in a coordinated manner without a shared understanding of "why."

- **"Who knows"** is an understanding about where knowledge and expertise resides within the team. Everyone can't know or be skilled in everything. Each team member has her own areas of expertise and knowledge and her own strengths and limitations. Do the members of your team know who to contact to learn about X or if they need help with Y?
- **"What if"** refers to contingencies. It is an understanding of what to do when particular events, cues, or conditions arise. If X happens, then what should we do? If Y happens, then what's the appropriate response? This shared cognition enables coordinated responses to emergent changes.
- **"What's up"** refers to situation awareness. We discussed the importance of maintaining situation awareness in the chapter on coordination. Do your team members have an accurate, shared understanding of what is currently going on?

A key point to keep in mind is that cognitions must be updated over time. Priorities change, work requirements change, and conditions change, so team cognitions need to be regularly updated and communicated. A study conducted by Sjir Uitdewilligen from Masstricht University in The Netherlands and his colleagues in Canada, showed that teams that update their "mental model" after a change demonstrate better subsequent performance.

In addition, a shared cognition need not be a formalized, rigid conclusion. For example, a team can have a shared understanding that it isn't possible to fully specify their priorities until they know the parameters of the new budget. Even though a definitive answer isn't available, it is beneficial for the team to collectively understand that their priorities are "in flux."

WHY SHARED COGNITIONS IMPROVE TEAM PERFORMANCE

The research clearly demonstrates that shared cognitions boost team performance. But *why* do they work? Fortunately, a few studies have given us a glimpse under the hood, revealing how shared cognitions enable a team to perform better. As shown in Table 8.2, shared cognitions: (a) increase team effort, (b) improve routine coordination, and

Table 8.2. The Results of Shared Cognitions

Shared Cognitions Can Lead To . . .	The Result of This Type of Shared Cognition
Increased effort	Vision, purpose, goals, priorities
Improved routine coordination	Roles, tasks, norms, interdependencies
Faster, smarter adjustments	Contingencies, if–then, expertise, situation, cues, rationale

(c) enable faster, smarter adjustments. The different types of shared cognitions contribute in different ways.

First, shared cognitions increase a team's level of effort. In a study of over 100 teams in a Canadian Public Safety organization, Caroline Aube and her colleagues found that team members were more motivated and exerted more effort when they believed their team possessed a shared understanding about priorities, goals, tasks, and roles. That increased effort, in turn, boosted their performance. In other words, knowing that you and your teammates are all "on the same page" enhances your team's collective efficacy and pumps everyone up. Over the years, we've asked thousands of people to describe a great team that they've been on, and one of the recurring themes is that great teams often share a common sense of purpose and direction. If you've had that experience, you know it can be both reassuring and energizing.

Second, shared cognitions enable coordination when performing routine tasks. The meta-analysis by DeChurch and Messmer-Magnus revealed that teams with stronger shared cognitions displayed better teamwork behaviors. When team members have a common understanding of how a task should be performed (task clarity), know who should be doing what and who they need to rely on (role clarity), and share a sense of "how things get done around here" (norm clarity), they can readily perform tasks that require coordination. It's also what allows for implicit coordination, or coordination with little or no communications. Remember the restaurant crew at L'Atelier? How they could prepare and plate food in a highly coordinated fashion, even while the kitchen was quiet? That's because they possessed shared cognitions.

In contrast, a lack of shared cognitions creates coordination problems. In a study of 300+ project teams in a large global company, Esther Sackett and John Cummings found that when team members have divergent perspectives on who needs to rely on whom, the team was far less likely to be successful. We suspect that's because it adversely affected their ability to seek assistance and back up one another, two hallmarks of team coordination.

Third, shared cognitions allow teams to make faster, smarter adjustments. For stable, routine tasks, basic role and task clarity is often sufficient. But to adapt on the fly requires a shared understanding of contingencies (e.g., "If this happens, then we might need to do X") and a shared awareness of the situation. It helps if the team also possesses a common understanding of "why" certain actions are needed, and not simply "what" to do, and knows who on the team has the most relevant knowledge or expertise. These types of shared cognitions allow a team to improvise in a synchronized manner, like a jazz quartet, or a football team like the Los Angeles Rams.

THE RELATIONSHIP BETWEEN MONITORING AND SHARED COGNITIONS

Consider the following questions. Do shared cognitions result from monitoring, or do they enable monitoring to work? The answer is both.

In a previous chapter, we discussed how monitoring enables a team to coordinate and adapt. Monitoring reveals what's going on and how team members are performing. When a team does an effective job of monitoring, team members are able to update their understanding about the situation and about their teammates. In that sense, shared cognitions develop as a product or result of monitoring. But there's more to the story. Michael Burtscher and Michaela Kolbe of ETH Zurich (a university in Switzerland), along with their colleagues Johannes Wacker and Tanja Manswer, examined medical teams performing anesthesia inductions. They found that when teams engaged in frequent monitoring but lacked shared cognitions about the task, team performance actually declined. This suggests that shared cognitions play a role in enabling monitoring to be effective. Team members can keep an eye on one another and monitor the situation, but if they don't have a common understanding of what to do with that information, additional monitoring may simply create noise that distracts the team. So while shared cognitions are formed and updated as a result of monitoring, they may also be a key to ensuring monitoring improves the team's performance.

Does working or spending time together help a team build shared cognitions? Does familiarity among team members help or hinder a team? As you'll see, familiarity can be an advantage, but not always.

When a new team is formed, if the team members haven't worked together previously, they're unlikely to possess a full set of shared cognitions. But they still may have a shared understanding about some things. Consider an airline flight crew. Over the years, we've talked with many crew members during our travels. If your coffee arrived late during a flight we were on, that may be because we distracted the flight crew. We're sorry, but flight attendants are fascinating people!

Most members of a flight crew have never worked together, but they all received similar training from their company where they learned about flight crew roles and tasks. They were taught that safety is the priority. They learned about behavioral norms, both during training and while flying with other flight attendants. For example, on Southwest Airlines, flight attendants learn that it is appropriate to use humor with customers; that's not the norm at many other airlines. Crew members have also been taught what to do in the event of an emergency or if a drunken customer become belligerent ("if–then" contingencies, such as when to contact the cockpit or alert police on the ground). However, they probably know nothing or very little about one another. They don't know who possesses deep expertise when the entertainment system isn't working or who is particularly adept at dealing with a crying baby. They don't know about one another's preferences or who may be exhausted because they were up late last night. In general, despite never having worked together, a flight crew enters with some useful shared cognitions and can do a good job handling a routine flight, but gaps in their shared cognitions could possibly limit them if they need to work together to resolve an unusual problem.

In contrast, consider a cross-functional project team that was formed in a large global company. The team was assembled to resolve a vaguely described problem and then disband. Team members were selected because they represented different regions of the world, different business units, and different areas of functional expertise. A few team members had received training in project management, but they participated in different programs. They hadn't worked together previously, and the project leader only knew one other person on the team. What type of shared cognitions did this team possess on day 1? Almost none. They didn't have a shared understanding about goals, priorities, or roles. They brought different norms to the team, were given somewhat different descriptions of the problem, and were likely to respond to emergent challenges in different ways. They didn't know which team members possessed key information and expertise. This was a team that really needed to focus on building shared cognitions during their first few meetings.

The flight crew and the project team were made up of people who were unfamiliar with one another. But what about a team that has been together for a very long time? They are far more likely to know each other well and to have developed shared cognitions. Does that mean they will be a better performing team than one that has less familiarity? What can the research tell us about familiarity and performance?

Familiarity Can Help a Team, Up to a Point

There appears to be an inverted U-shaped relationship between familiarity and performance. Too little or too much familiarity can inhibit team effectiveness. When team members first start working together, they may not have built a shared understanding, and performance can suffer. For example, in the aviation world, a disproportionately high percentage of aircraft accidents happen on the first day that a captain and first officer fly together as a team. At that point, they haven't developed good shared cognitions yet, so they are less likely to be ready to work seamlessly if a severe problem emerges.

Robert Huckman and his colleagues from Harvard conducted a study of teams at Wipro, a large Software Services Company headquartered in India. They discovered that when teammates were familiar with one another because they had worked together in the past, their team performed better. More specifically, a one standard deviation increase in team familiarity was associated with 18.6% fewer defects. Incidentally, average employment tenure of team members did not predict team performance. It wasn't having experience in the company that mattered; it was experience with fellow teammates that seemed to make a difference.

A similar pattern can be seen in Olympic hockey teams. Dev Dalal from the University of Albany, Kevin Nolan from Hofstra, and Lauren Gannon from the University of Connecticut studied the composition and performance of hockey teams during the 2014 Winter Olympics in Russia. They found that teams composed of players who had deeper connections with their teammates prior to the Olympics (e.g., they played together in a hockey league), performed better on a variety of metrics. Interestingly, this held for teams that had many teammates who "worked" together previously, but not for teams that had only a small cadre of teammates who had prior experience together.

Team member familiarity also appears to help medical teams. Researchers in Switzerland, including Anita Kurmann, studied teams performing major abdominal operations, with a specific focus on the senior and junior surgeon who would work together for a six-month period. The researchers found that patients exhibited significantly more postoperative complications when the surgical team was in their first month together than in their sixth month together. Intriguingly, senior surgeons also reported that they were better able to concentrate after the team had been together for a while (and that's a good thing!). We suspect that was because by the sixth month together, the senior surgeon knew that the junior surgeon would interpret situational cues the same way she does, which enabled the two of them to coordinate without a great deal of talking. In support of that premise, the researchers reported that noise levels in the operating room were lower during surgeries performed by experienced teams.

Familiarity can also enhance efficiency. Researchers at Brigham and Women's Hospital in Boston studied team familiarity in the operating room. In a study of over 750 mammoplasty procedures performed by 223 teams, surgical teams that had collaborated together at least 10 times previously were 16 minutes faster than other teams, even after accounting for the experience level of the attending and assisting surgeons.

So Familiarity Can Help, but Can Too Much Familiarity Be Detrimental?

Some studies suggest that you can have too much of a good thing. For example, Jamie Gorman and others at Arizona State University examined crews that fly uninhabited air vehicles (an aircraft without a human pilot on board). That study showed that crews that didn't have a long history together can at times be more adaptive. Yet many other studies have shown familiarity helps teams. How do we reconcile these findings?

Jost Sieweke from Heinrich-Heine University in Germany and Bin Zhao from Simon Fraser University in Canada were interested in seeing if familiarity exhibits a U-shaped relationship with team errors. They thought that when a team is first formed, they would make more errors, but as teammates became more familiar with one another, they would build a shared understanding and errors would decline. However, after a prolonged time together, team members might begin to rely on habitual functioning and not adjust as readily as needed. They tested their hypotheses by studying teams in the NBA. They examined mistakes that were attributable to team coordination errors and not to individual errors such as dribbling the ball out of bounds. About 42% of errors in NBA games can be considered team coordination errors. As they expected, the relationship between familiarity and errors was U-shaped. Team coordination errors were higher in teams with low familiarity, lower in teams with more familiarity, and higher in teams with very high familiarity. At some point, familiarity switched from being an asset to a liability.

PERSONAL OR PROFESSIONAL FAMILIARITY?

You'll recall that Google conducted a thorough study of their teams. One of their original hypotheses was that their best teams hung out and spent together. Spending time together outside work should increase familiarity. But that hypothesis was not supported. Hanging out together was unrelated to team performance at Google.

To understand how familiarity influences a team's performance, it is important to distinguish between **personal familiarity** (e.g., "I know about my teammates' hobbies and their family") and **professional familiarity** (e.g., "I know about their work-related strengths and weaknesses"). Our colleagues Travis Maynard from Colorado State University and John Mathieu from the University of Connecticut, along with Lucy Gilson, Diana Sanchez, and Matthew Dean, studied global virtual teams in an information technology company. These teams were responsible for managing the supply chain for various software and hardware products produced by the company. The research revealed that teams with higher levels of *professional* familiarity engaged in deeper information sharing and processing, which, in turn, enabled them to perform better. In contrast, *personal* familiarity didn't help. In other words, getting to know your teammates personally probably doesn't hurt and might build a little comradery (particularly if your team communicates mostly through technology), but it's unlikely to drive significant improvements in team performance. Learning about each other's capabilities, relative attention to detail, and other work-related factors is how familiarity can enhance team performance.

Collectively, the research tells us that shared cognitions boost motivation, facilitate coordination, and enable better adaptation. Working together can help a team develop shared cognitions, and professional familiarity is more important than personal familiarity. Hanging out together, while perhaps fun (if you have interesting team-mates!), is unlikely to build shared cognitions about priorities, roles, contingencies, etc.

Too much familiarity can create the risk of habitual functioning, where teams become complacent or calcify, resulting in more coord-ination errors, particularly in a dynamic environment. An intact team that has worked together for a very long time may be more prone to "everybody knows" bias, fail to share new unique information, overlook alternative solutions, and adapt too slowly to changing demands.

In our experience, most teams would benefit from developing stronger shared cognitions. But a few teams need to be concerned about having too much familiarity, too much comfort. If your team has been together for a long time, be careful about defaulting to "That's how we've always done it."

WAYS TO BUILD SHARED COGNITIONS

Working together can help boost familiarity, but shared cognitions won't always emerge naturally or be accurately updated simply as a result of working together. Sometimes you need to provide an appro-priate "nudge" to accelerate the process. What can you do to build the various types of shared cognitions your team needs to possess? There are at least 10 ways to build shared cognitions. Some can be imple-mented when a team is initially formed, some when there is a change in membership, and others can be used on an ongoing or as needed basis. They generally fall into four categories: direction setting, preparing, updating, and assimilating (Table 8.3).

Table 8.3. Ways to Build Shared Cognitions

Ten Ways to Build Shared Cognitions

Direction Setting
- Visioning
- Premortem
- Chartering

Preparing
- Role clarification
- Cross-training
- Scenario-based training

Updating
- Debriefs
- Huddles

Assimilating
- Onboarding
- New leader assimilation

Direction Setting

These are methods for helping a team look ahead to establish a common sense of purpose and focus. They are typically deployed when a team is initially formed. One example is visioning, which involves describing what a successful future looks like. A visioning exercise surfaces what the team expects to be doing, experiencing, and accomplishing in the future, if they are successful.

In contrast, a premortem anticipates potential problems. At the beginning of a project, the team considers a future where the project has failed and, working backwards, dissects why that might have happened. They then use those insights to establish a sense of direction that can mitigate or avert likely pitfalls.

Chartering is the process of developing a shared understanding about a team or project. A team charter is a written document that specifies a team's mission, objectives/goals, and boundaries and sometimes includes agreements about how the team will operate together. While a leader or sponsor may set some "nonnegotiable" boundaries, the team should usually be involved in finalizing the charter as a means of promoting a sense of ownership and common understanding. A team charter can be established for an ongoing team, while a project charter typically focuses on a specified, time-bound piece of work.

Preparing

A second set of methods is intended to prepare a team to coordinate their actions by establishing SMMs or building overlapping skills. Previously, we've alluded to the importance of role clarity. Exercises such as RACI charting are designed to build a shared understanding of who is responsible for what. In addition, cross-training can be provided to team members, ranging from full cross-training ("I'm trained to fill in for you"), to partial cross-training ("I'm trained to fill in or help out on a few tasks"), to interpositional knowledge training ("I learn about what you do so I'm more aware"). Each of the cross-training approaches are designed to build a common understanding about other team members' job requirements and make it easier to back up and support one another. Scenario-based training can also help. In the simplest version of this training, the team is presented with a future challenge and they discuss how they would handle it, including who would do what, with whom, why, and when. The trainer then provides additional information about the challenge, the team discusses what they would then do, and so on.

Updating

Third, several methods can be deployed to update shared cognitions. Debriefs and huddles are particularly useful for that purpose. For example, during a debrief, a team might discuss what happened during a recent work experience, what they did that worked well, what didn't work, and how conditions have changed. This allows them to recalibrate priorities and roles, update situation awareness, learn more about who knows what, and make modifications as needed. You'll find tips for conducting effective debriefs in the tools section at the back of the book.

Assimilating

Finally, there are methods that can be deployed to help bring on a new team member or leader. Team member onboarding can be used to communicate team norms, roles, and other factors to someone who joins the team "midstream," accelerating their understanding about the team's current shared cognitions. Talya Bauer and her colleagues from

Portland State University and the Army Research Institute conducted a meta-analysis of 70 prior studies that showed that effective onboarding creates greater role clarity and confidence, which, in turn, leads to better performance.

In contrast, when a new leader comes on board, they often bring their own approach to the team, which may be different than the existing shared cognitions. A new leader assimilation session is a facilitated meeting between a new leader and her team, in which team members generate questions for the new leader and the leader is given the chance to share her expectations and, if necessary, establish new shared norms.

IMPLICATIONS

Team cognitions are the shared, accurate, and complementary understandings that a team possesses. It doesn't mean everyone on the team knows exactly the same thing but that, collectively, they share a common "enough" understanding and they know who on the team possesses relevant knowledge and skills.

- Research shows that shared cognitions boost team performance because they enhance motivation, facilitate coordination, and enable smarter adjustments. It is worth the effort to ensure team members are on the same page.
- A shared cognition need not be a formalized, rigid conclusion. For example, if all team members are aware that priorities are in flux until the budget process is complete, that's a valuable shared cognition.
- Teams generally perform better when they can provide similar answers to the following questions, so consider discussing them as a team.
  - Where are we headed? (vision, purpose, goals)
  - What's important? (priorities)
  - Who should? (roles)
  - How to? (tasks, norms, interdependencies)
  - Why to? (rationale)
  - Who knows? (expertise)
  - What if? (contingencies, if-then)
  - What's up? (situation, cues)
- Determine what everyone must understand and what only some team members must understand. For example, everyone may need

to know where the team is headed, the current priorities, when to escalate a problem to "emergency" mode, and who is responsible if X occurs. But don't insist that everyone know everything if that's not needed.

- Be alert that SLTs are particularly susceptible to disconnects regarding their purpose and direction. Ruth Wageman, a psychology professor at Harvard, has written about the unique challenges they face. In the words of one of the leaders she studied, "So, our team purpose is really important, and it's going to be very tough to pull off . . . if only we knew what it was." We've found that SLT members often even disagree about how many people are on their team!

- There can be benefits to a team jointly establishing shared cognitions. But the team leader should communicate their expectations regarding any "nonnegotiables." By clearly stating what has already been determined and is unchangeable, a leader contributes to the formation of shared cognitions. Please don't assume that the team must jointly establish everything.

- If expertise and knowledge are distributed on the team, be sure team members know where that expertise resides. Who knows what? Who is really good at X?

- Too little or too much familiarity can inhibit performance. When team members first start working together, they may not yet have a shared understanding, so increasing familiarity helps. But after a prolonged time together, team members can rely on habitual functioning and not adjust as readily as needed. If you are on a long-tenured team, avoid defaulting to "That's how we've always done it."

- Professional familiarity (e.g., "I know my teammates' strengths and needs") is more important than personal familiarity (e.g., "I know their favorite hobbies"). So, simply hanging out together probably won't build the types of SMMs that really matter—even if you serve beer.

- Most teams need to spend a little more time building and updating their shared cognitions. Try using one or more of the direction-setting, preparing, updating, or assimilating approaches described in this chapter.

CHAPTER 9

Conditions

You Get What You Encourage . . . and Tolerate

Several years ago, a well-known, high-end retailer wanted to move toward more of a collaborative, team-oriented selling approach. Historically, each sales professional had been primarily an individual contributor. A meaningful part of their compensation was based on their own sales, and they tended to view certain customers as their own.

What happened when the sales professionals were first asked to work more collaboratively? We visited several of their stores and unobtrusively watched them in action. Here's an example of what we noticed.

A customer entered a store carrying a shopping bag with the store's logo on it, a good indication that she was there to return a previous purchase. As she approached one of the sales counters, the salesperson answered the phone, and as a result, he wasn't available to help process the return. Seeing this, the customer veered diagonally and approached a sales rep at the next counter. But there's a catch. We were close enough to notice that the phone had not rung! The first sales rep knew that if he spent time helping the customer return a prior purchase, he might miss the opportunity to make a sale to a paying customer. And if one of his big spending "regulars" came in during that time, he'd be unavailable and might miss a big sale. To avoid that risk, he pretended to answer the phone. Unsurprisingly, the phantom phone call ended the moment the customer approached the other counter.

Was the sales professional's behavior irrational? He might not have been doing what was best for the company (or the customer), and he certainly wasn't being a good team member, but his actions weren't irrational. In fact, he was responding in a manner that was consistent with the conditions in which the sales team operated. The store was staffed with capable people, but the cultural norm was that each person was primarily on their own. Moreover, the way rewards and promotions were distributed reinforced individualism. The salespeople with the greatest sales volume made the most money and were most likely to be promoted. Handling a return or taking the time to help another sales-person with "their" sale was not reinforced by either informal norms or formal human resource practices. As you might imagine, this frustrated those sales professionals who had a collective orientation and who ended up absorbing many "team first" tasks, such as handling returns, that adversely affected their own compensation.

Asking the sales professionals to work together as a team was insufficient to move the needle. They were well trained in their individual jobs and possessed most of the skills they would need to work as a team, but the conditions inhibited teamwork. Pulitzer Prize–winning author Upton Sinclair was fond of saying, "It is difficult to get a man to understand something, when his salary depends upon his not understanding it." It was only when the company modified the conditions that the sales professionals' behaviors started to change.

This chapter is about conditions—the context or environment in which a team operates. Conditions include tangible elements such as organizational policies and practices (e.g., that guide compensation and promotion decisions), resources (e.g., are enough people assigned to the team, does the team have access to the information they need, do they have ample time), and less tangible elements such as senior leader support and organizational culture.

No team works in a vacuum. Some of the conditions they experience may be favorable and serve to facilitate or enable team effectiveness. Others can act as constraints or inhibitors. We encourage you to monitor the conditions that can affect your team and to do all you can to ensure they are as favorable as possible. But let's also acknowledge that some things can't be changed. These are the "givens" that your team may need to learn to work around. As you'll see in this chapter, it is helpful to think about conditions as operating on two levels: the broader organizational or business unit level and the local, team-specific level.

WHY SHOULD YOU WORRY ABOUT CONDITIONS?

Conditions are probably the least studied of the drivers that we explore in this book. But based on our experience and drawing upon research that has examined organizational culture, human resource management practices, change management, and psychology, we conclude that conditions matter a great deal. They influence the extent to which people are willing and able to coordinate with one another, as well as the degree to which a team learns, adjusts, and innovates. They establish whether the team has adequate resources to accomplish their mission. When conditions are highly unfavorable, even good teams can fail.

When conditions are more favorable, teams exhibit significantly more learning behaviors as Chris Wiese of Georgia Tech and his colleagues discovered in their meta-analysis of 54 studies and over 4,800 teams. Learning behaviors help a team adapt and perform effectively over time.

Conditions also influence a team's creativity, innovativeness, and performance. In a study of 104 teams across 14 companies in South Korea, Yuhyung Shin and researchers from Seoul National University found that team culture played a key role in determining creativity and performance levels. And a study conducted by Doris Fay, Helen Shipton, Michael West, and Malcolm Patterson found that manufacturing teams in the United Kingdom were more innovative when conditions allowed them time to engage in thoughtful reflection.

When employees perceive their work environment to be supportive, positive things happens. James Kurtessis and a team of researchers conducted a meta-analysis on the effects of "perceived organizational support." When perceived support is higher, employees are more likely to trust their coworkers, leaders, and employer. They more strongly identify with the organization, and more employees go beyond their required job responsibilities to help the team and organization succeed (e.g., maybe they'll handle more customer returns!). Of course, trust and identity are enablers of teamwork. When trust is higher, it is easier to collaborate. When employees identify with the organization, they are less likely to think only about themselves. And when team members go above and beyond their own job requirements, it promotes team cohesion and effectiveness.

On a more tangible note, resourcing is a "condition" that directly impacts performance. If a team lacks access to critical information, necessary equipment, or other resources, performance will almost certainly suffer. And when a team is understaffed, even well-intended team members may lack the "bandwidth" to backup and help one another.

Collectively, the research on culture and the work environment confirms a well-known axiom in psychology—the social context creates potent forces that can constrain, encourage, or otherwise guide human behavior. That is true for teams as well as individuals.

Collectively, the research supports what we know intuitively— conditions have a significant impact on our behaviors.

SITUATIONAL STRENGTH

Psychologists like to say that behavior is a function of both the person and the situation. But how much does a situation influence behavior? That depends on the "strength" of the situation. Social psychologist Walter Mischel advanced the concept of situational strength to describe the relative power of a situation to control individual behavior and minimize the influence of personal attributes such as personality (you may know of Mischel as the Stanford researcher who conducted studies with children using marshmallows to explore delayed gratification).

To assess situational strength, you need to look beyond the objective characteristics of the situation and consider the way people "see" and interpret a situation. Perceptions may be consistent with objective reality, but not always. For example, in the same situation, two people can pick up on different cues, or they may see the same cues, but interpret them differently. From a psychological perspective, the perceptions and interpretations of the players are what matters.

Some situations are so strong they essentially mandate behaviors, others only offer hints or "nudges" about what to do, and weak situations may offer no clues about expected behaviors. A situation is considered to be "strong" when everyone involved is likely to see it and interpret how to behave in the same way and when it clearly incentivizes those behaviors. In other words, strong situations are much more likely than weak ones to induce conformity. The stronger the situation, the less behavior is determined by personal preferences or personality. For example, let's consider what happens when we drive a car.

You are driving along and approach a four-way stop sign at a busy intersection. What do you do? It doesn't matter if you have an assertive personality, you will almost certainly stop your car at that intersection. All drivers at the intersection are likely to interpret a stop sign in the same way. It evokes a similar understanding of what is expected ("I need to stop and wait my turn"), and the situation incentivizes stopping due to the physical and legal consequences of ignoring it. But what happens when a driver approaches a yield sign? The majority of drivers slow down or even stop, allowing others to proceed first. But assertive drivers may behave more aggressively, perhaps even speeding up to claim "their" spot as they merge into traffic. The situational cues are fairly strong, but not as strong as at the stop sign.

Now consider how people behave when driving on a multilane highway. Have you noticed how some people stay in the passing lane even though they are driving slower than everyone else? Eduardo does that quite often, much to Scott's dismay. Driving slowly in the passing lane is a rarely enforced infraction, and there are no tangible reminders to cue people to move over (unless you count the people who honk their horn at Eduardo), so personal preferences guide behavior on the highway much more so than at a stop sign or even a yield sign. The same is true for teamwork. Some situations send very strong signals that encourage or discourage people to collaborate with one another. Other situations send weak signals about what is expected.

In some instances, it is impossible to get things done without collaborating, so teamwork is essentially "baked into" the work, and a certain amount of coordinating will always take place. For example, on a manufacturing assembly line, where product moves from one person or station to another, these isn't much room for individual freelancing. Similarly, in underground long-wall coal mining, there are inherent coordination requirements that must be followed to ensure the safety of all involved. Everyone is aware of these requirements—they are baked in.

Even when teamwork isn't baked in, if coordination requirements are clear and teamwork breakdowns have serious consequences, the situation provides a strong nudge that encourages cooperation. For example, in deep-sea saturation diving, small teams of divers work together performing maintenance and construction tasks hundreds of feet below the surface of the sea. A dive team often consists of three divers, who descend together in a diving bell. One team member stays in the bell while the other two perform undersea work assignments. The "bellman" is the first line of defense to ensure the safety of the other divers. Team members rotate positions, so one day a person may be a diver and the next day, a bellman. Given the danger of the job and the fact that team members rely on each other so deeply (pun intended), monitoring and supporting one another doesn't feel optional. Even a naturally selfish person will collaborate when the cues are strong enough.

Keep in mind that "strong" doesn't mean positive; it means influential. You can have a strong situation in which many of the cues reinforce "me-first" behaviors. We've seen organizations where the policies (e.g., the use of a forced distribution rating system), social norms (e.g., managers won't eat lunch with "underlings"), and career-related decisions (e.g., promoting toxic employees because they generate revenue) encourage competition and discourage cooperation.

In most settings, the nature of the situation ("conditions") combines with the attributes of the people involved (e.g., "capabilities") to determine if a team will work together successfully. So, let's take a closer look at the conditions that matter, including ones that send signals (strong or weak) about whether being a team player is truly valued, whether it is okay to be a jerk, and whether it is acceptable for junior people to speak up. We'll also take a look at the conditions that can tangibly enable or constrain teamwork, such as the availability of resources and time. There are a dozen or so meaningful organizational and local, team-specific conditions that should be on your radar screen. You can read about these in the following discussion, and in the Tools section, you'll find a set of Diagnostic Questions you can use to review the conditions that currently exist within your organization.

Some conditions can influence many teams simultaneously. For example, company or business-unit wide policies and practices (e.g., about rewards) and senior leadership behaviors and communications (e.g., do senior leaders work well with one another) send widespread signals that can confirm or refute the importance of teamwork. In the following text, we describe these conditions and provide a set of questions you can use to assess current conditions and stimulate a conversation how to improve them.

As you read this section, we encourage you to reflect on the organization-wide signals that you experience. Do they support or inhibit teamwork? Which could be improved?

Policies and Practices in the Organization

When policies and practices are designed to work in an integrated manner and reinforce a common message, they can send a "strong" signal about expected behaviors. How do policies and practices influence teamwork? Let's look at five of the most salient ones.

1. **Hiring**. As job candidates go through the recruiting and screening process, they get their first glimpse at how teamwork is viewed in the organization. If they are never asked about their teamwork skills and experiences and instead are only assessed on their technical expertise and individual accomplishments, it sends an early signal that teamwork is relatively unimportant. The message is, "You don't get a job at our company because we think you'll be an effective collaborator, you get it because of your individual expertise." Do your interview protocols and assessment tools assess teamwork skills?

   In addition, managers and employees who actively participate in the hiring process learn about the pool of candidates and eventually see who was chosen. Each hiring decision can provide subtle signals about the importance of teamwork. For example, does your company seem comfortable hiring people with strong technical skills but who demonstrate no signs of being a team player? Do they ignore warnings about a candidate's selfishness or incivility? If this happens with some regularity, it doesn't matter if employees have been told,

"We value teamwork around here," because they see that hiring practices contradict that statement.

2. **Onboarding**. Every new hire goes through some type of onboarding experience, formal or informal. Formal onboarding is intended to communicate to a new hire what to expect and what is expected of them, so it sends initial signals about teamwork. But even if a new employee doesn't don't go through a formal orientation, they certainly will experience an informal onboarding process with their own team.

   Sometimes onboarding simply consists of the new team member being told by the team leader, "Here's your desk," which sends the message, "Don't expect teammates to help you." In contrast, if team members are involved, helpful, and supportive of the new hire during the first few weeks, it increases the likelihood that the new team member will conclude that working cooperatively and helping teammates is an expected norm.

3. **Promotions and opportunities**. People generally believe more of what they see than what they hear. One tangible manifestation of the relative importance of teamwork is seen when people get promoted.

   Show us who gets promoted in your organization, who gets the desirable developmental opportunities, and who is given choice work assignments, and we can tell you if teamwork is *really* valued. Employees pick up on these signals as well. If teamwork is important, then how well someone collaborates should make a difference when deciding if they are worthy of a promotion. When the "me-first" people get the choice assignments and promotions and great team players get overlooked, it sends a powerful message to everyone. As a character in Swedish novelist Fredrik Backman's book *Beartown* said, "Culture is as much about what we encourage as what we actually permit." Permitting selfish people to get ahead can define your culture in unintended ways.

4. **Performance management**. During the performance management process, employees receive feedback from and engage in discussions with their team leader. Some fairly strong signals get sent in that process, which conveys the "real" expectations about teamwork. Some of the signals surface during the formal performance review, while others occur during informal performance management discussions.

   Consider how the following elements might discourage teamwork. The company's rating form doesn't include any reference to teamwork or collaboration. The goals that get established are exclusively about individual accomplishments. Team members are never asked about who has been helpful to them. Performance review discussions focus strictly on individual performance. And a forced distribution rating system is used, where a certain percentage of employees must be designated as underperforming. Hmmm.

A company can say that teamwork is valued, but if the performance management process is all about "me" and not at all about "us," employees will learn what really counts. Australian software company Atlassan revised their performance review process to strongly weight how each employee impacts others on their team. Their intent is to signal that they will no longer tolerate brilliant jerks, employees who produce results by making things difficult for everyone around them.

5. **Rewards and recognition**. In "strong situations," behavioral expectations are clear and incentivized. Compensation and reward decisions, both financial and nonmonetary, are intended to clarify and reinforce behavioral expectations. In practice however, rewards can have unintended consequences. If a team member is told that he needs to contribute to the team but is only rewarded and recognized for his individual accomplishments, we can't fault him for concluding that teamwork isn't really an expectation. The message is, teamwork may be nice, but it's not what really matters around here.

Of course, many individuals are intrinsically motivated to collaborate, support their teammates, and think "we before me," but the way that rewards and recognition get distributed over time sends signals that can crush or enhance that motivation. We acknowledge that it is hard to design effective reward systems. At a minimum, we encourage you to consider if your company's reward and recognition system is inadvertently discouraging people from collaborating.

6. **Leadership development**. While teamwork isn't just about the leader, the team leader does play a disproportionately large role in determining a team's success. How do managers and project leaders learn how to become effective team leaders? While a few people may "naturally" figure it out, most need some guidance, so a key condition for driving effective teamwork is having the right leadership development practices in place to build key team leader competencies.

How does your organization prepare people to become effective team leaders? For example, does your leadership training teach people how to lead a team, or does it mainly focus on managing individuals and making business decisions?

What about the role of senior leadership? Even when senior leadership is hidden away on the top floor of corporate headquarters, their behaviors and communications can be surprisingly influential in establishing whether teamwork becomes an organizational norm. In some ways, senior leadership sets a cultural tone and creates the overarching conditions for teamwork throughout the rest of the company.

1. **Modeling of behaviors**. Although much of what senior leaders do on a day-to-day basis may be invisible to most employees, their behaviors still find a way of influencing people throughout the organization. A team of European researchers, led by Anneloes Raes, examined over 60 top management teams. They found that when members of the senior leadership team worked together in a cooperative manner, employee satisfaction and retention levels in the organization were significantly higher. This happened even though most employees didn't interact with the senior leaders! Apparently, what happens behind closed doors doesn't stay behind closed doors. Stories about senior leadership makes its way through the organization.

    Senior leaders also send signals through their personal behaviors. If a leader yells at subordinates or talks disparagingly about colleagues, it sends the message that incivility is acceptable. Peter Pisters, the CEO at the MD Anderson Cancer Center, recently told his employees that they will never see him raise his voice. He appears to understand the detrimental effect incivility can have on collaboration.

2. **Communications**. We've said that behaviors generally matter more than words, but senior leader communications are carefully scrutinized by employees for clues about what's important. The nature and content of senior leader communications can reveal insights about the importance of teamwork. Do they emphasize how teamwork is needed for the business to be successful? Do they tell stories that feature successful collaboration and teamwork, or do they only focus on individual accomplishments?

    Employees are sensitive to cues that indicate senior leaders are not on the same page, so consistency of communications also matters. For example, when members of a leadership team return from a planning meeting, and each leader delivers a different, unit-centric message to "their people," employees compare what they heard and uncover the discrepancies. When that happens, employees can easily conclude that senior leadership isn't unified and doesn't work as a team, leading them to think, "Why should the rest of us try to collaborate, if they don't?"

3. **Creating psychological safety**. Throughout the book we've emphasized the need to establish psychological safety, because the research provides a compelling picture of its importance. Psychological safety starts at the top. Senior leaders set the tone when it comes to psychological safety.

   To what extent do senior leaders make it easy for others to speak up, voice concerns, and offer divergent opinions? If top leaders typically crush dissent, chastise others for bringing bad news to them, or publicly berate people for making a mistake, that style of leadership trickles down level by level, making it harder for team leaders throughout the organization to establish psychological safety.

Other Signals about the Culture

Before we move on to team-specific conditions, we want to say a few words about two other subtle cues that send signals about teamwork. These cues are generally "weaker" than the ones we previously discussed, but they can provide nudges that encourage or discourage collaboration.

- **Who eats meals or drinks coffee together**? In many high schools, cliques of kids cluster together at lunch. The athletes don't sit with the science wizards, who don't sit with the musical kids, etc. As a result, you won't see much "cross-clique" communication or collaboration in high school.

  That same phenomena can be seen in some corporate settings. If the norm in your organization is for managers to only eat meals with other managers, it tends to reinforce the hierarchy. If employees only have lunch with members of their own department, it can reinforce silos, amplify a potential fault line, and make cross-team coordination just a little harder. Interestingly, Kevin Kniffen and his colleagues at Cornell University found that firefighting teams that shared meals together more frequently reported slightly higher performance. To be fair, the firehouse is a unique place, and we don't think eating together will help your team overcome performance problems. But who you spend time with at lunch or over coffee can send a subtle message to others about where the collaboration boundaries lie.

- **What does the physical workspace look like**? The configuration of the work environment can also send subtle but interesting signals about hierarchy and teamwork. For example, in some military meetings, there is a clear distinction made between the individuals who are and are not given chairs with wheels. The implied message is, if you don't have wheels, you should probably be quiet. When Scott led a session with senior leaders at the US Naval War College, he asked the people with wheels (high-ranking) to turn and face someone without wheels (lower ranks) and work together on a problem, which initially created some angst! As an aside, we've noticed that military leaders are every bit as competent as their counterparts in the private sector. Most of them have learned how to keep the hierarchical culture from inhibiting team performance.

  Chairs aren't the only physical features that send signals about hierarchy or can make collaboration a bit easier or more challenging. Michael Bloomberg, the former mayor of New York, and founder and CEO of the financial services and media company that bears his name, is also one of the wealthiest people on the planet. Yet at Bloomberg's new European headquarters in London, his desk is no larger than any other employee's desk. When designing that building, they also intentionally built in a large number of locations where small and mid-sized groups can assemble to work together. They were quite conscious of how the physical space can affect collaboration and tried to make it more of an enabler than an inhibitor.

LOCAL, TEAM-SPECIFIC CONDITIONS

Organizational conditions set the stage for collaboration and provide the overarching backdrop and big picture message about teamwork. But each team also operates within their own set of local conditions, experiencing differing degrees of resource availability, time availability, authority levels, and their own assigned mission. These team-specific factors can create a "strong situation," where in some cases, a team cannot be successful until conditions are improved.

Local conditions can be quite powerful. We've seen oases of outstanding teamwork within individualistic or punitive organizational cultures, as well as the opposite—teams that struggled to work together despite operating within highly collaborative organizational cultures. Here are four of the most salient team-specific conditions to keep an eye on:

1. **Resources**. While obvious, it is worth stating that if a team is understaffed, underbudgeted, and/or lacks access to critical information or equipment, it is almost assuredly going to struggle. Its resilience will be tested, and its performance will be adversely affected. It is really difficult, and in some cases impossible, to "team away" a severe lack of resources.

   A scarcity of resources can also lead to selfish behavior, as team members compete for what little is available, and subsequently trust often declines. In a highly constrained environment, a team needs to focus attention on garnering additional resources, prioritizing existing resources, and generating creative ideas for getting things done.

   While a lack of resources creates problems, an abundance of resources doesn't guarantee higher levels of team effectiveness. When Scott and a colleague conducted a study of state agencies, they found a curvilinear relationship between resources and innovation. When resource levels were very low or very high, innovation levels were lower. It seems that when resources were quite low, they were unable to adapt, and when resources levels were quite high, they didn't feel a need to adapt. So throwing additional resources at a team isn't always an effective way to improve team performance—but ignoring a significant lack of resources will almost always result in poor performance.

2. **Time availability**. You can think about time as a specific type of resource that can greatly influence teamwork. Consider the following thought experiment.

   Imagine that we have asked you to "team up" with two other people. We've given each of you two tasks to perform. If you focus and work briskly, each task should take around seven to eight minutes to complete. We tell you to "work together" and give you a total of 15 minutes to complete all the tasks. Your own tasks will take up virtually all the time allotted. How much coordination is likely to take place? Under those circumstances, the lack of any "free" time creates such a strong constraint, it is almost impossible for you and your teammates to coordinate. The moral of the story is, it is unreasonable to expect people to monitor, assist, and collaborate with their teammates when they have no time to do so. Recall the research with manufacturing teams in the United Kingdom; teams that had time to reflect performed better. Coordination takes some time.

3. **Autonomy/decision-making authority.** A team is typically granted a certain amount of autonomy to make decisions. The boundaries may be explicitly communicated, but not always. Some teams learn by making decisions and then getting "feedback" when they overstep the unstated bounds of their authority.

   Some organizations consistently attempt to push decision-making authority as far down the hierarchy as possible, and as a result, many of their teams feel empowered. Other organizations are more reluctant to delegate authority. When a team lacks adequate autonomy, they often spend an inordinate amount of time seeking approvals and "managing up" to decision makers. Insufficient decision-making authority can significantly constraint team performance.

   The question for any team is whether they have ample authority to make the decisions they need to make in a timely manner. If not, they should clarify where and why a little additional autonomy would help and make a case for it up the chain of command.

4. **Team mission/purpose.** Teams are typically formed with an intended purpose or mission. When the team has a mission that is compelling, engaging, and clear and when that mission can't be accomplished through individual excellence alone, it is likely to encourage team members to think and work more collaboratively.

   When a mission is compelling it makes it easier for team members to identify with the team. That's important. A meta-analysis conducted by Jessica Mesmer-Magnus and her colleagues revealed that when team members identify with their team, it has a positive influence on team effectiveness. If a team's mission is not obviously compelling, the team leader should help the team clarify the types of contributions they do or could make and attempt to establish a sense of team identity that they can all rally around.

   We've worked with teams that have big, compelling, team-oriented missions, including teams that treat cancer patients or help send astronauts into space. But a team's mission need not be that grand for the team to have a unifying sense of identity. For instance, we've seen accounting, manufacturing, and customer service teams that possess an engaging, unifying sense of purpose. Purpose and identity can help a team succeed.

We've highlighted 12 of the most influential organizational and team-specific conditions that can impact on team effectiveness. But it helpful to remember that organizations and teams exist inside a broader cultural context. Norms of behavior are not identical throughout the world, and those differences can impact how individuals work together. You can think of cultural norms as one of the conditions that a team must navigate.

Many researchers have examined cultural differences, including Daniel Balliet and Paul Van Lange, from the University of Amsterdam. They conducted a meta-analysis of 83 previous studies, examining how trust, punishment, and cooperation work in 18 different societies. One of their findings was that punishment was more likely to promote cooperation in societies where trust is high. We suspect that when trust is high, punishing someone is interpreted as being done for the larger good rather than to maintain personal power. While their meta-analysis examined societal rather than team-level behaviors, it was a useful reminder that norms vary around the world, and as such, team members may interpret situational cues and actions differently in different cultures.

For example, consider societal norms about "power distance." High power distance means that people with less power accept that others have greater power than they do, and as a result there tends to be greater deference to authority. In lower power distance cultures, such as The Netherlands, it is more readily acceptable for people with less authority to speak up. In contrast, countries such as Malaysia or Panama tend to demonstrate higher power distance. In general, it is usually easier to establish psychological safety in cultures with lower power distance than in cultures with a stronger deference to authority. But imagine the challenge of creating psychological safety when some team members come from cultures with high power distance and others have grown up in a low power distance culture.

On a more parochial level, the way cues are interpreted can vary across cultures. Remember the driving analogy? If you've ever driven in New York City, you may have noticed that traffic signals don't carry the same weight as they do in many other places. To a New Yorker, a red light might mean, "Squeeze one more car through the intersection," and a yellow light doesn't mean caution, but rather, "Hurry up before the light becomes red." When people from a more law-abiding location drive in New York City, confusion often occurs, typically accompanied by the sounds of New York drivers cursing. This is analogous to what can happen in cross-cultural teams when team members have grown up experiencing different norms about speaking up and deference to authority, but perhaps with less cursing.

A vast array of cultural norms can surface in a cross-cultural team. Some of these difference are relatively minor. For example, do we shake hands when we meet, should we engage in small talk at the start of meetings, and is it appropriate for me to ask about your family? Others can lead to more significant problems. For example, in some cultures it is rude to end a conversation before the other person is ready, which means I might be late to my next meeting out of respect for the person with whom I'm currently meeting. If all the parties at my next meeting share those cultural norms, they probably understand why I'm late. No problem. But, if the people in the next meeting are from a culture where a person is expected to end their prior meeting "on time" to arrive "on time" at their next meeting (e.g., in much of the United States), they will probably interpret my late arrival as a show of disrespect. My well-intended behavior probably cost me points from my trust account.

We saw first-hand how cultural differences manifest themselves when we facilitated a meeting of managers for a global company. Within the larger room, participants had been assigned to small working groups. The groups represented the way the company's business was structured, so people were assigned along geographical lines. For example, one table had managers from northern Europe, another from southern Europe, a third was from Japan, etc. We had them discuss a series of business challenges at their tables, with time allocated between topics for them to share their thoughts with the larger group. Here's what we observed. Whenever we ended a small group discussion period, participants at one of the tables loudly continued their conversation. They truly seemed to be enjoying the disagreements they were having! To stop them, one of us would walk to their table, put our hand on the shoulder of the person who was talking at the moment, and announce, "We're starting the large group discussion now." In contrast, at another table, we learned that we needed to give the managers time to warm up before they were comfortable tackling the problem. It was important for them to uncover who had the most seniority at the table. When they disagreed, they did so very carefully and quite respectfully. If you are aware of the different cultural norms around the globe, you might be able to guess which tables responded in which manner. There wasn't a right or wrong in this instance, and not everyone behaved consistent with the norms of their region, but it was easy to see the ways broader cultural expectations influenced how each team behaved.

We can't do an adequate job of covering the various cultural differences in this book. If you are working with a cross-cultural team or if you will be joining a team in a different part of the world, we encourage you to talk to your colleagues about the cultural norms you may experience. Recognize that your typical way of operating might be interpreted quite differently by your new colleagues!

BACK TO THE SALES PROFESSIONALS

Remember the story about the sales professionals at the start of this chapter? They were being asked to work as a team, but organizational and local conditions failed to support those expectations. In fact, some of the conditions, such as their compensation policy, were in direct conflict with the company's desire to promote a team-oriented sales approach.

Fortunately, when they made some changes, we started to see the emergence of more collaborative behaviors. One change they made was to establish a certification program for all their sales professionals. Each salesperson would maintain a portfolio that documented their sales performance as well as their contributions to the team, including indicators that they handled their fair share of returns and supported their colleagues. As the sales professionals attained higher levels of certification, their compensation percentage would increase, so there was a positive consequence to being recognized as a more complete contributor to the team.

Senior leadership communicated their support for the effort. And more important, their behaviors demonstrated their commitment. A tipping point occurred a few months into the change. One of the long-tenured sales professionals who generated a lot of revenue said that he didn't want to participate in the program. He felt that because he made a lot of sales and had been around a long time, he shouldn't need to do the "other stuff." To senior leadership's credit, they told him that they were confident he could succeed as part of a team, and they wanted him to be part of the company's future, but if he didn't participate in the certification effort, there wouldn't be a job for him. Period. He eventually decided that he could succeed in the team environment and completed his certification requirements. Most important, the rest of the organization learned that leadership would not tolerate "It's all about me" behaviors, no matter how much revenue a person generates. The conditions made the expectations clear and easy to interpret and incentivized teamwork behaviors. Teamwork had become baked into their job.

IMPLICATIONS

Conditions can have a major impact on teamwork behaviors and team effectiveness. We'd go as far as to say that organizations get the behaviors, cognitions, and attitudes that they develop, promote, tolerate, measure, and reinforce. Some conditions can affect many teams simultaneously (organizational conditions) and others may affect a single team (local, team-specific conditions). Here are a few implications from this chapter:

- The nature of the situation (conditions) combines with the attributes of the people involved (e.g., capabilities) to determine if a team will work together successfully When a situation is very strong, everyone involved is likely to see and interpret how to behave in the same way, and there are incentives for behaving appropriately.
- The stronger the situation, the more likely it is that people will behave as expected, regardless of personal preferences. Some conditions send strong signals about teamwork; others send weak ones. Some conditions send the message that teamwork is unimportant.
- We described several organizational conditions that influence team effectiveness—five policies and practices (i.e., hiring, onboarding, promotions and opportunities, performance management, rewards and recognition) and three related to senior leadership (e.g., modeling behaviors, communications, establishing psychological safety). These conditions can facilitate or inhibit teamwork throughout the organization, so it makes sense to monitor them centrally and engage senior leadership in addressing any gaps or unintended consequences that surface.
- We also described four local or team-specific conditions, three of which—resources, time, decision-making authority—can place significant constraints on a team's effectiveness. It is almost impossible to "team away" a significant lack of resources and unreasonable to

expect team members to monitor and support one another if they barely have ample time to complete their own assignments. Monitor these conditions locally and focus on how to remedy deficiencies. If you can't improve them, brainstorm how to work around them creatively, knowing that it is really hard to work around severe deficiencies!

- The fourth team-specific condition is mission/purpose. Having a clear, compelling mission provides the team with a common identity. That sense of identity can often stimulate teamwork, particularly if team members must work together to attain the mission. If your team doesn't have a clear, compelling mission, spend time clarifying the contributions the team does or could make and use that to create a sense of team identity.
- If you work with team members who may have learned different cultural norms (e.g., about deference to authority, timeliness), try to learn about those norms so you can be an effective contributor. People who have experienced different norms may act differently than you do and interpret your actions in ways you did not intend. Consider the broader societal norms that have shaped you and your fellow team members.

CHAPTER 10

Coaching

Leadership Isn't Just for Leaders

In prior chapters, we hinted about how leadership can affect a team, both positively and negatively. We'll explore that in greater depth in this chapter. But first, let's quickly revisit a few of the stories we shared earlier, highlighting the presence or absence of key leadership behaviors.

- **Being on the same page helps the Rams win**. Sean McVay, coach of the Rams, ensured that all members of the offense possessed a clear, common understanding (a shared mental model) of how to respond to certain situations. He ensured the team had clarity and alignment.
- **Lack of accountability means loss of future business**. In the Fifth Avenue retail store, the tailor attempted to hold the salesperson accountable for trying to sell Scott a poor-fitting suit. But because the team leader hadn't held the salesperson accountable in the past, the salesperson repeated his detrimental behavior. The customer experience suffered, and Scott never shopped there again (a sad ending to this story!)
- **You can't teach height—a failure to garner "resources."** Our graduate school basketball team faced a severe obstacle—a lack of height and talent. But no one on the team tried to find other players to join us. We didn't remove obstacles to success, and we didn't garner necessary resources. As a result, we lost.
- **It can be "lonely out in space."** During a space mission, crew members must keep an eye on their teammate's emotions, encourage one another, and handle conflicts effectively. A failure to manage

emotions and attitudes can erode the crew's resilience and jeopardize the mission.

- **The deadly consequences of poor psychological safety**. On the Mount Everest climb, five people died because the team leader didn't create psychological safety. (He told them, "My word will be absolute law.") As a result, team members felt they couldn't speak up when they needed to, and the lack of dissent was deadly.
- **Participation and empowerment saved Scott from old man underwear**. At Nordstrom's, everyone on the sales team was taught that together they "own" customer service, so it was easy for Stewart to step in and help when Sue became busy with another customers. Together they enabled Scott to avoid the dreaded "old man's underwear."
- **Truffles anyone? The best teams adapt and learn.** At L'Atelier in Las Vegas, the leader ensured that every kitchen crew member, new and experienced, was fully trained, which enabled them to work together seamlessly. And adaptation was encouraged, so when the boisterous customers rolled in requesting "lots of truffles," the team huddled up and quickly implemented a creative solution.
- **You get what you encourage and tolerate.** In a high-end retailer, a sales professional pretended to be on the phone rather than handle a customer return. It was only when leadership changed the conditions so they encouraged teamwork (and didn't tolerate selfishness) that the sales professionals started working as a team.

This chapter is about coaching or, more specifically, team leadership. Note that we didn't say the chapter focuses on "team leaders." Instead, we said it is about "team leadership," because team members other than the leader can at times demonstrate leadership behaviors that enable the team to succeed. We hope the chapter is useful to anyone in a designated team leader role, but it isn't just about officially appointed leaders.

A great deal has been written about leadership, and most of it is unsupported advice offered by leadership "gurus." Much of the leadership literature, and even most research on leadership, has concentrated on how to be a successful business leader or how to manage subordinates. In contrast, our focus in on team leadership.

Team leadership can be challenging, but fundamentally effective team leadership is about (a) ensuring the team has all the necessary "drivers" in place and (b) enabling the team to learn and adapt. So everything you learned previously applies here.

We begin this chapter by quickly referencing a few meta-analyses that highlight the importance of team leadership. We then identify seven essential team leadership functions that must be fulfilled on almost any team (we foreshadowed these in the opening stories). These functions, and related behaviors, describe much of what a good coach might do, and they move the needle on each of the other drivers. The functions tell us "what" needs to be done, but not "how" to do it.

Next, we provide a summary of four leadership approaches that suggest "how" to lead—three are based on strong research evidence (transformational, shared, and servant leadership) and one we derived based on our experiences (civil leadership). If you are familiar with these leadership approaches, feel free to skip that section and jump directly to the tips and implications at the end of the chapter. But we think you will discover some interesting insights about how to "show up" and maintain a healthy team leader mindset by reading about the four leadership approaches. Of course, we won't hold it against you if you jump right to the punchline!

DOES TEAM LEADERSHIP INFLUENCE TEAM EFFECTIVENESS?

The short answer is yes, of course, it does. If you've been on various teams in your career, you probably know that from experience. The difference between working with a good team leader and a poor team leader is intense and obvious. But what does the research say about the impact of leadership behaviors? A couple of meta-analyses examined how leadership affects team performance.

Meltem Ceri-Booms, along with her colleagues from The Netherlands and Romania, published a meta-analysis of 88 research studies that examined the relationship between leader behaviors and team performance. Similarly, Shawn Burke and researchers at the University of Central Florida (including Eduardo, who was a professor there at the time), conducted a meta-analysis that combined the results from 50 leadership studies.

Each meta-analysis found that that appropriate leadership behaviors were positively related to various measures of team effectiveness, both subjective and objective. They found that task-focused leadership behaviors (e.g., providing structure) and person-focused behaviors (e.g., empowering team members) both contributed to team effectiveness. The findings held true regardless of the degree of interdependency that existed among team members. The evidence confirms what of us know intuitively—leadership matters in almost any type of teams.

WHAT ARE THE ESSENTIAL LEADERSHIP FUNCTIONS THAT NEED TO BE FULFILLED ON A TEAM?

Think about a really good coach on any sports team. It could be a team you or a family member played on or perhaps a professional team that you follow. Next, think about a really good team leader from work. While the two leaders may lead in different ways, we would speculate that both of them ensured that the "essential team leadership functions" were performed, either by themselves or by others on the team. For example, any good coach holds team members accountable, ensures team members are developing, helps remove obstacles, ensures team members are on the same page, and so on. As illustrated in the examples at the beginning of the chapter, when the essential functions are completed consistently, the probability of a team's success increases significantly.

When we cut through all the noise, we see seven essential team leadership functions. You'll find them listed in the following text, followed by a few key leadership behaviors associated with each. You could use these as a checklist for your team. Are these being performed adequately?

THE SEVEN ESSENTIAL TEAM LEADERSHIP FUNCTIONS

Task-focused

1. Ensure clarity and alignment.
2. Hold teammates accountable.
3. Remove obstacles and garner support.

Team-focused

4. Manage team emotions and attitudes.
5. Foster psychological safety.
6. Encourage participation and empowerment.

Team and task-focused

7. Promote learning and adaptation.

> **Thought experiment**. As you review the leadership functions and behaviors, think about a team you are on and ask:
>
> - Are all the leadership **functions** being completed adequately? Which ones might merit **additional attention**?
> - Which of the **behaviors** are being **performed by team members** rather than (or in addition to) the leader?
> - Where else could team members help by **stepping up**?

TEAM LEADERSHIP BEHAVIORS

Based on what we know about the other drivers of team effectiveness, the right-hand column of Table 10.1 highlights a few key behaviors that a team leader (or other team members) can perform to ensure that each function is being completed adequately. Some of these behaviors should look familiar, as we alluded to them in prior chapters.

LEADERSHIP FUNCTIONS AND THE SEVEN DRIVERS OF TEAM EFFECTIVENESS

A key focus for any team leader should be to ensure the key drivers for their team are favorable. How does performing the essential leadership functions move the needle on the other drivers? Table 10.2 shows the primary impact each function has on the other drivers.

The essential functions and related behaviors describe the "what" of team leadership. Now, let's consider the "how." What can we learn about effective team leadership from a few evidence-based leadership approaches?

A BRIEF REVIEW OF RELEVANT LEADERSHIP APPROACHES

We're confident that leadership has been "studied" for as long as there have been leaders. When the first hunter-gathers formed a team, team members probably observed Ogg, their team leader and tried to grok (i.e., understand): "Why is Ogg assigning Rokk to the hunting party?" Historians have studied leaders through the ages, asking, for example, was Julius Caesar a good leader? Was Peter the Great actually great?

Table 10.1. Key Team Leadership Behaviors

Team Leadership Function	Key Behaviors
1. **Ensure clarity and alignment.** Teams are better able to coordinate and adapt when team members possess clear, shared, and accurate cognitions. Who is helping ensure the team has ample clarity and team members are aligned on things like roles and priorities?	• Providing a sense of direction and developing plans to attain results • Structuring and distributing work • Maintaining situational awareness (e.g., monitoring the situation, updating) • Ensuring the team has shared mental models about roles, priorities, vision
2. **Hold teammates accountable.** If no actions are taken to hold team members accountable for doing what they need to do, coordination and performance will suffer. Who keeps an eye on the team and recognizes when it may be starting to go off track? What happens when a team member isn't living up to expectations or is demonstrating incivility?	• Monitoring results and progress • Following up to ensure commitments are met • Ensuring team members are collaborating and communicating as expected • Dealing with jerks and underperformers
3. **Remove obstacles and garner support.** All teams face obstacles and challenges. Who is helping identify and remove obstacles? Who is representing the team to ensure they have adequate resources and support? Who is maintaining healthy relationships with people outside the team?	• Seeking necessary resources such as funding, talent, and support • Managing relationships with people outside the team (e.g., boundary spanning) • Helping solve problems • Monitoring the environment
4. **Manage team emotions and attitudes.** The research reveals that it is difficult, if not impossible, to sustain team effectiveness without the "right" cooperative attitudes. Who is monitoring the team's pulse and helping manage emotions and attitudes? Who is energizing and inspiring the team?	• Motivating and inspiring others (e.g., offering encouragement) • Fostering collaborative conflict (not avoidance or competitive conflict) • Building collective efficacy and cohesion • Demonstrating personal caring about team members
5. **Foster psychological safety.** If you don't recognize the importance of psychological safety by now, we have failed miserably! Without psychological safety, communication and performance suffers. Who is taking actions that help ensure team members feel comfortable speaking up and being themselves?	• Admitting mistakes or a personal lack of knowledge • Encouraging alternative points of view (e.g., thanking people for speaking up) • Building trust (e.g., living up to commitments) • Being clear about negotiables and non-negotiables
6. **Encourage participation and empowerment.** No one can see and do everything on a team. In effective teams, ideas and contributions emerge from throughout the team, and team members feel empowered to step up and help one another. Who is encouraging team members to participate and take ownership for the team's success?	• Actively seeking input from others • Ensuring team members are willing to back up one another • Encouraging shared leadership and "stepping up" • Building a sense of engagement and ownership
7. **Promote learning and adaptation.** The best teams become great by continually learning and adjusting. That is the only way to sustain team effectiveness. Who is helping individual team members learn and develop? Who is ensuring that the team learns and adapts over time?	• Monitoring team member's needs • Fostering individual learning (e.g., coaching, feedback) • Enabling team learning and adaptation (e.g., debriefing) • Ensuring team members have the competencies needed to coordinate effectively

Table 10.2. Leadership Functions and the Other Six Drivers

Leadership Functions	The Other Six Drivers					
	Capabilities	Cooperation	Coordination	Communication	Cognitions	Conditions
Task-focused						
Ensure clarity and alignment			✓		✓	
Hold teammates accountable			✓			
Remove obstacles and garner support	✓					✓
Team-focused						
Manage team emotions and attitudes		✓				
Foster psychological safety		✓		✓		
Encourage participation and empowerment		✓	✓	✓		
Team- and task-focused						
Promote learning and adaptation	✓		✓			

What about Steve Jobs? And employees in modern organizations have "studied" their leaders to decide if they want to keep working there and perhaps to ascertain how they too could become a leader someday.

In the 20th century, anecdotal study and reflection morphed into academic theorizing and research on leadership. Since then, we've seen a proliferation of ideas about how to be an effective leader, including trait theory, great man theory (introduced at a time when it was assumed women wouldn't be leaders), contingency theory, authentic leadership, charismatic leadership, leader–member exchange theory, ethical leadership, and situational leadership, to name a few. We won't bore you with an historical recap of all of these. Nor are we going to tell you to adopt a particular leadership approach. Instead, we've tried to extract what can be learned from a few empirically tested approaches to leadership (so you don't need to read it all!), starting with transformational leadership.

TRANSFORMATIONAL LEADERSHIP

Transformational leadership is about leading by inspiring, stimulating, engaging, and caring for people. It is often contrasted with transactional leadership, which relies more on the contingent provision of rewards, praise, and punishment. You can think of transactional leadership as more of a traditional carrot-and-stick style of leadership designed to engender compliance. As a transactional leader, I'll tell you what I expect, and if you do it, I'll reward you. In contrast, transformational leadership involves motivating and engaging people to believe in and contribute to a team's collective success. It is about building trust and commitment. Perhaps you've been the "recipient" of both styles of leadership in your career. Most leaders exhibit a bit of both, but tend to default to one more than the other.

Transformational leadership was originally introduced by presidential biographer James MacGregor Burns. The underlying elements of the theory were subsequently fleshed out by renowned leadership researcher Bernie Bass. According to Bass, some of the core behaviors of transformational leadership include communicating an inspiring vision and sense of meaning, challenging followers to question assumptions and live up to high standards, and encouraging them to believe that collective success is possible. It also involves attending to each team member's needs through listening and coaching, and connecting with people on an emotional level.

Theoretically, transformational leadership sounds good (who doesn't want to feel inspired), and it is certainly different than transactional leadership, but does it work? Several meta-analyses have examined that question. For example, Gang Wang, In-Sue Oh, Stephen Courtright, and Amy Colbert examined 113 transformational leadership studies. They found that transformational leadership was related to higher individual and team performance. At the individual level, people exposed to transformational leaders exhibited better basic task performance, but not necessarily better than those exposed to transactional leadership. Both leadership approaches seemed to yield conformance to basic expectations. Transformation leadership differentiated itself from transactional leadership in how it affected performance beyond basic task expectations. Transformational leadership seems to encourage individuals to go the extra mile, to voluntarily contribute in ways that extend beyond their basic job duties and role expectations.

How did transformational leadership play out at the team level? Transformational leadership was related to higher overall team performance. It yielded higher team performance even after accounting for transactional leadership behaviors (i.e., the use of contingent rewards). That feels right. Effective team performance is more than the sum of each person doing their basic job role adequately. It often requires coordination, helping teammates when needed, caring about the team's goals (and not just whether I'll get my reward!), and believing the team can "win." Aspects of transformational leadership align nicely with those teamwork requirements.

On the "softer" side, Diego Montano from the Institute for Medical Psychology and Sociology at the University of Göttingen in Germany and his colleagues conducted a meta-analysis that revealed transformational leadership was also related to employee mental well-being (e.g., less perceived stress and burnout). This suggests that there is a positive emotional component to working with a leader who exhibits a transformational leadership approach. Overall, there is strong evidence in support of transformational leadership. Here are a few useful lessons we can extract some from the research.

- If you need more than compliance, a transactional reward and punishment style of leadership isn't enough.

- Establish a positive, inspiring sense of direction and a collective purpose that the team can believe in (consider involving the team in its creation).
- Create high standards that team members care about and challenge them to determine (and redetermine as needed) how best to attain them.
- Listen attentively to uncover individual team member needs and ideas.
- Model what you expect from the team (e.g., collaborative behaviors, cooperative attitudes) and do what you say (trust is at the heart of transformational leadership).
- Remind them that the team can win.

We've see these transformational leadership behaviors in many organizations. One example was at SEFCU, a credit union with over 350,000 members and $3.5 billion in assets. Founded in 1934, they operated as a typical financial institution for many, many years. Then, in 2007, their CEO Michael Castellana encouraged the leadership team to change their focus and purpose from "dollars and cents" to "lives impacted." Castellana established a compelling sense of direction that emphasized making a big impact in the communities they serve, while still attaining financial success. He challenged his team (and, in turn, they challenged their teams) to attain some big goals, consistent with the vision. He involved the team in figuring out how to make that possible, and when the financial markets tightened, he reminded them about the importance of their mission and how the team could still succeed. Since adopting this approach, SEFCU has been voted the best financial institution in their region for 13 consecutive years.

SHARED LEADERSHIP

The term *shared leadership* is not intended to describe the assignment of multiple formal team leaders. Nor is it running the team as a democracy, with no leader. Rather, it reflects that in many teams, including those with a formal leader, different people may step up, often informally and dynamically, to perform some leadership functions and help the team succeed. Leadership expert Gary Yukl (who was a darn good team leader in his own right, as Scott experienced back in the day) said shared leadership is about "individual members of a team engaging in activities that influence the team and other team members." This is consistent with a central premise of this chapter—leadership isn't just for leaders.

Is it feasible for one person to see everything that is going on within and to a team? Can the leader recognize, guide, and respond to all emergent challenges and team needs? In most teams, the leader can't do that alone. Work has become increasingly complex and fast-paced. Organizational structures have become flatter, which means team leaders have more direct reports, widening the range of who and what must be "managed." There is often too much going on for one person to set direction, monitor the environment, check in on each team member, manage external "boundary" relationships, model team norms, mentor others, provide expert guidance, hold team members accountable, mediate conflicts, offer feedback, and so on. Even if one person could see it all, they probably wouldn't have the time to respond to it all. And even if they did have the time, they might not be the most qualified person on the team to perform each of those tasks. A leader would need to have superpowers to do it all well. That's why we're seeing more distributed or shared leadership, even within classic vertical leadership structures. In most teams, different members need to perform some "leader-like" actions.

What Happens When a Team Uses Shared Leadership?

Some degree of shared leadership will happen naturally in most teams, but should we be encouraging it? Does shared leadership benefit or weaken a team? Our friends, Lauren D'Innocenzo at Drexel University, John Mathieu at the University of Connecticut, and Mike Kukenberger at the University of New Hampshire conducted a meta-analysis of 50+ shared leadership studies, which revealed that teams that use shared leadership are more effective. Another meta-analysis of 40+ studies, conducted by Dani Wang, David Waldman, and Zhen Zhang reported similar results. While there were some subtle differences between the two meta-analyses (e.g., inconsistent conclusions about whether shared leadership becomes even more important when work is very complex), there is ample evidence that shared leadership can enhance team members' attitudes and the team's performance.

There is also reason to believe that it is harder for a team to adapt quickly when all leadership actions must flow through and be performed by a centralized, formal leader. Shared leadership should allow a team to adjust more rapidly to emergent needs. The musical world provides an interesting illustration of this.

A string quartet is typically comprised of a first and a second violin, a viola, and a cello. Traditionally, the first violinist is considered "the leader," but many quartets now operate with more of a shared leadership approach. Alan Wing from the University of Birmingham in the United Kingdom led a team of researchers in a study of two internationally recognized string quartets. Each quartet played an excerpt from Haydn's quartet Op. 74 no. 1, with intentional but unrehearsed variations in timing. In one quartet, team members adjusted only to the leader, and the leader rarely adjusted to the team. In the other quartet, adjustments were led by all four team members, and not simply the first violin. The differences in how the teams adjusted was attributed to their different leadership styles. The first quartet was a first-violin–led autocracy; the second quartet regularly operated in more of a shared leadership style.

Recently, Dominque Tremblay and a team of nurses, doctors, and researchers in Canada considered how shared leadership can apply to a "team of teams." They examined the case of a 47-year-old woman who underwent therapy to treat breast cancer, and the coordination and communication challenges that emerged as responsibility for the patient moved from oncology to primary care teams. The case highlighted the need for shared leadership not only *within* medical teams, but also *across* teams (including the "patient family team"). Shared leadership was applicable wherever there was a need to coordinate, communicate, and adapt together to ensure quality care for the patient.

What Makes Effective Shared Leadership Feasible?

In some cases, a leader can assign an informal leadership responsibility to a team member ("Jess, could you please coach Joe so he's prepared to handle that tricky Thompson account"). Often, however, shared leadership emerges more spontaneously when a team member recognizes and responds to a need. In either case, for shared leadership to be constructive, team members must be aligned on the team's purpose and norms and mutually aware of what's going on and where the team is headed. In other words, they need a foundation of shared cognitions. Otherwise, a team member who is genuinely trying to help can unintentionally derail the team.

Heather McIntyre and Roseanne Foti studied intact teams who exhibited shared leadership. They found that teams that possessed a common understanding about shared leadership performed better. That makes sense. If I think my leader is the only one who should give us guidance, I probably won't respond well to a teammate who tries to "help me" by providing feedback. Shared leadership works better when team members aren't surprised when one of their teammates "steps up" and performs what might normally be considered a task done by the formal leader.

A certain degree of vulnerability or exposure arises when a "non-leader" starts to act like a leader, so many team members may be reluctant to fill a leadership void without permission to do so. A team member might think, "Am I really supposed to represent our team when I interact with that senior leader? Perhaps it's best if I just listen quietly and take notes." The formal team leader can help by communicating where shared leadership is expected, where it is acceptable, and where it is off limits. When shared leadership is undefined and unbounded, we tend to see two extremes. On one hand, some team members will never step up, even when needed. They don't know that they should, so they are fearful of overstepping and getting in trouble (or alienating a team-mate). At the other extreme, some team members will step up inappro-priately, assuming it is okay to take an unacceptable action, such as making a commitment on behalf of the team that they should not have made. Shared leadership works best when boundaries are clear and team members are empowered within those boundaries. And sometimes, a leader needs to communicate individual boundaries, because what is acceptable for one team member should be off limits for another.

Actions that promote psychological safety can also create an envir-onment where shared leadership is possible. Psychological safety can increase the likelihood that a team member will voluntarily assume a leadership responsibility. It also makes it easier for a team member to be open to a teammate stepping up to fill a leadership need.

If you are a team member rather than a team leader, you might be thinking, "Sure, it can help my leader if I step up, but is it really in my best interest to help the team?" Robert Hirschfeld and his associates studied this for some time, differentiating between "team-oriented pro-activity" and "autonomous proactivity." The former is having an interest in making things better for the team, for example, by helping others per-form in better ways. We see this as being related to having a collective orientation. In contrast, autonomous proactivity involves a focus on improving oneself and one's own circumstances. Hirschfeld found that in team settings, individuals with team-oriented proactivity were seen as having greater advancement potential. Those with autonomous pro-activity were seen as having less potential. This suggests that in addition to helping the team, there can be a personal benefit to "stepping up."

SERVANT LEADERSHIP

In 1970, Robert Greenleaf published an essay titled, "The Servant as Leader," which introduced the concept of servant leadership into the modern vernacular. His work was philosophical in nature and eventually led to research efforts to test some of these concepts in work settings. Fundamentally, "servant-leaders" are genuinely concerned with serving their followers and creating opportunities for them to grow and thrive. They look beyond self-interest and put others first. Some proponents of this approach have emphasized the role of humility in servant leadership.

We recognize that, at first glance, servant leadership may feel too "soft" for some. If transformational leadership seemed soft to you, servant leadership will make you roll your eyes. You might think, "That's not leadership; that's followership," but servant leadership does not mean abandoning power, abdicating responsibility, or being submissive. It does, however, rely less on the formal power of being "the leader" and more on the trust that accrues from genuinely focusing on followers' needs.

To be clear, we are not advocating that you adopt servant leadership as your sole or primary guiding principle for effective team leadership. We do, however, believe a few insights can be gleaned from knowing about it. But first, let's confirm that there is ample research support for it.

Is Servant Leadership Effective?

Julia Hoch from Cal State University and her colleagues William Bommer, James Dulebohn, and Dongyuan Wu conducted an important meta-analysis of various leadership approaches, including transform-ational and servant leadership. They confirmed, with an even larger set of studies than in prior meta-analyses, that transformational leadership works. Transformational leadership is now one of the most studied and validated forms of leadership. So, Hoch and her team then examined the question, "If a leader is demonstrating transformational leadership, does servant leadership (or other forms of leadership) matter?"

There have been far fewer studies of servant leadership (41 studies) than of transformational leadership (over 150 studies!), but enough to conduct a reasonable meta-analysis. What did they find? Servant leadership demonstrated a positive relationship with employee job performance, a bit stronger positive relationship with employee organizational citizenship behaviors (i.e., going beyond one's basic job requirements), and a very strong positive relationship with employee commitment and trust in their leader. In addition, they found that servant leadership predicts those positive outcomes, even after accounting for transformational leadership. In contrast, other leadership approaches didn't add much to the mix. This suggests that there is a place for both transformational leadership and servant leadership and that adopting aspects of both could be beneficial.

To further compare these two approaches, Dirk van Dierendonck and his colleagues at Erasmus University in The Netherlands conducted a series of studies involving servant and transformational leadership. They found that both forms of leadership led to higher levels of employee commitment and engagement but that they operated in different ways. Servant leadership seemed to work because team members felt their needs were being satisfied, while transformational leadership seemed to work, in part, because team members viewed their leader as effective.

Similarly, Zhijun Chen from the University of Western Australia, along with Jing Shu and Mingjian Zhou, studied 238 hairstylists in 30 salons. They found that when the team leader demonstrated servant leadership behaviors, service quality was higher and customers felt their stylists were more customer-focused, even after accounting for transformational leadership behaviors. Our conclusion is that you're likely to have a better experience at a salon where the leader isn't a prima donna. Tell them Scott and Eduardo sent you.

How Can You Use Servant Leadership When You Are a Team Leader?

Servant leadership begins as a mindset. Acknowledge that you have a responsibility to look out for your team and your team members. That's a healthy perspective. If your team believes that you are driven mostly by your own self-interests, they are unlikely to trust you. In that case, you'll only be able to use transactional leadership, doling out rewards and punishments to coerce people to comply. Transactional leadership has its place, but you don't want that to be the only tool in your toolkit, particularly if you need your team to be engaged and adaptive and not simply compliant.

Be honest, if you are a leader and we were to interview your team members, would they say you are more concerned with their success or your own? We're not asking about your intent, but rather how your team perceives you. To use an American football analogy, from their perspective, do they see you acting like the star quarterback, with the rest of them working to ensure you can deliver the goods? Or are you more like an offensive lineman, trying to protect them and remove barriers so they can "score?" There is a meaningful advantage to being perceived as the obstacle remover, at least some of the time. In contrast, if the team perceives that "It's always about you," you'll find it hard to sustain long-term team success.

To apply servant leadership, take a genuine interest in the needs of your team members and at times put their needs above your own.

- Do something that is clearly not in your own best interest but visibly helps them. That builds trust and psychological safety.
- Show that you care about their personal growth. Listen intently.
- Look for obstacles that may be getting in their way and use the extra influence you have as a leader to help remove them.
- Roll up your sleeves and help out, occasionally doing something that might be perceived as "grunt" work. For example, Phillipe Cousteau, the President of EarthEcho International told *Fast Company*, "I still take minutes sometimes. Don't ask people to do anything you're not willing to do."

When thought of in this way, servant leadership isn't a radical approach, and it isn't inconsistent with transformational or shared leadership. It is simply a component of being a good team leader. Incorporate a servant leader mindset as part of your repertoire. Doing so can help promote the emergence of cooperative attitudes within your team—trust, psychological safety, cohesion, and collective efficacy.

CIVIL LEADERSHIP

Remember how, in our discussion about the dark side of destructive personalities, a team member who demonstrates narcissism or is generally a jerk can infect the rest of the team, through a form of emotional contagion?

It's even worse when the person demonstrating those negative attributes is the team leader! Our theory of civil leadership has two main tenets: (a) don't be a jerk and (b) don't tolerate incivility in the team.

We wish leader incivility was like a unicorn, so rare that we never see it. If that were true, we wouldn't need to discuss it here, but unfortunately we do. Christine Pearson and Christine Porath wrote a book on incivility at work, *The Cost of Bad Behavior*. They found that about 60% of incivility incidents are instigated by people with higher organizational status than the target. Top–down and leader-initiated incivility is actually more common than peer-to-peer incivility.

Leader incivility includes, for example, making demeaning or derogatory remarks about a person, putting someone down, or addressing someone in unprofessional terms. Hopefully you've never seen a team leader in your organization do those things (we can hear you chuckling). Amber Smittick from Hogan Assessments and her colleagues Kathi Miner and George Cunningham from Texas A&M gathered data from 52 NCAA Division I female college basketball teams. After controlling for past performance, they found that teams led by coaches who demonstrated more incivility won fewer games. Why? Because incivility lowered psychological safety, which you now know is a strong predictor of team performance. It turns out that leader incivility isn't the unicorn; the unicorn is the leader who can be uncivil and somehow still maintain high psychological safety and performance. It's almost impossible. So how can you apply civil leadership?

- Check yourself and don't be a jerk. When you need to be tough, do so without being rude. Monitor your team's emotions.
- Don't tolerate team members who act unprofessionally to other team members. Don't trick yourself into believing that a high-performing jerk won't infect the rest of the team. He will, and your team's "winning percentage" will eventually drop because of it.
- When team members disagree, which can be quite healthy, help them work through it collaboratively rather than competitively.

A FEW FINAL THOUGHTS ABOUT THE VARIOUS LEADERSHIP THEORIES

We're not suggesting that you adopt a single leadership approach. You don't need to declare that you are going to be a [fill in the blank] style leader. We described a few leadership approaches with strong research support and one that we invented but are fairly confident about. We think you can learn from each of the leadership approaches.

- **Transformational leadership** reminds us to inspire the team and not simply reward compliance.
- **Shared leadership** reminds us that if the leader is the only person showing leadership behaviors that's probably a red flag.
- **Servant leadership** reminds us to put the team first.
- **Civil leadership** reminds us not to be a jerk—and not tolerate incivility in others.

A FEW WORDS ABOUT SELF-ANCHORING

Proponents of any of the major leadership theories would probably agree that it is hard to be an effective team leader if you don't understand what your teammates are thinking and feeling. With that in mind, we want to alert you to a cognitive bias that you'll need to avoid whenever you serve in a team leader role. It's called self-anchoring bias.

Jennifer Overbeck from the University of Utah and Vitaliya Droutman from the University of Southern California published research that reveals what power can do to our perception of others. Across a series of studies, they showed that people in power are more likely to "self-anchor."

What does that mean? It means they are more likely to use themselves to infer what other people think or feel. More specifically, Overbeck and Droutman's research suggests that when people are in a position of power, they are more likely to assume that their team believes what they believe and feels what they feel. This doesn't happen consciously. A leader doesn't knowingly think, "I believe X, so my team must as well." When you are in a position of power, your self-anchoring can increase without your awareness. Some of it may even be physiological.

Researchers at Wilfrid Laurier University and the University of Toronto used transcranial magnetic stimulation to measure motor cortical output in the brain. They examined people who felt differing degrees of power. When they were in a position of power, they exhibited lower levels of resonance, suggesting reduced mirroring of other people. Apparently, something happens to us when we assume a position of power. We tend not to process as much information about others, particularly about those with less power than us. We have a harder time reading other's emotions. And, due to self-anchoring bias, our natural inclination can be to assume we are "reading the audience," when in reality we are merely reading ourselves.

Whenever you are in a team leader role, be on the lookout for self-anchoring. Ask yourself, "How confident am I that I *really* know what my team is thinking and feeling?" Then, acknowledge that you are likely to be overconfident and go talk to people on your team to learn their perspective. You may be surprised what you uncover!

IMPLICATIONS

Effective team leadership is primarily about (a) ensuring the team has the favorable drivers it needs and (b) enabling the team to learn and adapt. In this chapter, we described several research-tested approaches that have been shown to boost team effectiveness. We don't advocate picking one, but instead we encourage you to learn from each of them.

- Periodically review the seven essential leadership functions and determine if any merit additional attention. Remember, it isn't only the formal leader who can help fulfill these functions.
- If you need more than compliance, then a transactional reward and punishment style of team leadership will be insufficient.
  - But, to be clear, adopting lessons from the other leadership approaches does not mean abandoning power, running a team democracy, or being submissive. Those approaches offer ways of engaging the team to produce better results, not abdicating leadership responsibility.
- **Transformational leadership** offers ways to build trust and inspire the team. Actions you can take include
  - Establishing a positive, inspiring sense of direction and a collective purpose that the team can believe in (try to involve them in generating it, if possible).
  - Creating high standards that team members care about and challenging them to figure out how best to attain them.
  - Modeling the behaviors and attitude you expect from the team and doing what you say.
  - Reminding them that the team can win (to sustain a sense of collective efficacy).

- **Shared leadership** alerts us that if the leader is the only person demonstrating leadership, that's probably a red flag.
  - It is rare that one person can set direction, check in on each team member, manage external relationships, model team norms, provide guidance, hold team members accountable, etc.
  - Shared leadership works best when boundaries are clear and team members are empowered within those boundaries. Guide team members to "step up" in the right spots.
  - As a team member, stepping up is good for the team, and it can also enhance your reputation for future advancement.
- **Servant leadership** encourages us to put the team first. Actions you can take include
  - Doing something that is clearly not in your own best interest but visibly helps the team.
  - Showing that you care about a team member's personal growth.
  - Looking for obstacles and using the extra influence you have as a leader to help remove them.
  - Rolling up your sleeves and doing something that might be perceived as "grunt" work.
- **Civil leadership** reminds us not to be a jerk—and not tolerate incivility in others.
  - To lead others effectively, you need to know what your team is thinking. Beware of self-anchoring bias. Don't assume you know what they are thinking and feeling.
  - Make it a practice to talk to your team members and listen intently.

PART III

What Should I Do?

Using the Seven Drivers

CHAPTER 11
A Quick Refresher

In the prior chapters we shared findings and insights from an ever-growing science of teamwork. We hope you feel smarter and more confident that there are practical, doable, evidence-based ways to boost team effectiveness.

As we stated in the opening pages of this book, it is our belief that anyone who leads a team, works on a team, or supports teams in any way should know what really drives team performance. That knowledge enables us to make informed decisions about how to show up when we're on a team and how we can support the teams we care about. It keeps us from being unduly influenced by what sounds logical (but is wrong), is easy to understand (but is an oversimplification), or is consistent with what we have been led to believe (but is really a myth). People often "don't know what they don't know," so if you hear a friend or colleague talking about teamwork in a way that clearly conflicts with what you now know about the science of teamwork, perhaps you could lend them your copy of this book!

Knowing the seven drivers of team effectiveness—outlined in this book—is a start. But how can you best use that knowledge? That depends on whether you happen to be in a team leader role, a team member role, a senior leader role, or a consulting role (either inside the organization, such as in a human resources business partner or organizational development professional role or as an external consultant who supports teams). The next four chapters answer the question, "What should I do with my knowledge of how teams work?"

Each short chapter that follows provides 10 actionable recommendations about how to apply the science of teamwork in a specific role. You can choose to read all four chapters or zoom in on one that addresses a role you're currently filling. But before you go to those chapters, we want to offer you a super quick "refresher" about the science of teamwork that is applicable to everyone—and is essential reading if you skipped the middle section of the book!

TEAM EFFECTIVENESS AND HOW TEAMS VARY

Team effectiveness, as we view it, has three components:

- **Sustained performance**—Generating positive results over time.
- **Team resilience**—Working through challenges and bouncing back from adversity.
- **Vitality**—Maintaining energy, vibrancy, and resources needed for future success.

If team members are being burned out while trying to accomplish a milestone, and as a result, the team is no longer ready to handle the next challenge, we wouldn't consider that team to be highly effective.

TEAMS ARE NOT IDENTICAL

We wish we could tell you, "Here are three magical things that will make any team great." Unfortunately, as the research shows, teams aren't that simple.

Teams can vary in several important ways. For example, does the team consistently perform the same tasks or do work requirements change more dynamically? Is membership fairly stable or do members come and go? One of the most important ways that teams differ is with regard to reliance—to what extent do team members need to rely on one another to complete their work and accomplish the mission?

These differences can influence what matters most; throughout chapters 4 through 10, we highlighted how some aspects are more critical for certain teams. For example, when team members must consistently rely on one another, collective efficacy and team coordination are more important than in teams in which members work fairly independently (where civility and self-confidence become more important).

It helps to understand the nature of your team. Consider where it falls along the five dimensions in Table 11.1.

Table 11.1. Five Important Team Distinctions: How Would You Describe Your Team?

Reliance	Most work performed independently (**mostly independent**)	Split of work done independently and work that relies on others (**even split**)	Most members must rely on or coordinate with others much of the time (**mostly interdependent**)	Members consistently rely on or need to coordinate with others (**fully interdependent**)
Membership Stability	Almost all team members remain the same (**very stable**)	People leave or join the team on occasion (**fairly stable**)	People tend to leave or join fairly regularly (**fairly dynamic**)	People constantly leave or join the team (**very dynamic**)
Task Consistency	Work requirements remain constant over time (**consistent requirements**)	Work requirements change slowly over time (**evolving requirements**)	Work requirements change fairly regularly (**shifting requirements**)	Work requirements change rapidly and unpredictably (**unpredictable requirements**)
Proximity	All team members work in the same or a close location (**full co-location**)	Most of the teamwork in the same or a close location (**mostly co-located**)	Most of the teamwork in different locations (**mostly dispersed**)	All team members work in different locations (**full dispersion**)
Similarity	All team members share an overlapping area of expertise (**highly similar**)	Most team members share an overlapping area of expertise (**mostly similar**)	Most team members have unique areas of expertise (**fairly unique**)	All team members have unique areas of expertise (**highly unique**)

CAPABILITY

Capability refers to the individual and collective competencies that a team possesses. Does your team have the knowledge, skills, abilities, personality, and other personal attributes needed to complete assignments, overcome challenges, and adapt as needed to sustain performance? Capability is about having ample horsepower. If your team lacks essential competencies, it will have a tough time succeeding.

It is worth the effort to clarify the specific capabilities that are needed in your organization/team, and to use that information when hiring people and forming teams. As a starting point, consider looking for people with the following team-related capabilities in addition to any required job-specific or technical competencies:

- **Fundamental skills**: Giving/receiving feedback, communicating, conflict resolution, leadership, and interpersonal skills.

- **Teamwork savvy**: Understanding team dynamics and how to be a good teammate.
- **Personal attributes**: Cognitive ability (adequate to accomplish the work), collective orientation (enough team members possess it), adaptability (particularly in dynamic settings), and conscientiousness (but not everyone on the team must be highly conscientious).
- **Toxic traits to avoid**: Machiavellianism, narcissism, psychopathy, and very low levels of agreeableness—don't hire or tolerate toxic people no matter how strong their technical skills.

You can't miraculously "team away" a serious talent deficiency, so sometimes you may need to add or replace team members, to get the right people on the bus. But the research also revealed that simply adding another "star" won't always improve the team.

COOPERATION

Cooperation refers to the attitudes and beliefs about their team. What do they think about *this* team and the people on it? Do they think the team can succeed? Do they trust one another? Do they believe they can be "genuine" with other members on the team? Are they committed to the team and the work they do?

These attitudes and beliefs form as a result of experiences with the team (as well from their experiences with previous teams), and they are greatly influenced by the other drivers. They are based on perceptions, and perceptions don't always match reality. That is why you can't "make" someone trust you; you can only take actions that increase the likelihood that they will perceive you as trustworthy.

The research shows that four forms of cooperation are particularly important and should be the focus of your attention:

- **Trust**—Do I *expect my teammates to do the right thing*? Do I believe they have positive intentions?
- **Psychological safety**—Do I feel I *can be genuine and openly share my perspective*? Do I believe my teammates will give me the benefit of the doubt?
- **Collective efficacy**—Do we believe *our team can "get it done"*? Are we confident that our team will "win"?

- **Cohesion**—How do our team members feel about the team and our work? To what extent are we attracted or *committed to the team and the task?*

COORDINATION

Coordination is about teammates demonstrating the right teamwork behaviors at the right time. It is about actions, not attitudes. In highly effective teams, people monitor what's going on that might affect the team, they keep an eye on one another, and they help out as needs arise. In addition, the best teams become great by making ongoing adjustments. They make "in the moment" adaptations and they allocate time periodically to reflect and make longer term adjustments.

While specific coordination requirements vary by team, research suggests that the following four are among the most important teamwork behaviors:

- **Monitoring (maintaining situation awareness)**: Remaining aware of what is going on within and outside the team. Effective teams tend to monitor fellow team members, how well the team is performing, and the nature of the situation they are facing.
- **Providing back up/support**: Providing advice, support, or filling in for a team member when needed.
- **Adapting**: Learning from experience and making adjustments to address needs and improve performance.
- **Managing team emotions and conflict**: Dealing with conflicting points of view collaboratively (not competitively and not by avoiding disagreement), managing team members' emotions, and taking actions that maintain morale.

If team members aren't demonstrating teamwork behaviors, be sure everyone knows what is expected of them (the expected behaviors) and, as needed, provide them with feedback to ensure they live up to those expectations.

COMMUNICATION

Communication refers to the sharing of information and knowledge to accomplish work, maintain awareness, and foster positive relationships both within and outside the team. Of course, communication is essential for effective teamwork, but it isn't as simple as telling team members "to communicate more." When it comes to communication, quality is more important than quantity.

- At its most basic level, quality communication means sharing useful information clearly, accurately, and on time to the right people.
- But what drives team effectiveness is communicating unique information and knowledge that others may not possess or fully understand. For example, this might mean sharing a new piece of information or providing a "situation" update. Openly communicating information that others may not have is what builds shared awareness among team members.
- The most effective teams demonstrate closed-loop communications more frequently, where team members restate what they think they heard, allowing others to confirm or correct them. This significantly reduces miscommunications.

COGNITIONS

Cognitions refers to the extent to which team members possess a shared or at least a complementary understanding about priorities, roles, what's going on, and how to handle certain situations. All team members do not need to know exactly the same thing, but collectively they need to have a common "enough" understanding, and they should know who on the team possesses relevant knowledge. In other words, team members need to be "on the same page."

Teams generally perform better when its members can provide similar answers to the following eight questions. If they can't do that, you'll want to take actions that help them build a "shared mental model."

- Where are we headed? (vision, purpose, goals)
- What's important? (priorities)
- Who should? (roles)
- How to? (tasks, norms, interdependencies)
- Why to? (rationale)
- Who knows? (expertise)
- What if? (contingencies, if-then)
- What's up? (situation, cues)

CONDITIONS

Conditions refers to the context or environment in which a team operates, and they can greatly impact team effectiveness. Conditions, in conjunction with the attributes of the people involved (e.g., capabilities), determine if a team is equipped to work together successfully.

Some conditions can have a broad influence, for example, organizational policies and practices (i.e., hiring, onboarding, promotions and opportunities, performance management, rewards and recognition) and actions taken by senior leadership (e.g., modeling behaviors, communicating, and establishing psychological safety). Collectively, these help define your culture. Employees pick up on what is encouraged as well as what is tolerated (e.g., do you make excuses for toxic employees because they generate revenue?). Because these overarching conditions can facilitate or inhibit teamwork throughout the organization, it makes sense to monitor them centrally and take action to rectify any "gaps" or unintended consequences that surface.

Other conditions are more local or team-specific. Three of these—resources, time, and decision-making authority—can place significant constraints on a team's effectiveness. It is almost impossible to "team away" a significant lack of resources and unreasonable to expect team members to monitor and support one another if they barely have time to complete their own assignments. Monitor these conditions locally and focus on how to remedy deficiencies. If they can't be improved, brainstorm ways to work around them creatively.

COACHING

Coaching is the term we use to describe team leadership, but we aren't simply referring to the designated leader. More and more frequently we see the need for team members to step up and perform some leadership functions, what researchers refer to as "shared leadership." Shared leadership doesn't involve appointing an additional leader; it is more informal in nature.

What leadership is needed to ensure a team is successful? Research suggests that there are seven essential leadership functions that need to be fulfilled on almost any team. Some of these may be completed by the leader alone, but in other instances, various team members can "step up" and help out.

Task-focused:

1. Ensure clarity and alignment
2. Hold teammates accountable
3. Remove obstacles and garner support

Team-focused:

4. Manage team emotions and attitudes
5. Foster psychological safety
6. Encourage participation and empowerment

Team and task-focused:

7. Promote learning and adaptation

We also described four leadership approaches, each of which provides a helpful reminder to anyone who is a team leader.

- **Transformational leadership** reminds us to inspire the team and not simply reward compliance.
- **Shared leadership** reminds us that if the leader is the only person on the team who is showing leadership behaviors that's probably a red flag.
- **Servant leadership** reminds us to put the team first.
- **Civil leadership** reminds us not to be a jerk—and not tolerate incivility in others.

That concludes the high-level refresher. If you want more details on any of the Cs, you can always revisit the appropriate chapter. But now, let's turn to how to apply this knowledge. The next four short chapters each focus on a different role (Table 11.2). In each, you'll find 10 actionable recommendations for applying what's known about the science of teamwork.

Table 11.2. What to Expect in the Remaining Chapters

When you are a . . .	Consider how you can . . .
Chapter 12: **Team leader**	Help your team succeed.
Chapter 13: **Team member**	Be a more effective team member (and in so doing help the team and your career).
Chapter 14: **Consultant** (internal or external)	Support a team(s) or organization in need and enable them to improve.
Chapter 15: **Senior leader**	Promote teamwork and collaboration in your organization.

Team Leaders

Helping Your Team Succeed

Leading a team can be challenging, but fundamentally, effective team leadership is about (a) ensuring that your team has all the capabilities, cooperation, coordination, communication, cognition, coaching, and conditions it needs and (b) enabling them to learn and adapt as needed.

The following are 10 team leader tips for applying the science of teamwork. As you read through the recommended actions, we encourage you to identify at least two that you can use over the next few months to help your team succeed. You might decide to start doing something you don't currently do (or do enough) or instead focus on an action or two that you already know about but will commit to paying closer attention to over the next few months.

1. **Ensure that your team has the talent it needs to be successful.**
   a. Recognize that teamwork can rarely overcome very large talent deficiencies in core areas. A team needs ample talent.
   b. Be honest about your team's talent gaps and take action: provide individuals with targeted training or coaching to increase their capabilities; acquire, move, replace, or borrow talent to fill in talent gaps; or modify task assignments or work procedures to better fit team member capabilities.
   c. When hiring your next team member, clarify the competencies they need to possess, including both technical competencies and teamwork competencies.

2. **Staff your team with enough team members who think "team first" (i.e., who have "collective orientation").**
   a. Not every member of your team must be high in collective orientation, but you need enough who are. When hiring a new employee or assembling a team, assess more than technical expertise. Ask candidates about their prior team experiences and be alert for red flags, such as excessive complaining about or blaming of prior team members. Avoid people with toxic personalities even if they appear to be technically qualified.
   b. Be careful not to burn out your most team-oriented people by overrelying on them to fill in, help others, volunteer, work late, etc. If upon reflection, you realize that several of your most team-oriented people have left your teams in the past, it is possible that you either burned them out or failed to recognize their contributions to the team.
   c. Recognize and reward teamwork, and you'll gain a reputation as a leader for whom team players want to work. Tolerate jerks, and you'll gain a different reputation.
3. **Take actions that builds your team's "collective efficacy"—so they believe the team can win.**
   a. Teams that believe they can win are more likely to do so. While self-confidence is helpful ("I can succeed"), it is insufficient when team members must rely on one another. They need to believe in the team as well ("We can succeed").
   b. Boost your team's collective efficacy by discussing and celebrating team wins and accomplishments. Solving problems is important, but be sure to also spend some time on the team's successes. Ask, "How can we build on this success?" and "What did we learn from this win that we can apply elsewhere?"
4. **Act in a manner that consistently promotes a sense of psychological safety in your team.**
   a. Psychological safety is what enables team members to believe they can speak up, admit mistakes, ask questions, offer a dissenting opinion, seek feedback and be themselves—without the risk of being judged harshly. As team leader, you can greatly influence psychological safety, and it's among the strongest predictors of team performance.
   b. To help create psychological safety, admit when you don't understand something or made a mistake; encourage team members to voice concerns; and thank them when they have the courage to

offer a dissenting view. Treat mistakes as opportunities to learn, not opportunities for blame.

    c. But recognize that promoting psychological safety does not mean being weak or tolerating unacceptable behavior. You can address performance problems and still develop psychological safety in your team.

5. **Prepare your team members to back up one another.**

    a. Back-up behaviors (e.g., helping out, filling in, providing reminders) can be crucial for a team's success. For backup to occur, team members need to know when and how to do so and must possess the right skills.

    b. Clarify your expectations about when backup is needed and who should provide it, and selectively train people to know "enough" about other people's tasks to be able to help.

6. **Conduct periodic team debriefs to help your team "self-adjust."**

    a. The best teams are rarely great on day one. They become great by making small, ongoing adjustments.

    b. Get in the habit of conducting periodic team debriefs to discuss how the team has been working together. Ask what went well and where improvements might be beneficial. Discuss teamwork and task work, agree to one or more tangible adjustments, and then follow up to assess progress. You'll finds tips and an outline for leading a team debrief in Tool B toward the end of the book.

    c. When conducting a debrief, start by asking questions rather than telling your team what they should do. Teams adapt more effectively when they self-discover what they did well and can do better. After they've had the chance to share their perspectives, you can fill in anything they missed or redirect them as needed.

7. **Monitor and boost the quality of communications in your team.**

    a. How often are your team members "surprised" because they weren't told something or were unaware of an action or decision? Communications often suffer because people falsely assume "Everyone knows that." Get in the habit of asking team members, "Who else should know about this?"

    b. More communication is not always better. Simply talking more (or sending more emails) is not enough. Quality communication is a result of team members sharing unique information, in a timely manner, and restating what they heard to ensure clarity.

    c. If communicating with "outsiders" is critical, be sure that (a) the right people are handling that role (being "boundary spanners") and (b) they are well prepared to do so. When you need all team members to communicate a consistent message, be sure they all know the message. That won't happen by chance, so discuss with them, "What will we all tell people about X?"

8. **Be sure your team members are on the same page (maintain "shared cognitions").**

   a. Effective teams maintain shared cognitions about direction, priorities, roles, and ways to handle certain situations. If asked about these factors, would your team members provide the same answers? Don't assume this will happen naturally.

   b. Allocate time to review and discuss current priorities and direction. What does success look like for our team? What are our top priorities? To build shared understanding and future readiness, periodically discuss relevant scenarios. To anticipate if–then contingencies, ask, "If X happens, who should do what? Why?"

   c. Role clarity is critical. Role gaps (e.g., I assume you'll handle it, and you assume I will) and role conflicts (e.g., we each think we own a decision) create problems. List your team's major activities and decisions and, for each, clarify who is responsible for it, who should be asked for input about it, and who should be updated afterwards.

9. **Continue to sharpen your team leadership skills.**

   a. Leadership matters, but effective leadership doesn't mean being the most visible, forceful person in charge. Overreliance on rewards and punishment drives compliance but doesn't build commitment. Demonstrate that you are committed to your team members' success and not just your own—convey some sense of "servant leadership." Ask, "What can I do to help you and the team succeed?"

   b. Encourage team members to provide each other with constructive feedback, to offer advice, suggest new ideas, and hold each other accountable. You can't be there for everyone all the time, so some "shared leadership" will probably be needed for your team to thrive.

   c. Help your team establish an inspiring sense of identity. Discuss, "Why does our team exist"? "Who do we impact? Who relies on us?" and "How can we really make a difference?"

10. **Use your influence as a team leader to improve the environment in which your team operates.**

  a. Unfavorable conditions hinder team success—and no team operates under persistently favorable conditions. Does your team lack critical resources, access, time, information, equipment, or support?

  b. Be sure you know the difference between your team's needs (without which the team is truly unlikely to be successful) and wants (things that would be helpful but aren't essential) and spend most of your negotiating "chips" trying to acquire needs.

  c. Avoid making commitments to your team that you aren't sure you'll be able to keep. If a decision is outside your control, it is better to tell your team "I'll look into that problem, and let you know if it can be changed," than to say "I'll get that fixed" and then failing to deliver. Breaking your word is a big trust killer.

CHAPTER 13

Team Members

Being a Great Team Member

Hopefully you've had the chance to work with some great team-mates. If so, you've seen how they can elevate the people around them, without being "selfless." It is a myth that you can only be individually excellent *or* a team player—research shows you can be both! Strive for personal excellence *and* being a great teammate.

The following are a set of 10 recommended actions for applying the science of teamwork when you are part of a team. The recommendations reflect what great team members do that enables them and their teams to succeed. As you read through these, acknowledge the ones that you currently do well on a consistent basis. Bravo! Then identify at least two other actions that you intend to start doing, do more frequently, or do more effectively during the next few months, so they become part of your standard way of operating. Being a great team member is good for your career, your team, your teammates, and your organization!

1. **Stay alert and be aware of what's going on in your team, where its headed, and how you can help.**
   a. Be aware of your team's needs and priorities and how you can contribute. If you're unsure about where the team is headed, what's most important, or what is expected of you, ask. Don't guess. It's hard to contribute to the team's success without that understanding. Plus, if you don't know, it's likely that some of your teammates don't know either, so you'll be helping them by raising the question.

b. Learn about your teammates' capabilities and preferences, so you know who may need your help and who you can seek help from. Who is good at X? Who knows the most about Y? Who might benefit from your expertise?

2. **Ask "How can I help" and offer to provide support without waiting to be asked or told to do so.**

    a. Be generous with your support and expertise. That can be hard at times, but if you consistently help others, your teammates are more likely to view you as a trusted collaborator—and are more likely to help you when you need it.

    b. Be open to and willing to accept assistance. Thank your teammates when they offer to help. Do this even when you decline the assistance because you don't need it. If you make it hard for people to help you ("I don't need any help"; "I already know that"), you'll find that they aren't available when you do need them.

3. **Seek ways to adapt and improve—both personally and for the team.**

    a. The most successful teams aren't great on day 1. They become great because they learn and make adjustments over time. Continually look for and share ways that you and the team can improve.

    b. Demonstrate personal flexibility and a willingness to try new ways of working. Not every experiment will work, but it's hard to improve if you never try anything new.

    c. Don't get discouraged if you make a suggestion that your team leader ignores. You can't control that, but you can control whether you continue to try to help the team get better!

4. **Fulfill your commitments—do what you say you will do and complete your assignments.**

    a. Trust is essential in any team, and failing to do what you said you would do is among the top trust killers.

    b. People like working with teammates who they can count on. Don't say, "I will do X," if you are uncertain if you can. Be honest about what you can accomplish.

    c. If you start to anticipate a delay or a problem in something you are responsible for, give others a heads-up about it. Don't hope for a miracle, or you'll be likely to show up empty-handed on delivery day. If you recognize that there may be a problem, alert teammates who could be affected by it.

5. **Be an effective communicator.**
    a. Effective communicating isn't about talking or emailing more often; it's about communicating better. It starts with listening to what others are saying and then conveying back your understanding of what they told you (e.g., "So you're saying that this project is now more important than the other one we've been working on?"). That type of "closed-loop" communication gives them a chance to clarify or confirm what they said, which greatly reduces misunderstandings!
    b. It is easy to assume incorrectly that others know what you know. That happens so often that there's a name for it—it's called the "everybody knows" bias. When in doubt, share the information you have. You'll be surprised how often a teammate didn't know something you thought they did.
    c. One simple but effective way to improve team communications is to get in the habit of asking, "Who else should know this?"
6. **Care more about what is right than who is right.**
    a. Share your point of view, but your goal should be to ensure the best idea wins, not necessarily that your idea wins. Teams that disagree "collaboratively," who are trying to find the best answer, outperform teams that disagree competitively (where everyone defends their own ideas) and outperform teams that avoid disagreements. Don't pretend to agree and then complain about the decision later!
    b. If you find yourself continually defending your ideas and repeating your point of view, that's a sign that you may be more concerned with winning than with doing what's best for the team. Check yourself.
    c. Sometimes the best solution is one that combines ideas, so look for ways to connect different ideas to suggest an even better alternative.
7. **Acknowledge your mistakes and voice your appreciation.**
    a. No one is perfect; we all make mistakes. When you make a mistake or hurt someone's feelings, own it, genuinely apologize, and avoid repeating it in the future.
    b. Be willing to say, "I was wrong." If you've ever worked with (or lived with) someone who can never admit being wrong, you know how frustrating that can be.
    c. When a team member does something that is helpful or positive, say, "Thank you." Be honest: do you say "thank you" enough? *Thinking* "thank you" isn't the same as *saying* "thank you!"

8. **Provide and seek feedback within your team.**
   a. Make it easy for others to give you feedback. How? Thank them for sharing their perspective. Avoid acting defensively and attempting to explain why their feedback is wrong. And periodically ask teammates for their feedback ("How did I do?" "What am I doing that helps and what can I do better?"). Seeking feedback lets them know that you're open to input.
   b. Offer constructive feedback to teammates but know when to provide it in private. As a general guideline, if the feedback is likely to make the person uncomfortable, you probably shouldn't be giving it to them in front of others.
   c. Help your team leader be successful by providing them with your input. It can be harder to give upward feedback, so many leaders don't get enough of it. First, ask your team leader if they are open to hearing your input on a topic. Learn what they might consider to be off limits.

9. **Don't be a toxic teammate.**
   a. What do toxic teammates do? They say hurtful things, make inappropriate comments, act rudely, embarrass teammates, withhold effort, talk badly about teammates, are continually pessimistic, and/or drone on about the things that irritate them.
   b. If you've been around someone who consistently demonstrates some of these behaviors, you know how difficult it is to work with them. Don't be that type of teammate.
   c. Anyone can have a bad day. But if you exhibit any of these behaviors on a regular basis, you're hurting the team—and probably jeopardizing your career.

10. **Represent your team and team members when interacting with people who aren't on your team.**
    a. When you interact with people outside the team, look for the chance to help promote and position your team. It's okay to be a self-promoter, but great teammates also speak favorably about their team.
    b. Attempt to generate support, make connections, and garner resources for your team. At a minimum, be a positive ambassador for your team. Never complain about your team to outsiders!
    c. Be sure you're prepared to answer the question, "What is your team working on these days" in a concise, constructive way. If needed, get advice from your team leader.

CHAPTER 14

Consultants

Enabling Teams to Improve

Consultants are often asked to help boost teamwork and collaboration. Perhaps you are an internal consultant in a human resource business partner, organization development, learning and development, or quality role, or maybe you are an external consultant who supports teams across different organizations. As a consultant, you could be called upon to help a struggling team, to coach a team leader, or to advise a senior leader on how to promote greater collaboration throughout a unit or organization. To address any of these needs, it helps to understand what really drives teamwork.

The following are a set of 10 tips for applying the science of teamwork as a consultant. Depending upon your current role and client needs, some of the tips will be more immediately applicable, but we encourage you to find at least two that you can use in your consulting work over the next few months. Which of these tips could help you be a better consultant and, more important, which would help your clients be more effective?

1. **Attempt to uncover the *real* reasons why a team may be struggling (or what may be inhibiting collaboration in the organization).**
   a. Begin by trying to uncover what is helping and hindering teamwork. When someone says, "Our team members aren't getting along," what does that really mean? You'll usually need to dig a little deeper than the stated problem. Which of the seven drivers of team effectiveness that we described in this book may be

contributing to the problem? Consider using Tool D, the Quick Diagnostic, found at the back of the book.

b. When you uncover the real issues, use that understanding to guide the right course of action. No solution is universally applicable. For example, improving a team's attitude toward teamwork won't enable them to overcome a severe talent deficit. Review the Ideas Matrix (see Tool E at the back of the book) for a set of suggestions for addressing a wide range of specific deficiencies.

2. **Take action at the right level—individual, dyad, team, or organizational—and in the right setting.**

a. Recognize that the "right" solution might involve an intact team— but not always. Sometimes it is best to work with an individual or a couple of people rather than the entire team.

b. Never attempt to resolve an individual performance problem, a team leader issue, or a conflict between two team members in a team setting. Sometimes what is needed is to replace a team member, coach a team leader, or help two team members work through a conflict privately, rather than conducting an intervention that involves the entire team.

c. If you see recurring collaboration and team problems across the business, that's an indicator that broader organizational conditions may be inhibiting teamwork. It that case, it makes sense to consider more overarching solutions (e.g., to improve the culture, to ensure senior leaders are sending the right signals, to better align human resource practices), rather than continuing to put out fires, one team at time. The diagnostic questions found in Tool C at the back of the book can be helpful when thinking about these broader conditions.

3. **Avoid unrealistic expectations about feel-good exercises and experiences such as camping together or learning about each other's "type."**

a. While it's okay to arrange a fun event or entertain a team, don't expect those activities to rectify coordination breakdowns, communication problems, lack of shared cognitions, capability deficiencies, or unfavorable conditions. Similarly, don't expect an unvalidated personality style exercise to resolve significant team effectiveness challenges.

b. Research shows that it is far more beneficial for team members to become familiar with each other's work-related competencies, expertise, and knowledge than it is for them to become familiar with each other's personal lives. Work-related familiarity can boost team performance. Getting people to talk about their personal life is viewed as a fun "go-to" exercise by many facilitators, but it is unlikely to help a team overcome real problems (and it can make some team members feel uncomfortable.)

c. Be careful about finding a "favorite" approach that you end up applying to address most team problems. When all you have is a hammer, everything starts to look like a nail. One size does not fit all!

4. **Build your (and your organization's) toolkit of evidence-based team interventions.**

a. A few of the most effective evidence-based interventions include team debriefing, team training, role clarification, and team chartering. It makes sense to become proficient in those interventions.

b. Be sure you develop your toolkit to include ways to aid individuals (e.g., coaching a team leader), dyads (e.g., resolving a conflict), teams (e.g., leading a debrief), and organizational needs (e.g., reviewing key policies and practices).

5. **Teach team leaders how to help their teams adapt and "self-adjust."**

a. The most effective teams adapt over time. You can help them when you're with them, but you won't always be there to help. You should prepare team leaders to help their teams self-adjust without you.

b. Look for ways to educate team leaders about the science of teamwork. Be sure they are aware of the seven essential team leadership functions and how to use shared leadership effectively.

c. Teach team leaders about debriefs (including how to run them effectively). Then, facilitate a debrief for them and their team and encourage the leader to conduct the next team debrief on their own. Debriefing is a proven method that enables teams to adapt. The debriefing tool (see Tool B at the back of the book) contains useful tips and an outline for running effective debriefs.

d. When a leader knows what really drives team effectiveness and can lead team debriefs, their team will usually be able to learn and adapt to most challenges without you—and that's a good thing!

6. **Where appropriate, help teams build shared cognitions.**

a. Shared cognitions are when team members have a common or complimentary understanding about things like the team's priorities, team member's roles, and how to handle certain situations.

For example, if you were to ask each team member, "What are your team's top priorities?" "Who should do what in a particular situation?" or "Who on the team knows the most about X?" would they all provide similar answers? That's a pretty good diagnostic test you could conduct.

b. You can help teams develop clearer shared cognitions by using *direction-setting* techniques (e.g., visioning, chartering, premortems), *preparation* methods (e.g., role clarification exercises, cross-training, scenario-based training), *updating* approaches (e.g., debriefs and huddles), and *assimilation* methods (e.g., new member onboarding, new leader assimilation session).

7. **Help employees become better team members.**

   a. Teach them about the behaviors that great team members exhibit (as listed in chapter 13 of this book). Ask them to reflect on those behaviors. Which ones do they currently do well, and which ones could they do better or more often? You can introduce this during employee training or as part of a team development session.

   b. Help employees build transportable teamwork skills that they can use throughout their careers, as they move from team to team, including *communication, feedback, conflict, interpersonal,* and *leadership* skills (as described in Tool A). Be sure they know it is possible to be both individually excellent and a great team player.

8. **Promote the development of psychological safety.**

   a. Psychological safety is what enables team members to believe they can speak up, seek assistance, provide feedback, ask questions, and share expertise without being judged harshly. A lack of psychological safety is often a root cause of many teamwork problems.

   b. Become well-versed in how to build psychological safety and then train/coach team leaders how to develop psychological safety and trust in their teams. This will pay long-term dividends for the leaders and the teams they lead throughout their career.

9. **If you work with senior leaders, help them lead the way to better teamwork (or at least not get in the way!).**

   a. Coach senior leaders on what really drives teamwork and how they can help boost collaboration in the organization (e.g., share the senior leader tips provided in the next chapter!).

   b. Encourage them to act and communicate in ways that signal they value teamwork. Consider leading them through an exercise where they identify what they have "done and said" that would indicate they value teamwork and what they have done and said that could be perceived by others as inconsistent with that value.

c. Help senior leadership teams work together more effectively. When they work well together, they make better decisions and produce better results. Equally important, the way the leadership team operates sends a message to others throughout the organization about whether collaboration is the expected norm. Consider leading them through a team debrief.

10. **If you're trying to boost teamwork across the organization, examine relevant organizational policies and practices to ensure the right "conditions" are in place.**

a. Examine the organization's hiring, onboarding, performance management, and rewards practices, as well who tends to get promoted and offered better work assignments. How might these practices and decisions reinforce or inhibit teamwork and collaboration?

b. For example, are job candidates' teamwork competencies systematically assessed or just their technical expertise? Are the contributions an employee makes to their team evaluated as part of their performance review or just their individual accomplishments? Modify organizational policies and practices, as needed, to better support collaboration and teamwork. Consider using the diagnostic questions found in Tool C at the back of the book.

Senior Leaders

Promoting Teamwork in Your Organization

A s a senior leader, you set the tone for teamwork and collaboration for the rest of your organization. Although most employees may not see and talk with senior leaders on a regular basis, research shows that what happens among you and your colleagues somehow finds its way through the organization.

The actions you and other senior leaders take (and don't take) and the things you say (and don't say) send signals about whether collaboration is truly valued. If you believe that teamwork is an ingredient for business and personal success, you'll want to reinforce that message.

The following are a set of 10 senior leader tips for applying the science of teamwork. As you read through them, we encourage you to identify at least a couple that you will emphasize or focus on over the next few months. You might also find it of value to share and discuss the tips with your colleagues on the leadership team. Collectively, which are you doing well and where might additional attention be beneficial?

1. **Use teams wisely.**
   a. Don't overuse teams—they can be a great solution, but "Let's form a team to tackle (or research) that" isn't the correct answer to every problem.
   b. When you create a team, be sure to provide it with the resources it needs to succeed (people, talent, funding). If you are reluctant to dedicate ample resources to a team, you should be asking, "Do we really need that team?"

c. When you create a team, be sure their mission is clear and give them ample authority to accomplish it. If you've ever been on a team that has a vague sense of direction or that works on something for a while and later discovers that isn't what the sponsor intended, you know how frustrating that can be. To avoid this, ask the team to assemble a brief team charter, provide them with redirection as needed, and then give them the authority to do what they need to do.

2. **Make "talent" decisions that send the right signals about the value of teamwork.**
   a. Advocate for the promotion of employees who are personally competent *and* effective team players.
   b. When evaluating talent, continually ask the questions, "Does this person make others around them better or worse?" and "Do they have a legacy of team successes?"
   c. Do not put talented individuals who have no interest in or competency for leadership into positions where they are expected to guide teams to success.

3. **You get what you tolerate.** If you accept toxic or "all about me" employees in your organization, you should expect to see less collaboration.
   a. Don't make excuses for toxic employees—no matter how much revenue they generate or how smart they may be. If almost no one wants to work with someone, that's an indication that you've got a problem.
   b. Explore "how" your organizational stars have gotten ahead. Did they do so by stepping on others? Burning out their teams? Claiming all the credit? Are self-serving behaviors viewed as acceptable in your organization?
   c. Consider what happens to "knowledge/information hoarders." When hoarding is rewarded more than sharing ("He's the only one who knows that, so he must be smart"), people learn not to share what they know unless it is required or will make them look good.

4. **You get what you encourage.**
   a. Promote the value of collaboration—shine a light on instances where collaboration and teamwork have led to business successes. If the stories you tell always feature individual "heroes," it communicates that "me" is always more important than "we." Successes are rarely attributable to just one person, even if they appear that way at first glance.

b. Reflect on what you and other senior leaders have done or said (or perhaps didn't do or say) that sends a message—intentionally or inadvertently—about whether collaboration matters.

c. Walk the talk. People believe much more of what they see than what they hear, so if you want to promote teamwork and collaboration, demonstrate that through your day-to-day actions. At an absolute minimum, be civil. When you need to be tough, do so, but don't be rude.

5. **No badmouthing other senior leadership team members or other units or functions—period.**

a. You may think that what is said behind closed doors remains hidden, but somehow it travels through the organization, making it even more difficult for the people below you in the hierarchy to collaborate with their colleagues in other areas.

b. If you have a problem with another senior leader, talk with them directly. Nothing good comes from talking about them to others.

6. **Work to create "psychological safety."**

a. You can't see and know everything, so you need people to be willing to speak up, offer their point of view, seek assistance, provide feedback, ask questions, admit to errors, and share expertise. Psychological safety is what enables people to believe they can do those things without being judged harshly—and is one of the strongest predictors of team effectiveness.

b. A few behaviors can make a big difference—if you admit a mistake, acknowledge you don't know something, thank people for offering dissenting points of view, and treat errors as opportunities to learn (rather than to punish), then psychological safety will increase. When you "chew out" someone in front of others for admitting a mistake, they all learn not to speak up.

c. Psychological safety starts at the top and permeates an organization—so your behaviors set the stage.

7. **Allocate a little time to improve the way your senior leadership team (SLT) works together.**

a. When the SLT works well together, your business is more likely to succeed. Plus, it sends the right signal about collaboration to the rest of the organization. Most senior leadership teams don't work shoulder to shoulder each day, and each SLT member oversees a unique part of the business, so SLT coordination doesn't happen "naturally." It requires a little attention.

b. The best teams self-adjust, so allocate 60 minutes at least twice per year, to conduct a SLT debrief. Discuss "How are we working as a team? "What are we doing well?" "What could we do better?" and "What adjustments will we make?" Be sure that the discussion covers teamwork and not just task work. Ask question such as, "How well are we keeping each other informed?" "How useful are our meetings?" "Is it clear who owns certain decisions?" etc.?

c. One simple trick that will improve your meetings is to clarify, for each agenda item, whether the intent is to *update* the team, seek their *input*, or make a *decision* together. We suspect you've seen what happens when a team member thinks they are simply going to provide an update and other people start offering "unsolicited" advice or try to "take over" the decision. Clarity of intent helps.

8. **Be sure that the members of the SLT are on the "same page."**

   a. As previously noted, members of your SLT probably represent different parts of the organization and may not work together on a daily basis. Team members can start to interpret things differently, leading to disconnects. It can be hard for SLT members to maintain a "shared mental model."

   b. Be sure there is a common understanding among your team members about roles and priorities. Would each of you provide the same answer to the questions, "What are our organization's top priorities right now?" and "Who is responsible for X, Y and Z?" If not, spend time to clarify it.

   c. Consider allocating three minutes at the end of each SLT meeting to confirm any decisions or action plans that were made and agree what everyone will communicate to others. When SLT members communicate conflicting messages, it has a ripple effect that makes it harder for those below you to collaborate.

9. **Cultivate working relationships that cross functional boundaries and levels.**

   a. If you only spend time with, and are only seen with, people from your function or who are at your level, it sends a subtle message to others that silos are the norm.

   b. Recognize where silos or "fault lines" have formed or may emerge in your organization. Where are the main silos in your organization? Try to be a connector across those borders rather than a gatekeeper. If you can't be the connector, find someone who can; for example, someone who has had experience in two functional areas can often serve as effective bridge because they "speak both languages."

10. **Insist on a periodic review of organizational practices and policies that can send signals about teamwork.**

   a. For example, do your performance management and reward practices encourage or inhibit teamwork? Are teamwork skills systematically assessed during the hiring process? Who tends to get choice assignments and promotions in your organization? What messages are conveyed about the value of collaboration during the employee onboarding process? You will find a list of diagnostic questions for examining organizational "conditions" that can influence teamwork in Tool C at the back of the book.

Common Team Competencies List

Capability refers to the individual and collective competencies that a team possesses. This includes the knowledge, skills, abilities, personality, and other personal attributes needed to complete assignments, overcome challenges, work well with others, and adapt as needed to sustain performance.

Table A.1 provides a list of several capabilities that have been shown to influence team effectiveness. You can use this as a starting point to establish team member selection criteria (i.e., the characteristics you want to look for and avoid when you seek to hire new employees) and to target training and development efforts.

FUNDAMENTAL SKILLS

- **Communication skills**—to provide clear messages, ask effective questions, listen actively, and convey understanding.
- **Feedback skills**—to observe and monitor performance, provide constructive feedback to others, encourage feedback from others, and interpret feedback received.
- **Conflict skills**—to disagree productively, use constructive conflict styles, diagnose the cause of conflict situations, defuse and work through conflicts and help others do so.
- **Interpersonal skills**—to infer intent/emotions, convey empathy when appropriate, interpret non-verbal cues, regulate one's own emotions, and influence/persuade others.
- **Leadership skills**—to constructively hold others accountable, motivate and encourage teammates, share expertise/teach others, and clarify expectations and priorities.

Table A.1. Categories and Examples of Team Competencies

Category	Includes	Considerations
Fundamental skills	Giving/receiving feedback, communicating, conflict resolution, leadership, and interpersonal skills	These are transportable competencies that can be used in any team. You can look for these in potential team members and, because they can be developed, they are a logical target for training and coaching solutions.
Teamwork savvy	Understanding team dynamics and how to be a good teammate	This is transportable knowledge that can be assessed during hiring and can also be developed through training and coaching.
Personal attributes	Cognitive ability (adequate), collective orientation (enough), adaptability (particularly in dynamic settings), conscientiousness (but not everyone must be high)	These are relatively stable attributes that are difficult to change (particularly cognitive ability and conscientiousness). You can look for these during hiring. You can try to coach people to think "team," and to be more adaptable, but it isn't easy to move the needle on them.
Toxic traits to avoid	Machiavellianism, narcissism, psychopathy, and very low levels of agreeableness	These are very stable attributes and extremely difficult to change. You should try to avoid hiring people with these traits and take action if they surface in current team members.
Team- and task-specific competencies	Unique to the particular situation	These are unique for different teams. Try to specify which task specific competencies can be developed after joining the team and which are required at the time of hire. Team-specific competencies (e.g., knowing your colleagues' strengths) can only be developed posthire.

TEAMWORK SAVVY

- **Teamwork savvy** is knowing what drives team effectiveness and knowing what good team members do.

PERSONAL ATTRIBUTES

- **Cognitive ability** refers to the capacity to perform higher mental processes of reasoning, recalling, understanding, and problem-solving. It doesn't refer to what someone knows. Team members need adequate cognitive ability to perform their tasks but also to acquire new knowledge and skills, to communicate effectively, and to contribute to effective team decision making.
- **Collective orientation** is an underlying belief about working in teams. Individuals who are high in collective orientation typically prefer working in teams and think "team first." They are generally

predisposed to promote their team's interests. In laymen's terms, we might refer to them as "team players."

- **Adaptability** is the willingness and ability to adjust to fit changed circumstances; being flexible rather than rigid.
- **Conscientiousness** is a tendency to be dependable, organized, and dutiful. People with this trait typically prefer planned rather than spontaneous actions.
- **Agreeableness** is the tendency to be trusting, helpful, and cooperative rather than highly competitive and suspicious of others.

TOXIC TRAITS TO AVOID

- Someone with a **Machiavellian** personality believes manipulation is effective and acceptable, has a cynical view of human nature, and possesses a moral outlook that places expediency above principle.
- **Narcissism** is typified by an overinflated sense of self-worth, inaccurate beliefs about control and success, and a strong desire to have their self-love shared and reinforced by others. They typically see themselves as superior, even when others do not.
- Characteristics associated with **psychopathy** are a lack of concern for others, high impulsivity, and a lack of remorse after harming others. They are often great "impression managers" and can be charismatic.

TASK- AND TEAM-SPECIFIC CAPABILITIES

In addition to transportable teamwork-related capabilities that apply to almost any team there are some capabilities that are only apply when working with particular team members, when working on specific tasks, or both. A few of these are highlighted next.

Task-specific competencies include the skills and knowledge needed to perform certain tasks, regardless of who else is on the team. These can often be acquired through individual training and development activities and as a result of experience. Examples of these include

- Knowledge and skills needed to do one's own job effectively.
- Accurate "if–then" mental models, for example, the appropriate response to certain situations and problems ("If X happens, I am supposed to do Y").

- Knowledge of other people's roles as they relate to this task—sometimes referred to as interpositional knowledge, or IPK.
- Knowledge and skills needed to be able to fill in for, back up, or help others, as needed, related to a specific task.
- Awareness of specific coordination and communication protocols, including standard and emergency operating procedures.

Team-specific competencies include general knowledge about teammates and the team itself, not associated with any particular task. These are often acquired through team development and planning activities and through interactions with team members over time.

- Knowledge about teammates such as their general expertise, preferences, motivations, strengths, and limitations
- Knowledge about the bigger picture for the team including its mission, vision, and general priorities

Situation-specific competencies include shared understanding and common expectations for a set of people performing a particular task. These can be developed through team training activities with intact teams or over time through shared experiences.

- Shared task and role expectations—how this team, with its unique mix of team member capabilities and preferences, is expected to perform a particular task (e.g., a team-specific if–then model—who should do what when X occurs)
- Awareness of the task-specific expertise of team members
- Knowledge of who to contact when a particular task-related problem emerges

Team Debriefing Tips and Outline

CONDUCTING EFFECTIVE TEAM DEBRIEFS

Debriefs are a quick, simple, yet powerful tool for ensuring a team learns, gels, and improves over time. During a debrief, team members reflect upon a recent experience(s), discuss what went well and identify opportunities for improvement. They attempt to build a common understanding (e.g., clarifying priorities, roles, goals, or how to handle certain situations) and establish agreements to ensure future success (e.g., how they intend to work together in the future).

A debrief can occur after any team experience, for example, after a challenging situation or event, at any point during a project or work cycle, at the conclusion of a shift, or following a team activity.

> Research shows that teams that debrief outperform other teams by an average of 20%! And the actions you take as debrief leader can make a big difference.

DEBRIEFING TIPS

- **Conduct short periodic debriefs and not just end of project "postmortems."** While an end of project debrief may provide insights for future work, they are too late to make a mid-course correction. Get in the habit of conducting relatively quick, periodic team debriefs.
- **Schedule a time to debrief.** While it would be great if debriefs happened spontaneously, in our experience that rarely happens. Allocate 30 minutes for a quick debrief and 60 minutes if you want to take a deeper dive. While there isn't a magic frequency, a reasonable target

is to debrief once per month or every other month. However, if your team operates in a dynamic environment and works together constantly, you may want to conduct more frequent debriefs (that's why agile programming teams huddle up daily). For teams that only work together periodically, such as senior leadership teams, a more appropriate target may be to do quarterly or biannual debriefs.

- **If you are the team leader, be sure to use the following debriefing tips**:
  1. During the discussion, let your team members talk first.
     - If you respond first it, can discourage their input.
  2. Find a way to acknowledge a mistake you made or how you intend to change.
     - It makes it easier for others to do so.
  3. Encourage all team members to participate in the discussion.
     - Research shows that the best debriefs are those in which more team members contribute.
     - Simply "allowing" everyone to contribute often isn't enough for some members to speak up; you need to actively encourage people to share their perspective, in some cases asking directly. "Suzanne, what do you think?"
  4. If someone voices a concern or admits they could have done something better, do not chastise them—make it safe for them (and others) to speak up.
     - Otherwise, you discourage others from voicing a concern or admitting a misunderstanding.
     - You can't see everything, so you need your team to be willing to share their observations.
  5. Be sure to periodically ask, "Should we make an adjustment in how we do this?"
     - If so, explore how best to adjust (the forward look).
     - Capture any agreements and follow up on them during the next meeting.
- **Avoid the five debriefing "pitfalls."** We've observed five common problems that can derail or diminish the value of a team debrief. They are all avoidable if you're conscious of them.
  1. The leader talking too much and talking at the team ("telling" and not asking enough questions to engage the team).
  2. The focus is strictly on task work (e.g., technical aspects of work) and not on discussing teamwork issues (e.g., how well we are communicating and backing up one another).

3. Team members feel that they aren't able to weigh in (a common concern in hierarchical teams).
4. Time is wasted discussing areas of agreement and avoiding challenging topics (without guidance, almost all teams gravitate towards "safe" topics and defer the important issues to later, if ever).
5. The discussion looks backward (reflect/discuss) but not forward (action/agreements).

DEBRIEF LEADERS: DEBRIEFING MINDSET

To get the most value out of any debrief that you lead, be sure to have the following "mindset."

- **Participants first, you second**. When it is time for reflection and critique, let the team go first. If you begin by telling the team what you think they did wrong (or right), it may discourage them from speaking up and the team will be less likely to "own" any subsequent plans. So, avoid telling too much or too soon—either results in less learning.
- **Look back, then forward**. There are essentially two parts to a debrief. The first part is to reflect and understand what happened (the "look back"). Then, based on those observations, agree to specific action plans (the "look forward").
- **Ask and pause**. Let silence be your friend. Ask questions and give the group time to think and respond without "filling in the blanks" for them. You can't see and know everything about your team, so you and the team will learn more if team members speak up.
- **What's right, not who is right**. Avoid finger pointing or chastising. If team members feel they are being punished for admitting a problem they will stop speaking up. Moreover, other team members will be less likely to acknowledge anything that might make them look bad.
- **All aboard**. When possible, try to involve *all* team members. Invite all team members to participate. Ask quieter team members for their input.
- **Be the navigator, not the driver**—unless they aren't driving properly! It is helpful to think of yourself as the navigator for the debrief rather than the person driving all the answers.
- **Reinforce and thank**. Reinforce the team for what they did well. Thank people when they acknowledge a mistake, so they feel comfortable doing so next time.

- **Acknowledge something (work-related) you could have done differently or better**. When you acknowledge how you can improve it makes it easier for your team members to do so.

© The Group for Organizational Effectiveness, Inc. From gOEbase (www.gOEbase.com). Permission granted.

LEADING A QUICK TEAM DEBRIEF: SESSION OUTLINE

1. **Set the stage** (30 seconds).
   - Explain why you are conducting a debrief and what the team will be discussing.
   - "This is a quick opportunity to learn from our experience. Let's take a look at how we handled this [situation, project, event, meeting, shift, activity]. What we did well and could improve."
   - "Let's consider how we worked as a team, in addition to any technical issues."

> **Basic Assumption**: "We're all competent and well-intentioned people who want to do our best. This is about getting better at what we do."

2. **Ask the team for their observations** (5–20 minutes).

   - What **happened**?
   - What did we do **well**? What **challenges** did we face?
   - What should we do differently or focus on **next time**?
     - Do more or less frequently? Do faster? Do better? Stop doing? Start doing?
   - What could **help us** be more effective? Anything we need?

> **Tip**. Ask the team for their perceptions first. Then if possible, acknowledge one thing that **you** could have done differently or that you will focus on in the future. This will make it easier for team members to voice their own observations or concerns.
>
> **Tip**. If the team doesn't discuss teamwork, ask "**how well did *we work together* as a team**?" Perhaps ask one or two specific questions such as

- How well did we
  - Communicate or share info?, Ask for or offer help? , Prepare or plan?
  - Monitor and provide backup?, Handle conflict?, Speak up or challenge one another?
  - Coordinate with "outsiders? Share/allocate resources?
- How clear were our roles or assignments? Our goals and priorities?

3. **Add your observations/recommendations and confirm understanding.** (2–5 minutes)
   - Reinforce their observations, or if you noticed something different, share your view of what happened or needs to happen in the future.
   - Be sure your feedback is clear, actionable, and focuses on the work, not personal traits.

4. **Summarize any agreed upon actions or focus for the future** (2–3 minutes).
   - Confirm if the team will do anything differently going forward and, if so,
     - Be clear about who will do what, when, and how this will help the team.
     - Specify when and how you'll follow up to assess progress (e.g., when the next debrief will occur).

Conditions for Team Effectiveness: Diagnostic Questions

Organizational conditions set the stage for team effectiveness, either facilitating or inhibiting teamwork. For example, company or business-unit wide **policies and practices** (e.g., about rewards) and **senior leadership behaviors and communications** (e.g., do senior leaders work well with one another) send widespread signals that can confirm or refute the importance of teamwork. These conditions influence many teams simultaneously, so it makes sense to review these periodically at the organization or business unit level.

Each team also operates within their own set of local conditions, experiencing differing degrees of **resource availability**, **time availability**, **authority levels**, and their own assigned **mission**. These conditions are best reviewed at the team level.

Next are three sets of diagnostic questions you can use to assess current conditions and stimulate a conversation about how to improve them. The first two sets focus on organizational conditions, and the third focuses on team-specific conditions.

POLICIES AND PRACTICES

Use the following questions to review your company's policies and practices. To what extent are these contributing to or inhibiting teamwork? Which policies or practices may need to be modified?

Key Questions: Organizational Conditions—
Policies and Practices

1. Hiring
- Are candidates' teamwork skills and attitudes assessed systematically? Do interview protocols and other tools examine teamwork?
- Realistically, how much do teamwork and collaboration skills weigh into the hiring decision?
- To what extent are team members typically involved in the hiring process (or is the team leader usually the only person involved)?

2. Onboarding
- What messages are communicated (intentionally or unintentionally) to new employees about teamwork and collaboration during formal and informal onboarding?
- What messages should we be emphasizing to new employees about teamwork/collaboration? What are the expectations we want to convey?
- What is done to help prepare team leaders to onboard new team members effectively? Are they given any tools, tips, or talking points?

3. Promotions and Opportunities
- Who tends to gets promoted and has access to favorable opportunities? Strong team players? Individual stars? Selfish, "me first," people?"
- What happens to people who are good team players? Are they taken care of or overlooked? Do people get "credit" for being a strong collaborator?
- Do difficult people who are hard to work with but who produce good individual results get ahead despite their toxicity?

4. Performance Management
- To what extent are teamwork and collaboration assessed and discussed as part of the performance review process? What, if anything, do we do to encourage that focus?
- How much of the focus is on individual goals and accomplishments? Are any team or collaborative goals established?
- To what extent is team member input sought when assessing performance? For example, do we inquire about who is making contributions to the team and who is helping their teammates be successful?

5. Rewards and Recognition
- Who typically gets recognized and rewarded? How often do individuals who are great at teamwork get rewarded? Do teams that succeed get recognized?
- What types of people are publicly thanked and talked about as "successes?"
- Which, if any, reward and recognition practices may be inadvertently inhibiting teamwork and collaboration? How might they be getting in the way?

6. Leadership Development
- How do we prepare people to lead teams?
- What training do we provide to teach people how to lead a team? Or does leadership training focus mainly on managing individuals and making business decisions?
- Where do managers and project leaders learn how to be an effective team leader? Do we emphasize this enough?

SENIOR LEADERSHIP

Although most employees may not see or interact with senior leaders very often, senior leadership behaviors and communications can be surprisingly influential in establishing whether teamwork becomes an organizational norm. Use the following questions to identify potential opportunities for senior leaders to send a clearer signal about the value of collaboration.

Key Questions: Organizational Conditions—Senior Leadership
1. Modeling of Behaviors
- How well does the senior leadership team work together? Do they collaborate effectively? Are they able to disagree effectively?
- How do senior leaders typically behave? Do they model collaboration? Do they talk badly about one another or other departments? Are they "civil"?
- Do they make decisions that help break down silos or reinforce them?

2. Communications
- What do senior leader communications reveal regarding their beliefs about teamwork?
- Does senior leadership ever emphasize the importance of teamwork? Do they tell stories that feature successful collaboration or primarily individual accomplishments?
- When different senior leaders communicate, do they provide a similar message to the organization?

3. Creating Psychological Safety
- What has senior leadership done to build or reduce psychological safety? For example, how do they respond to well-intended dissent or to someone who provides them with "bad news"?
- What happens when they find out that someone has made an honest mistake?
- To what extent are they willing to acknowledge when they made a mistake, misunderstood something, or need to improve?

TEAM-SPECIFIC CONDITIONS

Each team also operates within their own set of local conditions that can exert a powerful influence on their ability to succeed. These conditions can help or hinder the team, and in some instances, they can make it almost impossible for the team to achieve its mission. Use the following questions to keep an eye on four of the most salient team-specific conditions.

Key Questions: Team-Specific Conditions
1. Resources
- Does the team have the necessary resources to accomplish its mission? If not, what do they need?
- How might the team attempt to garner additional resources?
- What resources are unchangeable? How can the team best work around or within those constraints?

2. **Time**
   - Do team members have adequate time to complete their "own" work? Any cushion?
   - Is there time for team members to back up and help one another and still get their own assignments done?
   - Is any time allocated for the team to work, learn, or innovate collaboratively? Are they ever given time to reflect on how they are working together?

3. **Autonomy/Decision Making Authority**
   - Is the team clear about where it needs the authority to make its own decisions? Does it have that authority?
   - Is the team able to work autonomously, when necessary, or do they spend too much time "managing up?"
   - How can they negotiate for greater autonomy, if needed?

4. **Team Mission/Purpose**
   - Is the team's purpose clear and compelling?
   - Do team members need to work together to accomplish the team's mission?
   - If the mission isn't naturally compelling, what can the team rally around to create a sense of identity?

Quick Diagnostic

Understanding Your Team: A Quick Self-Assessment

Driver	Key Questions	5 = Very strong 4 = Fairly strong 3 = Neither 2 = Fairly weak 1 = Very weak	Notes/Thoughts (e.g., What is a possible concern/opportunity? How might we build on a strength or improve a weakness?)
Capability	Does our team have the right **people** on it with the right **mix** of individual and team knowledge, skills, and attributes? (Do we have ample talent, any talent gaps or developmental needs, major personality problems, and enough team players?)	1 2 3 4 5	Where might a capability boost or change help us?
Cooperation	Do team members possess the right **beliefs** and **attitudes** about our team? (Do we trust one another, feel it is safe to speak up [psychological safety] think our team will "win" [collective efficacy], and believe the work we do is important?)	1 2 3 4 5	Which attitudes do we need to boost? How might we improve those?

Understanding Your Team: A Quick Self-Assessment

Coordination	Is our team consistently demonstrating effective **teamwork behaviors**? (Are we monitoring each other and the situation effectively, providing backup/support, adapting as needed, and managing conflict and emotions constructively?)	1	2	3	4	5	Where and when could we be better at monitoring, backing up, adapting, or managing conflict?
Communication	Are team members **sharing info** effectively with each other and with those outside the team? (Are we sharing unique info, communicating in a timely manner, confirming understanding, keeping others informed, and sending consistent messages to people outside the team?)	1	2	3	4	5	Where and when could be have better quality communications?
Cognition	Do team members possess a **shared understanding** about priorities, roles, vision, if–then, etc.? (Are we on the same page? Could we provide similar answers to the questions, Where are we headed? What are the current priorities? Who should do X? Who knows the most about X? and What's going on?)	1	2	3	4	5	What do we need to develop a clearer "shared understanding" about?
Conditions	Are the necessary **conditions** in place to enable our team to work together and succeed? (Do we have adequate resources, time, and support? Do policies, practices, and culture encourage teamwork?)	1	2	3	4	5	Which conditions would we hope to change? What is within our control?

Understanding Your Team: A Quick Self-Assessment

Coaching	Are our team leader and/or other members demonstrating **leadership behaviors** that help the team "win"? (Are we taking actions to hold each other accountable, improve clarity, remove obstacles, manage team emotions, encourage participation, and promote learning?]	1 2 3 4 5	What could our team leader or team members do more often or better?

IDENTIFYING OPPORTUNITIES FOR IMPROVEMENT

Limitations or breakdowns associated with any of the seven drivers can hinder your team's success. As you make a diagnosis, consider two key questions: "What if" and "Can we"?

"What if" refers to potential for **improvement**. How big is the current gap between the actual and the ideal (e.g., between the way your team communicates today and how you think they should)? If your team made an adjustment, what would be the likely benefits? In general, bigger gaps tend to have greater improvement potential.

- If your team made this adjustment, would you anticipate a **big, moderate, or small** boost?

"Can we" refers to change potential. How feasible is it to improve this area? Realistically, how difficult would it be to make an adjustment?

- **Easy to change**. A change is often easier when it is within the team's control and doesn't require external approval. In general, a change is easier when the necessary resources are likely to be available. An easy change may also be one that isn't elaborate; perhaps all that is needed is a little heightened attention. Think about "easy to change" solutions as low-lying fruit.
- **Challenging to change**. Some changes are more challenging to implement. For example, a proposed adjustment that requires

permission or support of others or that may necessitate currently unbudgeted time or money would be considered challenging. Such changes are likely to be more effortful than "easy" ones but still may be feasible.

- **Can't change**. Finally, it is important to recognize that some potentially useful changes may not currently be feasible. Some features of the team may be "locked" or at least unchangeable in a meaningful way for the near future. For example, perhaps you can't change the membership of your team—it is currently a "given." When a flight crew to Mars lifts off, membership is closed; no changes will be possible. Other proposed changes may be outside the team's control and require resources or support that are simply unavailable. You don't want to invest too much time and effort on ideas that fall into the "can't change" zone—instead you may want to seek alternative "work arounds."

Any change you contemplate is likely to fall into one of the nine cells in the following matrix. The matrix offers some basic advice to help you prioritize proposed solutions for boosting your team's effectiveness.

	Change Potential		
Improvement Potential	**Can't Change**	**Challenging to Change**	**Easy to Change**
Big boost	Create work arounds.	Worth trying	Do this now!
Moderate boost	Consider work arounds.	A solid maybe	Yes, do it.
Small or no boost	Let it go! (LIG)	Marginal	At some point

Team Ideas Matrix

PRACTICAL TIPS FOR ADDRESSING POTENTIAL CONCERNS

Capability (See Chapter 4 for Details)

Potential Concern	Ideas for Improvement
Team members need to **enhance their skills** or knowledge.	Determine who could benefit from **additional development** and be clear about the competencies they need. Provide **targeted coaching and individual training** to boost their capabilities.
	Assemble "how to" guides, **checklists**, and tip sheets. Use them to spread knowledge and expertise.
	If you have **experts** on the team, consider whether they can share their expertise and insights with others. For example, a "learner" may benefit from shadowing or observing the expert in action. If you do this, be sure they both know why this is happening and what the learner should be observing. It can help to provide the learner with a few targeted questions and tips, so they get the most out of the experience.
	If the concern is a lack of **"teamwork" skills or knowledge**, first clarify which competencies are needed (e.g., communication, giving and receiving feedback, teamwork savvy) and then identify individual or team training to help boost foundational teamwork skills.
Our team lacks an important type of expertise and **won't be able to develop current team members** to fill the gap.	Consider whether a temporary solution would work, for example, by **"borrowing"** someone from another team to work with your team for a period of time.
	If you know that an important missing capability will be needed on an ongoing basis and your current team members can't develop it, then **add, move, or replace team members** to fill the gap.
	If you won't be able to develop or acquire additional capabilities, consider if you can **modify task assignments or work procedures** to better fit current capabilities.
	If you can't mitigate the gap, proactively **manage your customers' and partners' expectations** because if your team lacks key capabilities it probably won't be able to deliver as quickly or effectively as it should.

There **aren't enough "team players"** on our team—people who think "team first."	When there is a shortage of team players, "teamwork" might not happen naturally. You may need to establish an agreement or **"ground rules"** about what it means to be a good team member. For example, you could conduct an exercise where your team members review a list of behaviors that good team members exhibit (see chapter 13), identify which ones they already do, and agree which they will do more consistently (or better) going forward.
	Looking ahead, be sure that the next person you add to the team is a good team player. Collective orientation is a fairly stable trait, so when screening potential team members, **ask them about their prior team experiences**. Look for red flags, such as excessive complaining about or blaming of prior team members, and avoid people with toxic personalities.
	Be careful about **overusing your best team players**. They are often the first to "volunteer" (e.g., to help out, stay late) and the first you turn to when you need something done, and as a result they can get burned out and leave the team.
	In general, be willing to advocate for and **promote your best team players**. When they leave for a position of greater responsibility or to a big opportunity, you lose a team player for now, but other team players will want to come work for you and your team.
We have a team member with a **toxic personality** (not just an occasional bad day).	Anyone can have a **bad day or two**, but if someone on the team consistently says hurtful things, makes inappropriate comments, acts rudely, embarrasses teammates, withholds effort, talks badly about teammates, is continually pessimistic, and/or drones on about the things that irritate them, they are a toxic teammate.
	Be sure that someone demonstrating any of those behaviors is **given clear expectations** that they need to change, **is given feedback** and is **held accountable**.
	Do not tolerate them. As a leader, consider this a **performance management issue**, and if they don't change their behavior, manage them out. No matter how good they are at their job, they are poisoning the team.
	Never attempt to deal with a toxic employee in a group setting—address the concern with them **privately**.

Cooperation (See Chapter 5 for Details)

Potential Concerns	Ideas for Improvement
Team members are reluctant to speak up, admit concerns, ask questions, or offer suggestions (because **psychological safety** is low).	Psychological safety is what enables team members to believe they can speak up, admit mistakes, ask questions, offer a dissenting opinion, seek feedback and be themselves—**without the risk of being judged harshly**.
	To **contribute to your team's psychological safety**, admit when you don't understand something or made a mistake, encourage team members to voice concerns, and thank them when they have the courage to offer a dissenting view.
	Focus more attention on what can be **learned from a mistake** ("Do differently next time") and less on assigning blame ("You really messed up this time").
	Don't tolerate team members **disparaging fellow team members**. When a teammate is criticized behind their back, other teammates wonder, "Is anyone saying bad things about me too" and "Would my teammates stick up for me?"

If you are the leader, **specify any nonnegotiables**, where team member input isn't valued (e.g., because it is unchangeable). Otherwise, when someone offers a suggestion about a nonnegotiable, and you shut him down, he and the rest of the team can falsely conclude that you don't want their input on anything. Make it clear that you're open to input in everything except the nonnegotiables.

The team doesn't believe that it can "**win**" (low collective efficacy).	Take time to reflect upon and **discuss your team's successes**. Consider the lesson's learned from those accomplishments—how can we build on that success? If you are always focused on finding and fixing problems, it is easy for the team to dwell on the negative and start feeling that they can't win.

Celebrate wins and accomplishments, of individuals on the team, and, equally important, of the team as a whole. What should our team be proud of?

When faced with a challenge, draw a line of sight between the current challenge and a time when **the team overcame a somewhat similar challenge**.

A failure can be a great learning opportunity for the team, but don't dwell on it. Review what happened, figure out how it can be avoided in the future, and **move on**. Focus on things your team can do to win next time rather than wallowing about things that happened in the past.

Don't overpromise on what your team can deliver. If you **overcommit**, the team will often come up short and start to believe, not unreasonably, that they aren't capable. This leads to a downward performance cycle of doubt, poor performance, more doubt, etc.

If you are the leader, take actions to **improve or remove persistently low-performing team members**. When team members see poor performers on the team and no signs of improvement, collective efficacy drops precipitously.

The level of **trust** in our team is low.	**Educate the team** so they understand how trust works, including what influences it, the behaviors that matter, and the value of monitoring your "trust accounts."

Trust often emerges from doing other things well. You can't make someone trust you, but you can take actions that increase the likelihood that people will see you as trustworthy. Ask yourself, "How might my teammates perceive my ability to deliver, my concern for them, and my interest in doing what's right?" Why **might a team member fail to trust you**?

On a personal level, be very careful about making commitments that you may not be able to keep. **Living up to commitments** is essential for trust. And when you make a mistake (which we all do at times), own it, apologize genuinely, and avoid making it again in the future.

Get in the habit of thanking team members when they help you. It is a small gesture but contributes to trust and cohesion. Sometimes we think, "Thank you," but we don't say it. Make sure your teammates know that you **appreciate** them.

Want to add points to the trust account? Taking actions that are **in the best interest of another person** and not necessarily best for you shows that you care about them. If you are always angling to get what's best for you, you'll be perceived as less trustworthy.

Our team may be "splintering" into **subgroups** or silos.	Splinters often occur along a "**fault line**," an invisible dividing line that splits a group into two or more subgroups. When team members identify more closely with some members of their team due to shared characteristics—age, seniority, culture, gender, ethnicity, education, nationality, occupation, or physical location—that's a fault line.
	To combat silos, establish and **emphasize shared goals, priorities, needs, and/or identity** that all team members can embrace.
	Connectors can often help. In this context, a **connector** is someone who shares something in common with both groups (e.g., a salesperson who is trained as an engineer). Research shows that having even one connector can help reduce the detrimental effects of a fault line. Who could be a constructive connector on your team?
	If the team is fairly new, start by **focusing on what the team needs to do and accomplish collectively**. An early focus on task requirements tends to emphasize commonalities and de-emphasize demographic differences. After task requirements and roles have been established, you can shift towards more relationship focused considerations.

Coordination (See Chapter 6 for Details)

Potential Concerns	Ideas for Improvement
We aren't **filling in, helping out, and backing up** one another.	Determine **why this may be happening**. Sometimes it is because team members don't know that are expected to fill in and help out. In other cases, it is because they don't know how to do so. Another potential cause is low psychological safety, which inhibits people from admitting when they need help. Be sure the solution addresses the cause.
	Be sure that everyone knows when they should help or step in. Clarify **expectations** about when backup is needed and who should provide it. While we should all "support" one another, **not everyone on the team can be expected to fill in** for every other team member. Who should I be ready to back up?
	Selectively prepare team members so they **know "enough" about other people's tasks** to be able to help or fill in. What do I need to know to fill in effectively?
	When someone helps you, fills in, or reminds you about something you need to do, **thank them**. When you fail to acknowledge or you dismiss someone's help, they are less likely to help you again.
We aren't doing a great job of **monitoring** what's going on **outside** the team.	Identify prior "**surprises**" and determine what your team needs to monitor more effectively to avoid future surprises (e.g., customer needs, market trends, supply chain, budgets, product changes, competitors, organizational changes).
	Determine **what** should be monitored, **who** should do it, and how discoveries will be **shared**. Consider allocating time for team members to provide situational updates—"Tell us what you have learned about X."
	If there is a lot to monitor, **divide** up the task. Who should keep an eye on what?
	If you think the team could be better at interpreting the signs, engage the team in periodic, "**What might that mean?**" conversations to boost their collective understanding.

We could do a better job of **coordinating** with one another.	There are times when our team members need to **rely on one another**, for example, when working together on a task, coordinating related tasks, or completing a work product that another teammate needs to do their job. To understand more about those dependencies, conduct a **coordination requirements analysis**. That is simply looking ahead to anticipate where collaboration is most likely to be needed and where it is most important.
	Consider conducting **team training** to practice particularly important coordination tasks. Team training can range from a full simulation (where team members physically perform the task in a training environment) to a simple mental walk through. In the simplest version, assemble the people who need to coordinate and verbally walk through key coordination points step by step. Ask what would be happening, surface where problems have emerged in the past (and why), and confirm what we can do to coordinate smoothly in the future.
	After a challenging coordination point, huddle up to conduct a **quick debrief**. Discuss what happened, what went well, and what we could do differently next time. Try to do this while the experience is still fresh in everyone's memory.
We could do a better job of **learning and adapting** as a team.	Schedule and conduct **periodic team debriefs**. These don't need to be lengthy and you don't need to wait until an end of a big milestone or the conclusion of a project to conduct them. Discuss how we are working together, what's going well, and what could we do better. Establish agreements about any changes you'll make as a team. Review the team debriefing tips in the tools section of the book.
	Encourage team members to be **alert for new ideas and ways of doing things** and to speak up about them. Ask, "Does anyone have any new ideas for the team to consider?"
We could do a better job of managing **disagreements and conflict.**	Ensure that everyone on the team understands what is meant by **collaborative conflict**, where the goal is to collectively seek the best solution, not to push "my" ideas. When people only argue for and hold onto their own ideas, that's competitive conflict, which research shows isn't as effective as collaborative conflict.
	If you find yourself clinging to your ideas, for example, repeating your point of view rather than looking for the potential merits of what others are saying, you are defaulting into competitive conflict. Catch yourself and try to find a way to **integrate another point of view into your suggestion**. Sometimes the best solution combines aspects of different ideas.
	If you find that team members are reluctant to disagree or offer a different perspective, you may have a psychological safety issue. **Avoiding conflict is not healthy** and hurts the team's effectiveness. Make it easier for team members to speak up. Ask, "Who has a different perspective on this?" Or, "What else should we consider?" Thank people when they offer a different perspective, even if you don't agree with them.
	Consider appointing a "**devil's advocate**," who is expected to offer a dissenting point of view, even if they agree. Rotate the role. This sends the message that it is healthy to disagree.

Our **team meetings** are ineffective.	An effective team meeting can help promote subsequent team coordination. But meetings need to be run properly and with the right frequency for that to happen. As a starting point, consider whether you may be **meeting too often** (e.g., feels like there is a lot of redundancy) or **too infrequently** (e.g., things that should be discussed during a meeting are happening prior to the meeting) and adjust your schedule accordingly. It is okay to experiment with this until you find the "right" timing.
	Be sure that your meetings are well-organized, with an **agenda** and meeting **objectives** established and, if possible, shared in advance. Seek input from participants.
	Ensure that key **decisions and action plans** (including who is responsible and when it will be done) are clearly understood by everyone. Summarize these at the end of the meeting and give people a chance to confirm or ask questions. A good practice is to capture these in writing and circulate it to team members after the meeting.
	Clarify how team **members who couldn't attend** will be "brought up to speed."
	Occasionally allocate 15 minutes to discuss what could be done to **make your meetings better**. Ask questions such as "Are we covering the right topics?" "Do we have the right people in the room?" "Are we meeting with the right frequency?" and "Are we spending our time wisely (e.g., should we be doing less updating and more problem-solving)?"

Communication (See Chapter 7 for Details)

Potential Concerns	Ideas for Improvement
There are frequent **miscommunications**; for example team members are often "**surprised**" that they weren't told something sooner.	If team members are often caught off guard because they weren't told something or were unaware of an action or decision, that's an indication of a communication problem. One common reason for this type of problem is when people falsely assume "everyone knows that." Get in the habit of asking one another, "**Who else should know about this?**"
	Identify **where communication breakdowns have happened** most frequently in the past. For example, whenever a handoff needs to occur (e.g., of information, responsibilities), there is greater risk. After identifying the risk points, agree on ways to ensure effective communications, for example, by building a checklist of information that should be shared at handoff points (e.g., at a shift change).
	Ensure that the team knows that more communication is not always better. Simply talking more (or sending more emails) is not enough. Quality communication means team members are sharing information that others need, in a **timely** manner.
	To ensure clarity, teach and encourage everyone on the team to use "the convey" to restate what they thought they heard, allowing the other person to confirm or correct their intent. This **closed-loop communication** technique will greatly reduce miscommunications.

Our team members should be communicating a more **consistent message** to people outside the team.	When team members communicate divergent messages to people outside the team, it creates **confusion** and can lead to dysfunctional conflict. At a minimum, it can hurt your team's reputation.
	Allocate a few minutes at the end of each meeting (or at the end of the week or the end of a shift) to **confirm any agreements** that were reached, because you can't communicate a similar message if you don't have a common understanding about what you agreed to do. Then, ask the question, "**What should we be telling people** about this, and **who** needs to hear it?"
	For very important communications, you may want to help the team prepare. For example, huddle up and ask one team member to **pretend they are responding to someone outside the team** who asked them, "What is going to happen?" Afterwards, point out what they said that was useful and offer suggestions about what else we might say. Then give another team member a chance to practice out loud, and so on.
We need to do a better job of communicating with and maintaining relationships with **key stakeholders outside our team.**	Conduct a **stakeholder analysis**. Stakeholders could include the people your team relies upon ("suppliers") as well the people who rely on your team ("customers.") For each stakeholder, clarify the following. What do they need from us? What do we need from them? What are their big concerns about us? What are our big concerns about them? What do we need to keep them informed about? What do we need them to keep us informed about?
	For important stakeholders, be sure that (a) the right people are focused on maintaining the connection (serving as "**boundary spanners**") and (b) they are well prepared to do so. Be clear about who will be responsible for communicating and managing the relationship on both side of the boundary.
	When team members should be providing the **same message to different stakeholders**, be sure everyone knows the intended message. That won't happen by chance, so discuss with them, "What will we each tell our key contacts about X?"
Team members work in **different locations**, which creates communication problems.	Communicating is particularly challenging when team members work at a distance, in part because there are typically **fewer opportunities to talk informally** and in part because you may not be able to see nonverbal cues.
	Be smart about the communication technology you decide to use. It is easy to misinterpret intent in written communications, so **don't over rely on emails or texts**, particularly for "emotional" topics. When you first start to communicate with someone at a distance, set up a video conference (see and hear) or at least a phone call (hear), rather than defaulting to an email or text (neither see nor hear).
	Double down on the use of the "**convey**." Get in the habit of summarizing what you've heard—and consider it a win when the person you're talking to says, "That is not what I meant." It is much better to discover that on the spot than to operate on an incorrect assumption.
	Be aware that team members who work on their own in remote locations (e.g., from home) can experience a **sense of isolation**. Make sure the team stays connected with them. Recognize that you may need to spend a little time engaging in "small talk" when a team member is feeling isolated.

Communication and trust go hand in hand. When one erodes, the other is likely to follow. Trust is trickier at a distance, so it is even more critical to **do what you say you will do**. Trust is based, in part, on a belief that someone is capable of doing a task. Don't commit to doing something you know you won't be able to complete.

If you get "stuck" and can see you'll be **unable to meet a commitment** that will affect a teammate at another location, communicate that as soon as possible and, if appropriate, ask for assistance.

Cognitions (See Chapter 8 for Details)

Potential Concerns	Ideas for Improvement
There appear to be disagreements or lack of clarity among team members about the team's **purpose, direction, and/or priorities.**	Engage in a discussion about the team's **purpose and direction**. Why does our team exist? What would success really look like for our team? Where are we headed?
	Allocate time to **review and discuss the team's current priorities.** What are our current top priorities? Why are these a priority? Revisit the team's priorities periodically, as they are likely to change over time.
	Create a **team charter** that summarizes your team's mission, objectives/goals, and boundaries. If possible, engage the team in formulating the charter to promote ownership and common understanding. Once established, a team charter can also be a helpful tool for bringing a new team member up to speed.
Team members aren't in full agreement about roles—there are **role gaps, conflicts**, and/or **ambiguities.**	Conduct a **role clarification** exercise. Generate a list of the major actions and types of decisions the team makes and, for each, establish who does it, who is accountable for it, who should be consulted in advance, and who should be notified afterwards.
	Document role expectations in a way that is clear and makes sense to team members. A document of this type is also quite helpful when a new person joins the team. Update role expectations, as needed, over time.
	When an organizational change is introduced it can disrupt existing expectations and introduce role ambiguity. Discuss, **What is the impact of this change** on our team, and how will that effect our work? Will we need to modify our role expectations?
Team members don't share a common understanding of **how to respond** to certain situations.	As a team, conduct a **scenario-based walk through.** Identify a situation that may happen in the future and generate a scenario based on that. Assemble the team, present the start of the scenario, and ask, "At this point, who should be doing what? Why? Who should be talking with whom? What are team members thinking?" Then provide more information about how the scenario is unfolding ("Now X just happened") and, again, ask the group to discuss what should be happening. At the end of the scenario discussion, capture lessons learned and agreements about how the team should handle that type of situation in the future.
	Sometimes it can be helpful to document how to handle particular tasks or situations in the form of a **standard operating procedure** or **checklist**.

Our **membership changes** regularly, so it is hard to sustain a shared perspective.	When someone new joins the team, they are unlikely to have a shared understanding with the other team members. If your team regularly brings in new members, spend some time ensuring that your **onboarding** process bring people up to speed quickly.
	Provide new team members with **relevant materials** such as role descriptions, standard operating procedures, checklists, team goals, scenario summaries, and the team charter.
	Consider **assigning a buddy** to a new team member to help them learn about the team and get up to speed more quickly. This isn't just for junior hires. A very experienced hire may have deep content expertise but won't know "how things get done on our team." Even a seasoned hire can benefit from a buddy.
Team members work in **different locations** (or have different backgrounds), so it is hard to sustain a shared perspective.	Be sure everyone knows the team's **purpose** and are generally aware of one another's **responsibilities**. Clarify **how decisions will be made**, including the types of decisions that should involve the entire team and the type that can be made by team members at a specific location.
	If there are national, geographic, professional, or cultural differences across locations, remember that people may **be accustomed to different norms and expectation**. For example, norms about risk tolerance, speed of decision-making, or willingness to disagree openly can vary across cultures. Diversity of background can contribute to a team's success, but they can also lead to fault lines and silos if they aren't recognized.
	Establish and communicate a set of **team norms** about how you want to work together; for example, how quickly are we expected to reply to a message or request from a teammate? What is a reasonable amount of time?
	Establish agreements about how the different locations will stay on the same page. How **frequently will we meet as a full team** (virtually or at a single location)? How can we schedule calls to accommodate people in **different time zones** fairly? What should we be **updating** one another about on a regular basis?
	Find a way to intentionally share **lessons learned** across locations. Take advantage of naturally occurring differences in the way things are done and transport the best ideas across locations.

Conditions (See Chapter 9 for Details)

Potential Concerns	Ideas for Improvement
We **lack resources** that may keep us from being successful (e.g., budget, equipment, access, information, visible support).	Be clear about what you are asking for and why you are requesting it. Then actively **seek the resources** your team needs. Tool C in the book includes a few targeted questions for diagnosing and thinking about resource availability.
	Differentiate between team **"needs" and "wants."** A need is something that will almost certainly keep your team from being successful if you don't get it. A want is a nice to have but the team can get by without it if necessary. Spend most of your "chips" trying to get the needs addressed.

Ideally, articulate your requests in a way that resonates with the person who can provide them. For example, "We're concerned that without access to the customer data set, we won't be able to complete the report on time, and I know how important that is to you." If your request sounds like it is "all about you," you are less likely to get it than if your request **draws a line of sight to what is important** to the person who can provide the resources.

When you determine that a lack of resources is unchangeable, discuss ways to succeed given the limited resources. What are potential **trade-offs**? Where might we be able to renegotiate or lower our stakeholders' expectations?

An organizational **policy** or **practice** is inhibiting teamwork.	Recognize what is **within your control** (blue), what is outside your control but perhaps can be influenced (yellow), and what you neither can control nor influence (red).
	Change what is within your control. Seek to influence what is in the yellow area but recognize that the final decision isn't yours. Do not spend too much time talking about things in the red zone. It is frustrating and fruitless. Identify how best to **work around or within** those things you cannot change.
	Use the diagnostic questions in Tool C to **stimulate a conversation** about how various policies and practices may be facilitating or inhibiting collaboration.
We are **starting a project** and are concerned that the conditions for success may not be in place.	Conduct a **premortem** exercise. Imagine that the project is over and that your team failed. Work backwards and discuss what may have derailed the project. Develop plans to try to avoid, minimize, or mitigate those problems before they arise.
	Flag potential **obstacles** and seek the sponsor's (or another appropriate stakeholder's) help in removing them. Don't wait and hope for a miracle.
I don't think our **senior leadership** supports teamwork and collaboration.	Determine if there is an opportunity to provide them with **constructive feedback**. If so, be prepared to share your perspective with them. As leaders move up the organizational hierarchy, they tend to get less feedback, so they may be unaware of how they are "showing up" to others.
	Tool C in the book contains some targeted questions for examining how senior leadership may be encouraging or discouraging teamwork in the organization. Use this to do a **quick assessment** and engage in a conversation about opportunities.
	Recognize that the actions of senior leadership are outside your control and, in many cases, may even be outside your influence. If so, focus your team's attention on what is **within your control or influence**. Fortunately, your team can choose to work together collaboratively, even when senior leadership isn't showing their support.

Coaching (See Chapter 10 for Details)

Potential Concerns	Ideas for Improvement
Our team would benefit from greater **guidance** and **support from our team leader.**	Consider the seven **essential leadership functions** (i.e., ensuring clarity, removing obstacles, encouraging participation, promoting learning, managing team emotions, holding teammates accountable, and fostering psychological safety). Are all seven being performed adequately on our team? Which ones might merit additional attention from our leader?

Leaders are particularly prone to **self-anchoring bias**, or incorrectly believing that others think and feel the same way they do. If you are a leader, don't fall prey to this bias. Be sure to spend time **talking with team members**, one on one, to learn what is really on their mind.

People aren't born team leaders; they need to learn how to be an effective team leader. Many people get promoted to team leader because of their technical competence, but that doesn't equip them to be in the team leader seat. Many team leaders could benefit from a little **training** and/or **coaching** on team leadership—and they all should know about the science of teamwork!

We aren't holding one another **accountable.**	People who practice accountability do their part, are considered to be reliable and trustworthy, and are viewed as good teammates. But it is difficult to act accountably, and to hold other people accountable, without clear behavioral and performance expectations. So, one way to boost accountability to **ensure that everyone knows what is expected of them**. Role ambiguity can mean things "slip through the cracks." What do you expect me to deliver and how are we all supposed to behave on this team?

If you are a team leader, holding people accountable is one of your primary functions, so set aside time to **check in**, follow up to **assess progress**, and provide useful **feedback**. If a team member repeatedly fails to live up to their commitments and there are no consequences, not only are they unlikely to change, but it also sends a message to the rest of the team that accountability doesn't matter. This is particularly true for team members who act in **toxic** ways. Toxic behavior must be dealt with or the entire team will suffer.

Ideally, team members also **hold one another accountable**, offer encouragement to help teammates live up to their commitments, and provide constructive feedback when they aren't. Be sure that everyone on the team **knows what is acceptable** when it comes to holding each other accountable.

We would be better if members **helped out the team leader** a bit more frequently, for example, to give each other feedback and advice or hold one another accountable.	Recognize that a leader can't see everything and handle all a team's needs, so team members also need to help ensure the team's success. Identify how members of our team can **best support** any of the leadership functions (i.e., ensuring clarity, removing obstacles, encouraging participation, promoting learning, managing team emotions, holding teammates accountable, and fostering psychological safety)?

Equally important, be clear about those areas that should be considered **"leader-only."** For example, the team leader may be the only one who should be providing formal performance feedback.

Clarify where team members are **expected** to contribute, where it is **acceptable** but not required, and where it is **off limits**.

We could probably be better at **learning from our experiences** as a team.	One of the essential leadership functions is **promoting learning**. Simply experiencing something doesn't mean that the team will learn from it. Learning happens best when there is intentional reflection, feedback, and interpretation of experiences. In other words, what did we experience, what did we do, how did that work, and what can we learn from it?

Conduct **"lesson learned" debriefs** after key experiences. Review what happened, what the team did well, and what it could have done differently. Summarize the lessons learned and agree how the team will work together in related situations in the future.

BIBLIOGRAPHY

CHAPTER 1

Boothby, E. J., Clark, M. S., & Bargh, J. A. (2014). Shared experiences are amplified. *Psychological Science, 25*(12), 2209–2216. doi:10.1177/0956797614551162

Committee on Quality of Health Care in America, Institute of Medicine. (2000). *To err is human: Building a safer health system* (L. Kohn, J. Corrigan, & M. Donaldson, eds.). Washington, DC: National Academies Press.

Corporate Executive Board. (2012). Breakthrough performance in the new work environment: Identifying and enabling the new high performer. Retrieved from https://www.cebglobal.com/content/dam/cebglobal/us/EN/top-insights/executive-guidance/pdfs/eg2013ann-breakthrough-performance-in-the-new-work-environment.pdf

Cross, R., Rebele, R., & Grant, A. (2016). Collaborative overload. *Harvard Business Review, 94*(1), 16.

Davey, L. (2013). *You first*. Hoboken, NJ: Wiley.

Duhigg, C. (2016, February 25). What Google learned from its quest to build the perfect team. *New York Times*. Retrieved from https://www.nytimes.com/2016/02/28/magazine/what-google-learned-from-its-quest-to-build-the-perfect-team.html

Eddy, E. R., Tannenbaum, S. I., & Mathieu, J. E. (2013). Helping teams to help themselves: Comparing two team-led debriefing methods. *Personnel Psychology, 66*(4), 975–1008.

Global Human Capital Trends. (2016). The new organization: Different by design. Deloitte University Press. Retrieved from https://www2.deloitte.com/content/dam/Deloitte/global/Documents/HumanCapital/gx-dup-global-human-capital-trends-2016.pdf

Hackman, J. R. (2009). Why teams don't work: Interview by Diane Coutu. *Harvard Business Review, 87*(5), 98–105.

Hughes, A. M., Gregory, M. E., Joseph, D. L., Sonesh, S. C., Marlow, S. L., Lacerenza, C. N., & Salas, E. (2016). Saving lives: A meta-analysis of team training in healthcare. *Journal of Applied Psychology, 101*(9), 1266–1304. doi:10.1037/apl0000120

LePine, J. A., Piccolo, R. F., Jackson, C. L., Mathieu, J. E., & Saul, J. R. (2008). A meta-analysis of teamwork processes: tests of a multidimensional model and relationships with team effectiveness criteria. *Personnel Psychology, 61*(2), 273–307.

Podsakoff, N. P., Whiting, S. W., Podsakoff, P. M., & Blume, B. D. (2009). Individual- and organizational-level consequences of organizational citizenship behaviors: A meta-analysis. *Journal of Applied Psychology, 94*(1), 122–141. doi:10.1037/a0013079

Salas, E., DiazGranados, D., Klein, C., Burke, C. S., Stagl, K. C., Goodwin, G. F., & Halpin, S. M. (2008). Does team training improve team performance? A meta-analysis. *Human Factors*, 50(6), 903–933.

Schawbel, D. (2013, February 19). Po Bronson: How to become the top dog in your industry. *Forbes*. Retrieved from http://www.forbes.com/sites/danschawbel/2013/02/19/po-bronson/

Schoenfeld, G. (2014). 2014 global management education graduate survey report: Curriculum insight. Retrieved from https://www.gmac.com/-/media/files/gmac/research/curriculum-insight/2014-gmegs-report-webrelease.pdf

The top 20 reasons startups fail. (2018, February 2). https://www.cbinsights.com/research/startup-failure-reasons-top/

Wilson, E. O. (2013). *The social conquest of Earth*. New York, NY: Liveright.

CHAPTER 4

Aguinis, H., & O'Boyle Jr, E. (2014). Star performers in twenty-first century organizations. *Personnel Psychology*, 67(2), 313–350. doi:10.5465/AMBPP.2013.35.

Bell, S. T. (2007). Deep-level composition variables as predictors of team performance. *Journal of Applied Psychology*, 92(3), 595–615.

Bell, S. T., Brown, S., Colaneri, A., & Outland, N. (2018). Team composition and the ABCs of teamwork. *American Psychologist*, 73, 349–362. doi:10.1037/amp0000305

Bennett, R. J., & Robinson, S. L. (2000). Development of a measure of workplace deviance. *Journal of Applied Psychology*, 85(2), 349–360.

Brown, R. (2017, February). Lessons in leadership. *Fast Company*, p. 58. Retrieved from http://www.fastcompany-digital.com/fastcompany/feb_2017?pg=58#pg58

Cannon-Bowers, J. A., Tannenbaum, S. I., Salas, E., & Volpe, C. E. (1995). Defining competencies and establishing team training requirements. *Team Effectiveness and Decision Making in Organizations*, 333, 333–380.

Capretto, L. (2015, October 30). The reason Smokey Robinson wrote '"My Girl" had nothing to do with a girl. *Huffington Post*. Retrieved from https://www.huffington-post.com/entry/smokey-robinson-my-girl_us_56327f22e4b0c66bae5bc14e

Czarna A., Wróbel, M., Dufner, M., & Zeigler-Hill, V. (2014). Narcissism and emotional contagion: Do narcissists "catch" the emotions of others? *Social Psychological and Personality Science*, 6(3), 318–324. doi:10.1177/1948550614559652

Dezecache, G., Conty, L., Chadwick, M., Philip, L., Soussignan, R., Sperber, D., & Grèzes, J. (2013). Evidence for unintentional emotional contagion beyond dyads. *PloS One*, 8(6). doi:10.1371/journal.pone.0067371

Foulk, T., Woolum, A., & Erez, A. (2016). Catching rudeness is like catching a cold: The contagion effects of low-intensity negative behaviors. *Journal of Applied Psychology*, 101(1), 50–67.

Gayton, S. D., & Kehoe, E. J. (2015). Character strengths and hardiness of Australian Army Special Forces applicants. *Military Medicine*, 180(8), 857–862. doi:10.7205/MILMED-D-14-00527

Groysberg, B. (2010). *Chasing stars: The myth of talent and the portability of performance*. Princeton, NJ: Princeton University Press.

Groysberg, B., Linda-Eling, L., & Nanda, A. (2008). Can they take it with them? The portability of star knowledge workers' performance. *Management Science*, 54(7), 1213–1230. doi:10.1287/mnsc.1070.0809

Harada, T., Hayashi, A., Sadato, N., & Iidaka, T. (2016). Neural correlates of emotional contagion induced by happy and sad expressions. *Journal of Psychophysiology*, 30(3), 114–123. doi:10.1027/0269-8803/a000160

Mathieu, J. E., Tannenbaum, S. I., Kukenberger, M. R., Donsbach, J. S., & Alliger, G. M. (2014). Team role experience and orientation: A measure and tests of construct validity. *Group & Organization Management*, 40(1), 6–34. doi:10.1177/1059601114562000

Morgeson, F. P., Reider, M. H., & Campion, M. A. (2005). Selecting individuals in team settings: The importance of social skills, personality characteristics, and teamwork knowledge. *Personnel Psychology*, 55, 583–611.

O'Boyle, E. H., Forsyth, D. R., Banks, G. C., & McDaniel, M. A. (2012). A meta-analysis of the Dark Triad and work behavior: A social exchange perspective. *Journal of Applied Psychology*, 97(3), 557–579.

Peteraf, M. A. (1993). The cornerstones of competitive advantage: A resource-based view. *Strategic Management Journal*, 14(3), 179–191.

Rhoads, C. (2008, August 22). Questions for Jerry Colangelo. *Wall Street Journal*. Retrieved from https://www.wsj.com/articles/SB121939315839463251

Swaab, R. I., Schaerer, M., Anicich, E. M., Ronay, R., & Galinsky, A. D. (2014). The too-much-talent effect: Team interdependence determines when more talent is too much versus not enough. *Psychological Science*, 25(8), 1581–1591. doi:10.1177/0956797614537280

CHAPTER 5

Anicich, E. M., Swaab, R. I., & Galinsky, A. D. (2015). Hierarchical cultural values predict success and mortality in high-stakes teams. *Proceedings of the National Academy of Sciences*, 112(5), 1338–1343. doi:10.1073/pnas.1408800112

Beal, D. J., Cohen, R. R., Burke, M. J., & McLendon, C. L. (2003). Cohesion and performance in groups: A meta-analytic clarification of construct relations. *Journal of Applied Psychology*, 88(6), 989–1004.

Breuer, C., Hüffmeier, J., & Hertel, G. (2016). Does trust matter more in virtual teams? A meta-analysis of trust and team effectiveness considering virtuality and documentation as moderators. *Journal of Applied Psychology*, 101(8), 1151–1177. doi:10.1037/apl0000113

Chiocchio, F., & Essiembre, H. (2009). Cohesion and performance: A meta-analytic review of disparities between project teams, production teams, and service teams. *Small Group Research*, 40(4), 382–420. doi:10.1177/1046496409335103

Colquitt, J. A., Scott, B. A., & LePine, J. A. (2007). Trust, trustworthiness, and trust propensity: A meta-analytic test of their unique relationships with risk taking and job performance. *Journal of Applied Psychology*, 92(4), 909–927.

De Jong, B. A., Dirks, K. T., & Gillespie, N. (2016). Trust and team performance: A meta-analysis of main effects, moderators, and covariates. *Journal of Applied Psychology*, 101(8), 1134–1150. doi:10.1037/apl0000110

Dirks, K. T., & Ferrin, D. L. (2002). Trust in leadership: Meta-analytic findings and implications for research and practice. *Journal of Applied Psychology*, 87(4), 611–628.

Duhigg, C. (2016, February 25). "What Google learned from its quest to build the perfect team." *New York Times*. Retrieved from https://www.nytimes.com/2016/02/28/magazine/what-google-learned-from-its-quest-to-build-the-perfect-team.html

Edmondson, A. (1999). Psychological safety and learning behavior in work teams. *Administrative Science Quarterly*, 44(2), 350–383. doi:10.2307/2666999

Frazier, L. M., Fainshmidt, S., Klinger, R. L, Pezeshkan, A., & Vracheva, V. (2016). Psychological safety: A meta-analytic review and extension. *Personnel Psychology*, 70(1), 113–165. doi:10.1111/peps.12183

Gino, F., Ayal, S., & Ariely, D. (2009). Contagion and differentiation in unethical behavior: The effect of one bad apple on the barrel. *Psychological Science, 20*(3), 393–398.

Gully, S. M., Incalcaterra, K. A., Joshi, A., & Beaubien, M. J. (2002). A meta-analysis of team-efficacy, potency, and performance: Interdependence and level of analysis as moderators of observed relationships. *Journal of Applied Psychology, 87*(5), 819–832.

Krakauer, J. (2009). *Into thin air: A personal account of the Mount Everest disaster.* New York, NY: Anchor.

Mayer, R. C., Davis, J. H., & Schoorman, D. (1995). An integrative model of organizational trust. *The Academy of Management Review, 20*(3), 709–734.

Pearsall, M. J., & Ellis, A. P. J. (2011). Thick as thieves: The effects of ethical orientation and psychological safety on unethical team behavior. *Journal of Applied Psychology, 96*(2), 401–411. doi:10.1037/a0021503

Schein, E. H., & Bennis, W. G. (1965). *Personal and organizational change through group methods: The laboratory approach.* New York, NY: Wiley.

Simons, T., Mclean Parks, J., & Tomlinson, E. (2018). The benefits of walking your talk: Aggregate effects of behavioral integrity on guest satisfaction, turnover, and hotel profitability. *Cornell Hospitality Quarterly, 59,* 257–274.

Stajkovic, A. D., Lee, D., & Nyberg, A. J. (2009). Collective efficacy, group potency, and group performance: Meta-analyses of their relationships, and test of a mediation model. *Journal of Applied Psychology, 94*(3), 814–828.

Thatcher, S. M. B., & Patel, P. C. (2012). Group faultlines: A review, integration, and guide to future research. *Journal of Management, 38*(4), 969–1009. doi:10.1177/0149206311426187

CHAPTER 6

Barnes, C. M., Hollenbeck, J. R., Wagner, D. T., DeRue, D. S., Nahrgang, J. D., & Schwind, K. M. (2008). Harmful help: The costs of backing-up behavior in teams. *Journal of Applied Psychology, 93*(3), 529–539.

Bowers, C. A., Pharmer, J. A., & Salas, E. (2000). When member homogeneity is needed in work teams: A meta-analysis. *Small Group Research, 31*(3), 305–327.

Bradley, B. H., Klotz, A. C., Postlethwaite, B. E., & Brown, K. G. (2013). Ready to rumble: How team personality composition and task conflict interact to improve performance. *Journal of Applied Psychology, 98*(2), 385–392.

Bradley, B. H., Postlethwaite, B. E., Klotz, A. C., Hamdani, M. R., & Brown, K. G. (2012). Reaping the benefits of task conflict in teams: The critical role of team psychological safety climate. *Journal of Applied Psychology, 97*(1), 151–158. doi:10.1037/a0024200

Bunderson, J. S., & Sutcliffe, K. M. (2003). When to put the brakes on learning. *Harvard Business Review, 81*(2), 20–21.

Burke, S. C., Stagl, K. C., Klien, C., Goodwin, G. F., Salas, E., & Halpin, S. M. (2006). What type of leadership behaviors are functional in teams? A meta-analysis. *The Leadership Quarterly, 17,* 288–307. doi:10.1016/j.leaqua.2006.02.007

Christian, J. S., Christian, M. S., Pearsall, M. J., & Long, E. C. (2017). Team adaptation in context: An integrated conceptual model and meta-analytic review. *Organizational Behavior and Human Decision Processes, 140*(C), 62–80. doi:10.1016/j.obhdp.2017.01.003

DeChurch, L. A., Mesmer-Magnus, J. R., & Doty, D. (2013). Moving beyond relationship and task conflict: Toward a process-state perspective. *Journal of Applied Psychology, 98*(4), 559–578. doi:10.1037/a0032896 de Wit, F. R. C., Greer, L. L., & Jehn, K. A. (2012). The paradox of intragroup conflict: A meta-analysis. *Journal of Applied Psychology, 97*(2), 360–390. doi:10.1037/a0024844

Jehn, K. A., & Chatman, J. A. (2000). The influence of proportional and perceptual conflict composition on team performance. *International Journal of Conflict Management, 11*(1), 56–73. doi:10.1108/eb022835

Lehmann-Willenbrock, N., & Chiu, M. M. (2018). Igniting and resolving content disagreements during team interactions: A statistical discourse analysis of team dynamics at work. *Journal of Organizational Behavior, 39*(9), 1142–1162.

LePine, J. A. (2005). Adaptation of teams in response to unforeseen change: Effects of goal difficulty and team composition in terms of cognitive ability and goal orientation. *Journal of Applied Psychology, 90*(6), 1153–1167.

LePine, J. A., Piccolo, R. F., Jackson, C. L., Mathieu, J. E., & Saul, J. R. (2008). A meta-analysis of teamwork processes: Tests of a multidimensional model and relationships with team effectiveness criteria. *Personnel Psychology, 61*(2), 273–307. doi:10.1111/j.1744-6570.2008.00114.x

Salas, E., Nichols, D. R., & Driskell, J. E. (2007). Testing three team training strategies in intact teams: A meta-analysis. *Small Group Research, 38*(4), 471–488. doi:10.1177/1046496407304332

Schippers, M. C., West, M., & Dawson, J. (2015). Team reflexivity and innovation: the moderating role of team context. *Journal of Management, 41*(3), 769–788. doi:10.1177/0149206312441210

Siassakos, D., Crofts, J. F., Winter, C., Weiner, C. P., & Draycott, T. J. (2009). The active components of effective training in obstetric emergencies. *BJOG, 116*(8), 1028–1032. doi:10.1111/j.1471-0528.2009.02178.x

Smith-Jentsch, K. A., Kraiger, K., Cannon-Bowers, J. A., & Salas, E. (2009). Do familiar teammates request and accept more backup? A test of transactive memory in commercial Air Traffic Control. *Human Factors, 51*, 181–192.

Tannenbaum, S. I., & Cerasoli, C. P. (2013). Do team and individual debriefs enhance performance? A meta-analysis. *Human Factors: Journal of Human Factors and Ergonomics Society, 55*, 231–245.

Tannenbaum, S. I., Smith-Jentsch, K., & Behson, S. J. (1998). Training team leaders to facilitate team learning and performance. In J. A. Cannon-Bowers & E. Salas (Eds.), *Making decisions under stress: Implications for individual and team training* (p. 247–270). Washington, DC: American Psychological Association.

CHAPTER 7

Ancona, D. G., & Caldwell, D. F. (1992). Bridging the boundary: External activity and performance in organizational teams. *Administrative Science Quarterly, 37*(4), 634–665.

Duffy, K. A., & Chartrand, T. L. (2015). The extravert advantage: How and when extraverts build rapport with other people. *Psychological Science, 26*(11), 1795–1802. doi: 10.1177/0956797615600890

El-Shafy, I. A., Delgado, J., Akerman, M., Bullaro, F., Christopherson, N. A., & Prince, J. M. (2018). Closed-loop communication improves task completion in pediatric trauma resuscitation. *Journal of Surgical Education, 75*(1), 58–64.

Faulmüller, N., Mojzisch, A., Kerschreiter, R., & Schulz-Hardt, S. (2012). Do you want to convince me or to be understood? Preference-consistent information sharing and its motivational determinants. *Personality and Social Psychology Bulletin, 38*(12), 1684–1696. doi:10.1177/0146167212458707

Kanki, B. G., Folk, V. G., & Irwin, C. M. (1991). Communication variations and air-crew performance. *International Journal of Aviation Psychology*, *1*(2), 149–162. doi:10.1207/s15327108ijap0102_5

Marlow, S. L., Lacerenza, C. N., Paoletti, J., Burke, C. S., & Salas, E. (2018). Does team communication represent a one-size-fits-all approach? A meta-analysis of team communication and performance. *Organizational Behavior and Human Decision Processes*. *144*, 145–170.

Mesmer-Magnus, J. R., & DeChurch, L. A. (2009). Information sharing and team performance: A meta-analysis. *Journal of Applied Psychology*, *94*(2), 535–546.

CHAPTER 8

Aubé, C., Rousseau, V., & Tremblay, S. (2015). Perceived shared understanding in teams: The motivational effect of being "on the same page." *British Journal of Psychology*, *106*(3), 468–486.

Austin, J. R. (2003). Transactive memory in organizational groups: The effects of content, consensus, specialization, and accuracy on group performance. *Journal of Applied Psychology*, *88*(5), 866–878.

Bauer, T. N., Bodner, T., Erdogan, B., Truxillo, D. M., & Tucker, J. S. (2007). Newcomer adjustment during organizational socialization: a meta-analytic review of antecedents, outcomes, and methods. *Journal of Applied Psychology*, *92*(3), 707–721.

Burtscher, M. J., Kolbe, M., Wacker, J., & Manser, T. (2011). Interactions of team mental models and monitoring behaviors predict team performance in simulated anesthesia inductions. *Journal of Experimental Psychology: Applied*, *17*(3), 257–269.

Christian, J. S., Christian, M. S., Pearsall, M. J., & Long, E. C. (2017). Team adaptation in context: An integrated conceptual model and meta-analytic review. *Organizational Behavior and Human Decision Processes*, *140*(C), 62–80. doi:10.1016/j.obhdp.2017.01.003

Dalal, D. K., Nolan, K. P., & Gannon, L. E. (2017). Are pre-assembly shared work experiences useful for temporary-team assembly decisions? A study of Olympic ice hockey team composition. *Journal of Business and Psychology*, *32*(5), 561–574. doi:10.1007/s10869-016-9481-6

DeChurch, L. A., & Mesmer-Magnus, J. R. (2010). The cognitive underpinnings of effective teamwork: A meta-analysis. *Journal of Applied Psychology*, *95*(1), 32–53. doi:10.1037/a0017328

Dismukes, R. K., Berman, B. A., & Loukopoulos, L. (2017). *The limits of expertise: Rethinking pilot error and the causes of airline accidents*. New York, NY: Routledge.

Gorman, J. C., Amazeen, P. G., & Cooke, N. J. (2010). Team coordination dynamics. *Nonlinear Dynamics, Psychology, and Life Sciences*, *14*(3), 265–289.

Huckman, R. S., Staats, B. R., &, Upton, D. M. (2009). Team familiarity, role experience, and performance: Evidence from Indian software services. *Management Science*, *55*(1), 85–100.

Kurmann, A., Keller, S., Tschan-Semmer, F., Seelandt, J., Semmer, N. K., Candinas, D., & Beldi, G. (2014). Impact of team familiarity in the operating room on surgical complications. *World Journal of Surgery*, *38*(12), 3047–3052.

Maynard, T. M., Mathieu, J. E., Gilson, L. L., Sanchez, D. R., & Dean, M. D. (2018). Do I really know you and does it matter? Unpacking the relationship between familiarity and information elaboration in global virtual teams. *Group & Organization Management*, *44*(1), 3–37. doi:10.1177/1059601118785842

Sackett, E., & Cummings, J. N. (2018). When team members perceive task interdependence differently: Exploring centrality asymmetry and team success. *Group Dynamics: Theory, Research, and Practice, 22*(1), 16–31.

Sieweke, J., & Zhao, B. (2015). The impact of team familiarity and team leader experience on team coordination errors: A panel analysis of professional basketball teams. *Journal of Organizational Behavior, 36*(3), 382–402. doi:10.1002/job.1993

Tannenbaum, S. I., Beard, R. L., & Salas, E. (1992). Team building and its influence on team effectiveness: An examination of conceptual and empirical developments. In K. Kelly (Ed.), *Issues, Theory, and research in industrial/organizational psychology* (pp. 117–153). Amsterdam, The Netherlands: North-Holland.

Uitdewilligen, S., Waller, M. J., & Pitariu, A. H. (2013). Mental model updating and team adaptation. *Small Group Research, 44*(2), 127–158.

Wageman, R., Nunes, D. A., Burruss, J. A., & Hackman, J. R. (2008). *Senior leadership teams: What it takes to make them great.* Boston, MA: Harvard Business Review Press.

Xu, R., Carty, M. J., Orgill, D. P., Lipsitz, S. R., & Duclos, A. (2013). The teaming curve: a longitudinal study of the influence of surgical team familiarity on operative time. *Annals of surgery, 258*(6), 953–957.

CHAPTER 9

Balliet, D., & Van Lange, P. A. M. (2013). Trust, punishment, and cooperation across 18 societies: A meta-analysis. *Perspectives on Psychological Science, 8*(4), 363–379. doi:10.1177/1745691613488533

Fay, D., Shipton, H., West, M. A., & Patterson, M. (2015). Teamwork and organizational innovation: The moderating role of the HRM context. *Creativity and Innovation Management, 24*(2), 261–277. doi:10.1111/caim.12100

Hernandez, C., Burke, C. S., Howell, R., & Wiese, C. W. (2018, April). *Team learning behaviors: A meta-analysis of direct effects and moderators.* Poster presented at the 33rd annual meeting of the Society for Industrial Organizational Psychology, Chicago, IL.

Kniffen, K. M., Wansink, B., Devine, C. M., & Sobal, J. (2015). Eating together at the firehouse: How workplace commensality relates to the performance of firefighters. *Human Performance, 28*(4), 281–306. doi:10.1080/08959285.2015.1021049

Kurtessis, J. N., Eisenberger, R., Ford, M. T., Buffardi, L. C., Stewart, K. A., & Adis, C. S. (2015). Perceived organizational support: A meta-analytic evaluation of organizational support theory. *Journal of Management, 43*(6), 1854–1884. doi:10.1177/0149206315575554

Mesmer-Magnus, J. R., Asencio, R., Seely, P. W., & DeChurch, L. A. (2018). How organizational identity affects team functioning: The identity instrumentality hypothesis. *Journal of Management, 44*(4), 1530–1550.

Raes, A. M., Bruch, H., & De Jong, S. B. (2013). How top management team behavioural integration can impact employee work outcomes: Theory development and first empirical tests. *Human Relations, 66*(2), 167–192.

Shin, Y., Kim, M., Choi, J. N., & Lee, S-H. (2015). Does team culture matter? Roles of team culture and collective regulatory focus in team task and creative performance. *Group & Organization Management, 41*(2), 232–265. doi:10.1177/1059601115584998

Tannenbaum, S. I., & Dupuree-Bruno, L. M. (1994). The relationship between organizational and environmental factors and the use of innovative human resource practices. *Group and Organization Management, 19*, 171–202.

CHAPTER 10

Burke, C. S., Stagl, K. C., Klein, C., Goodwin, G. F., Salas, E., & Halpin, S. M. (2006). What type of leadership behaviors are functional in teams? A meta-analysis. *Leadership Quarterly, 17*, 288–307.

Ceri-Booms, M., Curşeu, P. L., & Oerlemans, L. A. (2017). Task and person-focused leadership behaviors and team performance: A meta-analysis. *Human Resource Management Review, 27*(1), 178–192.

Chen, Z., Zhu, J., & Zhou, M. (2015). How does a servant leader fuel the service fire? A multilevel model of servant leadership, individual self identity, group competition climate, and customer service performance. *Journal of Applied Psychology, 100*(2), 511–521.

D'Innocenzo, L., Mathieu, J. E., & Kukenberger, M. R. (2014). A meta-analysis of different forms of shared leadership: Team performance relations. *Journal of Management, 42*(7), 1964–1991. doi:10.1177/0149206314525205

Hirschfeld, R. R., Thomas, C. H., & Bernerth, J. B. (2011). Consequences of autonomous and team-oriented forms of dispositional proactivity for demonstrating advancement potential. *Journal of Vocational Behavior, 78*(2), 237–247.

Hoch, J. E., Bommer, W. H., Dulebohn, J. H., & Wu, D. (2016). Do ethical, authentic, and servant leadership explain variance above and beyond transformational leadership? A meta-analysis. *Journal of Management, 44*(2), 501–529. doi:10.1177/0149206316665461

Hogeveen, J., Inzlicht, M., & Obhi, S. S. (2014). Power changes how the brain responds to others. *Journal of Experimental Psychology: General, 143*(2), 755–762.

McIntyre, H. H., & Foti, R. J. (2013). The impact of shared leadership on teamwork mental models and performance in self-directed teams. *Group Processes & Intergroup Relations, 16*(1), 46–57. doi:10.1177/1368430211422923

Montano, D., Reeske, A., Franke, F., & Hüffmeier, J. (2017). Leadership, followers' mental health and job performance in organizations: A comprehensive meta-analysis from an occupational health perspective. *Journal of Organizational Behavior, 38*(3), 327–350.

Overbeck, J. R., & Droutman, V. (2013). One for all: Social power increases self-anchoring of traits, attitudes, and emotions. *Psychological Science, 24*(8), 1466–1476. doi:10.1177/0956797612474671

Pearson, C., & Porath, C. (2009). *The cost of bad behavior: How incivility is damaging your business and what to do about it.* London, England: Portfolio.

Smittick, A. L., Miner, K. N., & Cunningham, G. B. (2019). The "I" in team: Coach incivility, coach gender, and team performance in women's basketball teams. *Sport Management Review, 22*(3), 419–433. doi:10.1016/j.smr.2018.06.002

Tremblay, D., Latreille, J., Bilodeau, K., Samson, A., Roy, L., L'Italien, M. F., & Mimeault, C. (2016). Improving the transition from oncology to primary care teams: A case for shared leadership. *Journal of Oncology Practice, 12*(11), 1012–1019.

Van Dierendonck, D., Stam, D., Boersma, P., De Windt, N., & Alkema, J. (2014). Same difference? Exploring the differential mechanisms linking servant leadership and transformational leadership to follower outcomes. *The Leadership Quarterly, 25*(3), 544–562.

Wang, D., Waldman, D. A., & Zhang, Z. (2014). A meta-analysis of shared leadership and team effectiveness. *Journal of Applied Psychology, 99*(2), 181–198. doi:10.1037/a0034531

Wang, G., Oh, I. S., Courtright, S. H., & Colbert, A. E. (2011). Transformational leadership and performance across criteria and levels: A meta-analytic review of 25 years of research. *Group & Organization Management, 36*(2), 223–270. doi:10.1177/1059601111401017

Wing, A. M., Endo, S., Bradbury, A., & Vorberg, D. (2014). Optimal feedback correction in string quartet synchronization. *Journal of the Royal Society Interface, 11*(93). doi:10.1098/rsif.2013.1125

Yukl, G. A. (1998). *Leadership in organizations.* Boston, MA: Pearson Education.

INDEX

Page references to tables and figures and boxes are indicated by *t's, f's* and *b's* respectively.

For the benefit of digital users, indexed terms that span two pages (e.g., 52–53) may, on occasion, appear on only one of those pages.